A Sufi Message of S

Volume

THE ALCHEMY OF HAPPINESS

Revised Edition

By the same author

The Way of Illumination Volume I
The Mysticism of Sound and Music Volume II
The Art of Personality Volume III
Health and Healing Volume IV
Spiritual Liberty Volume V
The Alchemy of Happiness Volume VI
In an Eastern Rosegarden Volume VII
Sufi Teachings: The Art of Being Volume VIII
The Unity of Religious Ideals Volume IX
The Path of Initiation Volume X
Philosophy, Psychology and Mysticism Volume XI
The Vision of God and Man Volume XII
Sacred Readings: The Gathas Volume XIII
Sufi Teachings: The Smiling Forehead Volume XIV

A SUFI MESSAGE
OF SPIRITUAL LIBERTY
VOLUME VI
(revised edition)

THE ALCHEMY OF HAPPINESS

HAZRAT INAYAT KHAN

East-West Publication (UK) Ltd.
London
in association with
The International Headquarters of
the Sufi Movement, Geneva

First published by Barrie and Rockliff (Barrie Books Ltd) 1960
Subsequent reprints by Uitgeverij Servire BV, Katwijk,
Netherlands.

Revised edition first published in Great Britain in 1996 by East-West Publications (UK) Ltd., London.
in association with
The International Headquarters of the Sufi Movement, Geneva

Cover design by Max Fairbrother
Printed and bound in Belgium by Arte-Print

British Library Cataloguing in Publication Data
Inayat Khan, Hazrat 1882-1927
A Sufi Message of Spiritual Liberty-Rev. ed.
Vol.VI - The Alchemy of Happiness
1. Sufi life
I. Title

ISBN 0-85692-217-X

CONTENTS

PREFACE

THE READER who is familiar with the 1962 edition of this volume in the series "The Sufi Message of Hazrat Inayat Khan" will notice that the present volume contains the same subject matter as its predecessor which proved so extraordinarily successful. However, on closer inspection it will become clear that the text of many individual chapters differs somewhat from the earlier text. This is due to a change in editorial policy, as explained in the preface to the revised edition of Volume VIII of the present series (1991). The majority of the changes follows the decision to return to the original integrity of the lectures of Hazrat Inayat Khan. This has meant the omission of interpolated elements derived from other lectures; the appending of questions put to Hazrat Inayat Khan with his answers, as such, after the lecture, rather than incorporating them in the main body of the text; and a preference to adhere as closely as possible to the lectures' original wording, keeping to a minimum the editorial amendments inevitable in any transition from oral discourse to printed page.

This search to reproduce authenticity of expression with its gain of original freshness, however, also implies that a certain duplication becomes difficult to avoid, especially with regard to the many stories that Hazrat Inayat Khan liked to tell in order to illustrate a particular point or to stimulate comprehension by a lightening of tone. It may be argued that undue repetition ought to be avoided, yet the stories appear to be worded differently each time - be it ever so slightly - and they seem to 'belong' exactly there where the Master tells them. On a deeper level the repetition is no longer a repetition: it increases the understanding of the reader. It was therefore decided to leave in all the stories.

Readers wishing to consult the original records of Hazrat Inayat Khan's lectures, are referred to the edition of source materials entitled Complete Works of Pir-o-Murshid Hazrat Inayat Khan, Original Texts: Lectures on Sufism, an ongoing publication under the auspices of the Nekbakht Foundation (East-West Publications, London - The Hague, 1989).

CHAPTER I

The Alchemy Of Happiness

THE SOUL in the sanskrit language and in the terms of Vedanta is called *Atman*, which means happiness or bliss itself - not that happiness belongs to the soul, but the soul itself is happiness. Today we often confuse happiness with pleasure. Pleasure is only an illusion of happiness, a shadow of happiness, and in this delusion man perhaps passes his whole life, seeking after pleasure, and never finding satisfaction. There is a Hindu saying that man looks for pleasure and gets pain. Every pleasure which is seeming happiness in outward appearance promises happiness, for it is the shadow of happiness, but just as the shadow of a person is not the person and yet represents the form of the person, so pleasure represents happiness but is not so in reality.

According to this idea one finds that there are rarely souls in this world who know what happiness is; they are constantly disappointed in one thing after another, but the nature of life in the world is such; it is so deluding that if man were disappointed a thousand times he would still take the same path, for he knows no other. The more we study life, the more we realize how rarely there is a soul who can honestly say, "I am happy". Almost every soul, whatever his life's position, will say that he is unhappy in some way or another, and if you ask for a reason he will say perhaps, "I cannot attain to the position, power, property, possessions or rank, for which I have worked for years". He is craving for money perhaps, and does not realize that possessions give no satisfaction; or perhaps he says he has enemies, or those whom he loves do not love him; there are a thousand excuses for unhappiness that the reasoning mind will make.

But is even one of these excuses ever entirely correct? Do you think even if people gained their desires they would be happy? If they possessed all, would these things suffice? No; for still they would find some excuse for unhappiness, and all these excuses are as coverings before man's eyes, for deep within is the yearning for the true happiness which none of these things can give. The one who is really happy is happy everywhere: in a palace or a cottage, in riches or poverty, for he has discovered the fountain of happiness which is situated in his own heart; so long as a person has not found that fountain, nothing will give him real happiness. The man who does not know the secret of happiness often develops avarice. He wants thousands; and when he gets them they do not satisfy, and he wants millions; and still he is not satisfied - he wants more and more. If you give him your sympathy and service he is still unhappy; all you possess is not enough - even your love does not help him, for he is seeking in a wrong direction, and life itself becomes a tragedy.

Happiness cannot be bought or sold, nor can you give it to a person who has not got it. Happiness is in your own being, your own self, that self that is the most precious thing in life. All religions, all philosophical systems, have taught man in different forms how to find it by the religious path, or the mystical way, and all the wise ones have in some form or another given a method by which the individual can find that happiness for which the soul is seeking.

Sages and mystics have called this process Alchemy. The stories of the Arabian Nights which symbolize these mystical ideas, are full of the belief that there is a philosopher's stone that will turn metals into gold by a chemical process. No doubt this symbolic idea has deluded men both in the East and West; many have thought that a process exists by which gold can be produced. But this is not the idea of the wise; the pursuit after gold is for those who are as yet children. For those who have the consciousness of reality gold stands for light or spiritual inspiration. Gold represents the colour of light, and therefore an unconscious pursuit after light has made man seek for gold. But there is a great difference between real gold and false. It is the longing for true gold that makes man collect the imitation gold, ignorant that the real gold is within. He satisfies the craving of his soul in this way, as a child satisfies itself by playing with dolls.

But a man does not depend upon age for this realization. A person may have reached an advanced age and be still playing with dolls: his soul may be involved in the search for this imitation gold, while another in youth may begin to see life in its real aspect. If one studied the transitory nature of life in the world, how changeable it is, and the constant craving of everyone for happiness, one would certainly endeavour, whatever happened, to find something one could depend upon. Man placed in the midst of this everchanging world yet appreciates and seeks for constancy somewhere - he does not know that he must develop in himself the nature of constancy; the nature of the soul is to value that which is dependable. But think, is there anything in the world on which one can depend, which is above change and destruction? All that is born, all that is made, must one day face destruction. All that has a beginning has also an end; and if there is anything one can depend upon it is hidden in the heart of man, it is the divine spark, the true philosopher's stone, the real gold, which is the innermost being of man.

A person who follows a religion, and has not come to the realization of truth, of what use is his religion to him if he is not happy? Religion does not mean depression and sadness. The spirit of religion must give happiness. God is happy. He is the perfection of love, harmony and beauty. A religious person must be happier than the one who is not religious. If a person who professes religion is always melancholy, in this way religion is disgraced, the form has been kept, but the spirit is lost. If the study of religion and mysticism does not lead to real joy and happiness, it may just as well not exist, for it does not help to fulfil the purpose of life. The world today is sad and suffering as the result of the terrible war; the religion which answers the demand of life to-day is that method of morals which invigorates and gives life to souls, which illuminates the heart of man with the divine light which is already there, not necessarily by the outer form, although for some a form is helpful, but the first necessity is the showing forth of that happiness which is the desire of every soul.

Now as to the question of how this method of alchemy is practised, the whole process was explained by the alchemists in a symbolical way. They say gold is made out of mercury;

the nature of mercury is to be ever moving, but by a certain process the mercury is first stilled, and once stilled it becomes silver; the silver then has to be melted, and on to the melted silver the juice of a herb is poured, and then the melted silver turns into gold. Of course this method is given in outline, but there is a detailed explanation of the whole process. Many child-souls have tried to make gold by stilling mercury and melting silver; they have tried to find the herb, but they were deluded, they had better have worked and earned money.

The real interpretation of this process is that mercury represents the nature of the ever-restless mind. This is realized especially when a person tries to concentrate; the mind is like a restive horse, when it is ridden it is more restive, when in the stable less restive. Such is the nature of mind, it becomes more restless when you desire to control it, it is like mercury, constantly moving.

When by a method of concentration one has mastered the mind, one has taken the first step in the accomplishment of a sacred task. Prayer is concentration, reading is concentration, sitting and relaxing and thinking on one subject are all concentration. All artists, thinkers, and inventors have practised concentration in some form; they have given their minds to one thing, and by focusing on one object have developed the faculty of concentration; but for stilling the mind a special method is necessary, and is taught by the mystic, just as singing is taught by the teacher of voice production; the secret is to be learnt in the science of breath.

Breath is the essence of life, the centre of life, and the mind which is more difficult to control than a restive horse, may be controlled by a knowledge of the proper method of breathing. For this, instruction from a teacher is a necessity; since the mystical cult of the East has become known in the West, books have been published, and teaching, which had been kept as sacred as religion has been discussed in words which cannot truly explain the mystery of that which is the centre of man's very being. People read the books and begin to play with breath, and often instead of receiving benefit they injure both mind and body; there are also those who make a business of teaching breathing exercises for money, and so degrade a sacred thing. The science of breath is the greatest mystery there is, and for thousands of years in the schools of the mystics it has been kept as a sacred trust.

When the mind is under complete control, and no longer restless, one can hold a thought at will as long as one wishes. This is the beginning of phenomena; some abuse these privileges, and by dissipating the power, before turning the silver into gold they destroy the silver. The silver must be heated before it can melt, and with what? With that warmth which is the divine essence in the heart of man, which comes forth as love, tolerance, sympathy, service, humility, unselfishness, in a stream which rises and falls in a thousand drops, each drop of which could be called a virtue, all coming from that one stream hidden in the heart of man, the love element. When it glows in the heart, the actions, the movements, the tones of the voice, the expression, all show that the heart is warm. The moment this happens the man really lives; he has unsealed the spring of happiness which overcomes all that is jarring and inharmonious: the spring has established itself as a divine stream.

After the heart is warmed by the divine element, which is love, the next stage is the herb, which is the love of God; but the love of God alone is not sufficient, knowledge of God is also necessary. It is the absence of knowledge of God which makes man leave his religion, because there is a limit to man's patience. Knowledge of God strengthens man's belief in God, throws light on the individual and on life. Things become clear; every leaf on a tree becomes as a page of a holy book to one whose eyes are open to the knowledge of God. When the juice of the herb of divine love is poured on to the heart, warmed by the love of his fellow man, then that heart becomes the heart of gold, the heart that expresses what God would express. Man has not seen God, but man has then seen God in man, and when this is so, then verily everything that comes from such a man comes from God Himself.

CHAPTER II

The Aim of Life

1

THE MAIN object of life can be but one object and the external objects of life are as many as there are beings. There is one object of life for the reason that there is one life - although outwardly it appears to be many lives. It is in this thought that we can combine and it is from this thought that true wisdom is learned. No doubt that main object of life cannot be understood at once. Therefore the best thing for every person is to pursue his object in life first and in the accomplishment of his personal object, someday he will arrive at accomplishing that inner object. When man does not understand this he thinks there is something else to accomplish, and he thinks of all that is before him that is not yet accomplished, and so he remains a failure.

The person who is not definite about his object has not yet begun his journey on the path of life. One should therefore first determine one's object for oneself, however small that object is; once it is determined one has begun life. We find in the many lives of people that, sometimes all through their lives, they do not find their life's vocation. What happens then is that in the end they consider their life a failure. All through their life they go from one thing to another, yet as they do not know their life's object they can accomplish so little. When people ask, "Why do I not succeed?" my answer is, "Because you have not yet found your object". As soon as a person has found his life's object he begins to feel at home in this world where before he had felt himself in a strange world. No sooner has a person found his way than he will prove to be fortunate because all things he wants to accomplish will come by themselves.

Even if the whole world were against him, he will get such a power that he can hold on to his object against the whole world. He will get such patience that when he is on the way to his object no misfortune will discourage him.

There is no doubt that as long as he has not found it he will go from one thing to another and again to another; and he will think that life is against him. Then he will begin to find fault with individuals, conditions, planets, the climate, everything. So, what is called fortunate or successful is to have the right object. When a person is wearing clothes which were not made for him, he says they are too loose or too short, but when they are his clothes he feels comfortable in them. They are his. The real thing therefore is to give freedom to every soul to choose his object in life and if he finds himself at home in it, then to know that he is on the right path.

When a person is on the path, certain things have to be considered. When he has a knot to unravel, to loosen and he is given a knife to cut it, he has lost a great deal in his life. It is a small thing, but by not accomplishing it a person has gone backward, he has taken a step back. This is a little example, but in everything one does, if one has not the patience and confidence to go forward, one loses a great deal. However small a work a person has undertaken, if he accomplishes it, he has accomplished something great. It is not the work that the person has accomplished, it is the very fact of accomplishing which gives him power.

As to the main object of every soul, that object may be called spiritual attainment. A person may go all through his life without it, but there will come a time when although he may not admit it he will begin to look for it, for spiritual attainment is not only an acquired knowledge, it is the soul's appetite. There will come a day in life when a person will feel the soul's appetite more than any other appetite. No doubt every soul has an unconscious yearning to satisfy his soul's appetite, but at the same time one's absorption in everyday life keeps one so occupied that one has no time to pay attention.

The definition of spiritual attainment can be found in studying human nature, for the nature of man is one and the same, be he spiritual or material. There are five things that man yearns for: life, power, knowledge, happiness and peace, and the continual appetite which is felt in the deepest self yearns for one or the other of these five things. In order to answer his appetite what does man do? In order to answer the desire to live, he eats and drinks and protects himself from all dangers of life. Yet the appetite is not fully satisfied because all dangers he may escape except the last one which man calls death.

In order to answer the next thing which is power, a man does everything to gain physical strength, influence, rank; every kind of power he seeks in order to be powerful. He always knocks against disappointments because he sees that if there is a power of ten degrees there is another power of twenty degrees to knock against. Just think of the great nations whose military power was once so immense that one could not have believed that in a moment they would fall down. One could have thought, "If they will fall down it will take thousands of years to do so", so great was their power. We need not look for it in history, we have just seen this happen in the last few years; we have only to look at the map.

The third kind of appetite is for happiness. Man tries to answer it by pleasure, not knowing that pleasures of this world do not answer that happiness which his soul really seeks after. Man's attempts are in vain; he will find in the end that every effort he made for pleasure brought greater loss than gain. Besides, that which is not enduring, which is not real in its nature, is not satisfactory.

Then there is the desire for knowledge. This knowledge gives a tendency to study. A man might study and study all through his life but even if he read all the books in the great libraries, there would still remain the question "why"? This "why" will not be answered by the books he studies, by exploring the facts which belong to outer life. In the first place the depth of nature is so profound that man's limited life is not long enough to probe its depths. Comparatively or relatively one may say that one person is more learned than another; but no one reaches true satisfaction by the outer study of life.

Lastly there is the appetite for peace. In order to find peace one leaves one's environment which troubles one, one wants to get away from people, one wants to sit quietly and rest. But he who is not ready for that peace would not find it even if he went to the caves of the Himalayas, away from the whole world.

When explaining these five appetites, which are the deepest man has, one finds that all the efforts man makes to satisfy them seem to be in vain. They can only be satisfied by spiritual attainment; for that is the only thing which answers these five different appetites. The desire to live can only be satisfied when the soul realises its eternal life, for mortality exists in conception rather than in reality. From a spiritual point of view mortality is the lack of the soul's understanding of its own self. It is like a person who had lived all his life in the conception that his coat was himself and when that coat was torn he thought that he died. One experiences the same in life. The soul gets from the physical body a kind of illusion and identifies itself with this mortal being. It is just like identifying oneself with one's overcoat and by the loss of it one thinks that one is lost. As an intellectual knowledge of this is but of little use, wise people of all times have practised meditations to give the soul a chance to find itself independent of the physical body. Once the soul has begun to feel itself, its own life, independently of its outer garb, it begins to have confidence in life and is no longer afraid of what is called death. As soon as this phenomenon is vouchsafed a person no longer calls death "death"; he calls death a change.

Coming to the idea of power, the true power is not in trying to gain power, the true power is in becoming power. But how to become power? It requires an attempt to make a definite change in oneself and that change is a kind of struggle with one's false self. When the false self is crucified, then the true self is resurrected. Before the world this crucifixion appears to be lack of power, in truth all power is attained by this resurrection.

As to knowledge, it has two aspects. One knowledge is what one learns by knowing the names and forms of this life; it is what we call learning. That cannot be the answer to this appetite, it is only a steppingstone to it. This outer learning only helps one to come to the inner learning, but the inner learning is quite different from the outer one. How is it learned? It is learned by studying the self. One finds that all the knowledge one strives after and all that exists to study, is in oneself. One finds a kind of universe in oneself and by the study of the self one comes to that spiritual knowledge which really is the soul's appetite. Then, there is the question of happiness. A person thinks that when his friends are kind to him, when people respond to him or when he gets money, then he will be happy. But that is not the way to become happy. It is a mistake. The lack of happiness makes him blame others, believing they are standing in the way of his becoming happy. In reality that is not so. True happiness is not gained, it is discovered. Man's way itself is happiness, that is why he longs for it. What keeps happiness out of one's life is the closing of the doors of the heart and when the heart is not living, happiness is not living there. Sometimes the heart is not fully alive but only a little; at the same time it expects life from the other heart. But the real life of the heart is to live independently in its own happiness. And that is gained by spiritual attainment.

The person who has found his peace within himself may be in a cave of the mountain or among the crowd, in every place he will experience peace.

Now the question is how these five things can be gained. As I have said, the first thing needed is to accomplish the object which is immediately standing before one, however small it is does not matter. It is by accomplishing it that one gains power. As one goes further in this way through one's life, always seeking for the real, one will come to reality. Truth is attained by the love of truth. When a person runs away from truth, truth runs away from him. If not, truth is nearer to a person than that which is without truth. There is nothing more precious in life than truth itself, and in loving truth and in attaining to the truth one attains to that religion which is the religion of all people and of all churches. It does not matter then what church one belongs to, what religion one professes, what race or nation one belongs to. Once a person realizes the truth he is all, because he is with all. There is disagreement and misunderstanding before a person has attained to the truth. Once he has attained to the truth there is no misunderstanding. It is among those who have learned the outer knowledge that disputes arise, but those who have attained to the truth, whether they come from the North or the South, from whatever country, it does not matter; for when they have understood the truth they are in at-one-ment.

It is this object that we should keep before us in order to unite the divided sections of humanity, for the real happiness of humanity is that unity which can be gained by rising above barriers which divide men.

2

I wish to speak on the same subject of which I spoke last evening. The reason is that when a subject is treated before a large public one cannot very well touch upon the intimate points. Therefore I ask your indulgence for some remarks which go rather into the details of the same subject. I had said that there are five aspects in which the appetite of the soul shows itself. Those aspects are the desire to live, the desire for knowledge, the desire for power, the desire for happiness and the desire for peace. One person perhaps shows one desire more than another person. Nevertheless, every person has these five aspects of the soul's appetite just the same.

If we study the desire to live profoundly we shall find that we cannot have a desire if it is not in our nature. If there is a desire there is an answer to it. The desire to live continually is a desire of the spiritual person as well as of the material person. A spiritual person will perhaps hope for the next life and a material person is pessimistic against his own desire, but the desire is there all the same. How does one attain to this continuity of life? It does not only depend upon a belief although belief helps a person to the realization of that experience. When there is no belief a person does not find the way. Nevertheless, the continuity of life is possible logically because every person desires to live. It is natural that no one will desire what is not possible. A natural desire has its possibility there already. If there were no possibility one would not desire.

In saying this I do not speak about a mad person. Such a person can desire anything. But a person with reason will only desire what is possible to accomplish.

The secret of this question can be found by analysing oneself. By studying the self one will find that one's body is only a cover over one's real self. But by a still more profound study one will find that even one's mind is a cover over one's real self. As soon as one finds this out, one will become independent of the body to live. Also one will become independent of the mind to live. "But", one might ask, "if there is no body, then what is life"? One asks this because man has limited himself by experiencing life through the body and has not tried to experience life without its help. When man is not conscious of his body, then he is conscious of his mind. When his eyes are open he is looking at things before him. When his mind is closed then he is pondering upon what his mind has gained. In both cases he is dependent either upon his body or upon his mind to experience that he is living. This dependence makes the soul limited. It does not only limit it but it mortalizes the soul. I do not mean by this that the soul is mortal, but even for the soul to believe in mortality is like being mortal.

Now there is the question of the desire for power. Man desires power because it is natural for him to gain. Somewhere the power is hidden in him, he cannot help it. Man is powerless, in spite of that power which is hidden in him. The powerlessness, the experience of being powerless is his ignorance of the power which is in him. In order to open the doors, in order to see the power he has in store it is necessary to seek the kingdom of God as it is said in the Bible. Because then he will find his divine heritage which is all power.

Next comes the desire for knowledge. In order to acquire that knowledge which cannot be studied one must try to meditate and to dive into the sea of knowledge. It is by diving deep into the water that one gets that knowledge which cannot be taught by study. In this way one divides two aspects of knowledge, one aspect is intellect, the other is wisdom.

Therefore a wise man is not a clever man nor a clever man a wise man. Coming to the explanation of happiness, happiness comes by digging deep into our own heart. It is a great mistake to look for happiness in the outside world. The true happiness is our own self, our deepest self. The more conscious we become of our real self, the more true happiness comes from that. Coming to the desire for peace, what happens is that in order to get peace we always blame the other person who walks upon our nerves. But true peace can only come by being so firm against all influences around us that nothing can disturb us.

Question: Do you believe in the immortality of the soul?
Answer: Well, my whole lecture has been on that subject.

Question: On which basis is your belief in the immortality of the soul founded?
Answer: There cannot be a better basis than one's own realization.

Question: I do believe but I want to be fortified in my ideas. I would like to get a reason for the immortality of the soul.
Answer: All the religions of the world support this idea. Therefore for a believer there is everything to support it.

Question: Is there any instruction in Sufism that can fortify that belief?
Answer: Yes, our whole instruction is to realize this, not only to fortify it. Our work, the work of the Sufi philosophy is not only to strengthen a person's belief but to make his belief his conviction. Therefore we do not teach people any belief.

Question: Murshid, how do you propose to realize the knowledge of oneself?
Answer: There are four ways by which one comes to the realization of selfknowledge. By the way of knowledge, by the way of good action, by the way of meditation and by the way of devotion, whatever be the temperament. When one of these four ways is near to your nature, walk on that path

and in the end you will find the answer of your soul.
Question: Meditation is the principal I think; the other three are interesting but please give an explanation of the fourth.
Answer: Devotion is the original nature of man. As the Bible says, "God is love", so the person in whom there is love there is God.

Question: If an atheist has devotion, love, how can one reconcile that?
Answer: He cannot be any longer an atheist when he has devotion or love, because that love-principle in its development will make him believe, if not in God, then in a person he loves. If a person truly loves one person, he must in the end love all persons. When a person says, "I love one person but I hate another person", he does not yet know what love is. For love is not limited, it is divine and unlimited. By opening the love-element in oneself one opens a divine element in oneself. When the divine fountain begins to rise from the heart, then all realizations which are divine must rise as a fountain. The great saints, who had love even for the smallest insect and living being, had divine realization without great study or meditation. Only their love taught them so.

Question: How to conceive this divine element?
Answer: Love is divine from its beginning in all its aspects. The great poet of Persia, Rumi, says, "Whether you love a person or whether you love God, if you journey all through the way of love, in the end you will arrive in the presence of the Sovereign of love".

Question: Is the realization of the knowledge of oneself the realization of the spirit or of the soul?
Answer: Self is the soul. Therefore it is the realization of the soul as well as of the body and mind, of the whole being. Even in the realization of the self God-realization comes.

Question: Everyone in life has to have an object, everyone has to find his way and in finding one's way one must put all

one's intelligence. Is there a means of finding one's way in life?
Answer: Yes, if one lives a straight life, a natural life intuitively one finds the straight way to go. Beside that, when a person has got his object, which is for him, then he feels himself, he feels at home. Then he feels that everything helps him, he feels hopeful and courageous.

Question: Is there a means to find the object? I have not yet found an object in life.
Answer: One must develop intuition.

Question: How can one develop intuition in somebody who does not possess it?
Answer: Self-confidence. A person must be ready to risk mistakes because he may not always have the right intuition; if he disbelieves the intuition, then he will not have it at all.

Question: Then it is a great risk?
Answer: Nothing is attained without risk. When people say that in something there is a risk, I often tell them that in not taking a risk there is a greater risk still.

Question: Is intuition superior to intelligence?
Answer: Superiority and inferiority are relative terms. Of course, intuition sometimes comes from a deeper source than intellect. By intelligence is meant the capacity of knowing and by intellect what one knows. Intelligence is the capacity, intellect the knowledge. Intelligence is a pure substance, something most pure. Therefore intelligence is the divine substance that one can trace in oneself. If there is any sign of the soul in a person, it is the intelligence. Therefore the more intelligent a person is, the more brilliant a soul that person has. By this I do not mean that an intellectual person has no intelligence.

Question: Is the will not nearest to divinity?
Answer: Yes, if I were to give a definition of will I would call it love. "I will to do it" means "I love to do it", it is poetic.

Question: I have done many things which I did not like to do.
Answer: In that case a person does not will to do them. Then he is a machine, there is no will. When a person wills to do then he loves to do. For me willpower and lovepower are one thing.

Question: Is doing what one does not like to do still a way of developing one's will?
Answer: Yes, we develop our power by doing it. We develop power over a part of ourself which is unwilling. That only means that one part of ourself does not love to do something which another part of our self loves to do. And therefore we call the part which conquers: the will.

Question: If I give good for bad, the first impulse is not to do it.
Answer: I would call it love, love in the form of forgiveness, of tolerance. If you are not willing to do it, it is another thing. I would rather have a man not practise a certain virtue than to practise it without love. Practising it unwillingly is not good. For instance, someone visits you and upon leaving asks to borrow your raincoat. You say, "allright", but as it happens you have to go out also. Suppose you then say, "What a nasty man, he took my raincoat". I would have preferred you not to have given it but to have said, "I am very sorry, I cannot give it, sir"!
Every good action only has its virtue if it comes by our love. If not, it is a dead action, it is not living.

Question: Does the Sufi philosophy in its essence believe in reincarnation?
Answer: The philosophy of the Sufis does not give any belief and does not oppose any belief. It interprets to its best ability every belief as favourably as its followers do. For instance, if a person asks a Sufi a question about Buddhism, Brahmanism or the Christian religion, the Sufi stands for that person as the lawyer would stand in the tribunal, giving his argument before the law. But Sufism does not give any belief as its own belief. That is why one Sufi perhaps believes in one doctrine

and another does not understand that just now. In order to become a Sufi it is not necessary to have this or that belief, this or that doctrine. The Sufi only helps one to rise above things and to look at life from a higher point of view. Sufism follows exactly the idea written in the Bible, "Seek ye first the kingdom of God and all these things shall be added unto you". Instead of troubling about beliefs the Sufi first goes straight to that central idea and when he stands there he sees the truth of all things. It is the mystery of life that whenever he takes the divine lantern in hand all things become clear. Sufism gives freedom to every adept to believe for himself and to find out things for himself. Now I wish to say one word and that is that our life's greatest need is God. To our great disappointment we find that this very ideal is lost. Whether it is a spiritual gain or a material gain, all inspiration and power is in the love of God, in the knowledge of God and in the realization of the self and God.

CHAPTER III

The Purpose of Life

1

EVERY LIVING being has a purpose in life and it is the knowing of that purpose that makes every soul able to fulfil it. As it is said in the *Gayan*, "Blessed is he who knoweth his life's purpose".

Do not be surprised if you find many groping through the darkness all through life, doing one thing and going from one thing to the other, always dissatisfied, always discontented; and nothing they undertake has the desired result. The reason is the absence of that knowledge, the knowledge of the purpose of life.

Individuals apart, every object has its purpose. The mission of science is to discover the purpose in objects. It is from that discovery that science has come; be it medical science or philosophy, all the different aspects of science are the result of discovering the purpose of things. But mysticism is to find the purpose in the lives of human beings the purpose in one's own life and the purpose in the life of others. As long as man has not found this purpose he may have success or failure, he may seemingly be happy or unhappy but in reality he does not live; for life begins from the moment a person has found the purpose of his life.

You will find people with all riches, with position, with comfort and conveniences in life and yet they are missing something, missing the main thing which alone can make them happy: the knowing of the purpose of their life. This is the very thing they miss and at the same time mankind is ignorant of this. Man will be interested in a thousand things, in one thing and then in another thing and so on, but he will never come to that point where he finds the purpose of his life. Why? First of all because he does not look for it.

Now coming to children's education, the education of youth, very often the parents never think about this problem. Whatever seems to them beneficial for the child they recommend him to do. They do not pay attention to the fact that the child, the youth has to find the purpose of his life. How many lives have been ruined for this reason! A child may have been brought up with every facility and yet always kept away from the purpose of his life. Sa'di says, "Every infant is born for a certain purpose and the light of that purpose is kindled in his soul". It is a psychological and mystical secret that however unhappy man may be, the moment he knows the purpose of his life a switch is turned and the light is on. He may not yet be able to accomplish it, but the very fact of knowing the purpose gives him all the hope, vigour, inspiration and strength to wait for that day. If he had to strive after that purpose his whole life, he would not mind as long as he knew that that was the purpose. Ten such persons have much greater power than a thousand people working from morning till evening, not knowing the purpose of their life.

Besides, what we call wrong and right, good or bad is also according to our purpose in life. There is for instance a person whose vocation in life is to write plays and there is another person who is studying medicine. Both have their examination before them. There is a play advertised which makes them both feel, "I want to go and see it". The medical student thinks, "My examination is near, I must study at home but this is an attractive play" and then he says, "I must go and see it". The student who is a playwriter thinks, "To go and see the play might be beneficial". Both act in the same way, both see the same play but one loses the sense of studying and the other is inspired.

Now we come to the purpose of all, the ultimate purpose. We begin our lives with an individual purpose but we come to a stage where the purpose of every soul is one and the same. And that purpose can be studied by studying the inclination of man. Every soul has five inclinations hidden in the depth of his heart. Being absorbed in the life of the world man may forget that ultimate purpose, but at the same time there is a continual inclination towards it; which shows that the ultimate purpose of the life of all persons is one and the same.

One of these five inclinations is the love of knowledge. It is not only the intellectual and intelligent beings who seek after knowledge. Even an infant wishes to know what every little noise is. Every child in seeing a beautiful colour and line in a picture asks what it is. And so - it may be more or less - every individual is striving after knowledge. No doubt in life as it is to-day many are placed in a situation where they never have a moment in which to gain that knowledge which they seek after. From morning till evening they have their duty to perform, they are so absorbed in it that after some time that hunger for knowledge is gone and their mind becomes blunted. It is not one person, there are thousands of people whom life has placed in a certain situation where they cannot help but put their mind to their work and never have time to think about things that they would like to think, that they would like to know. We have made this life. Can we call it progress? We call it freedom, but it is not freedom of mind. The mind is thrown into a limited horizon and we call it a sphere.

Besides that, in education we can see everyday that the examinations for different things are becoming more and more difficult, not with regard to the knowledge but in order to make less people fit for it. I happened to ask the captain of a ship if they had to pass an examination. "Yes", he said, "and every year it becomes more difficult". I asked, "What is the reason"? He answered, "We have to read so much and not all of it is useful for our work, it is only to make it difficult. There are so many candidates for this examination that learning is made more difficult for them". If all think, "Life consists in studying something only in order to earn one's bread and butter" then when can they give thought and mind to what their soul is seeking after?

Among those who have a little freedom in life, who have time for seeking after some knowledge, there are many who seek after novelty. They think that to learn means to get to know something they did not know before. There are very few seekers who will find, who will see that in every idea, however simple, when they put their mind to it a revelation rises from it which begins to teach them more and more things they had never known. I have experienced this myself: there was a couplet of a Persian verse I had known for twelve years. I liked it, it was a simple everyday's outward expression, but after twelve years one day a glimpse of inspiration came and the very couplet became a revelation. It seemed as if once there had been a seed and then came from it a seedling which turned into a plant and from that plant sprang fruits and flowers.

The difficulty with socalled truth-seeking people is that when they have a little time to look for truth they are restless. One thing does not satisfy them, so they go from one thing to another and so on. Instead of coming to the real idea, they get into confusion because every new idea confuses them again.

Someone asked an artist, "Can you make a new picture"? "Yes", he said, "I can". He put two horns and two wings on the body of a fish and people said, "How wonderful, this is something no one has ever seen"! Everyone has seen wings on birds and horns on beasts, but there are many souls who need such a novelty. Many are the souls who admire it and few think that - as Solomon has said - there is nothing new under the sun, especially when we come to the domain of wisdom, of knowledge. For one does not arrive at concentration, contemplation or meditation by studying many things and by going from one idea to another.

The next inclination is the love of life. Human beings apart, even little insects escape if you want to touch them. Their life is dear to them. What does this show? It shows that every being wishes to live, however unhappy he may be, however difficult his life may be. Perhaps in the sadness of a moment a person might wish to commit suicide, but if he were in his normal condition he would never think of leaving this world. Not because the world is so dear to him, but because the soul's inclination is to live. As is said in the *Gayan*, "Life lives, death dies". Since life lives, life longs to live, and nobody wishes for one moment that death should ever take him. The great prophets, masters, saints, sages, philosophers, mystics what was their striving? Their striving was to find some remedy to cure man from mortality. But was his mortality his conception or his condition? It is a condition when seen outwardly; in reality it is a conception. The soul wears the physical body as its garb and when it cannot carry it any longer then the purpose of the garb is fulfilled and the soul wishes to leave it; for no one wishes always to carry his heavy coat. Even the king feels more comfortable when the crown is put in the cupboard.

It is the soul's happiness to be free from its physical burden, but it can only be happy when it can be itself. As long as man thinks he is his body, he is a mortal being, only conscious of his mortal existence. What is it? It is a garb. But this, intellectually understood, will not help. The soul must see itself, the soul must realize itself. How to do it? In the Scriptures it is said, "Die before death". What is this dying? This dying is playing death. The mystics have through their life on earth practised playing death; by playing it they were able to see what death is. Then it is not only intellectual knowledge; they actually see that the soul stands independently of this physical garb. Buddha has called it *Jnana*, which means realization. The absence of it is called *Ajnana*, the lack of realization. Buddha was asked to give an example of this, and he told about a person clinging to a branch of a tree in the darkness of the night. Every moment he was trembling for fear of falling and did not know what was there beneath his feet, water, a ditch or a rock. After the break of morning he saw that his feet were not very far from the ground, he had trembled in vain. He said, "Alas, if only I had known". And so it is with every person.

Every thoughtful person, when he thinks of the day when he will have to depart from this earth where he has his friends whom he loves and his treasure, feels very sad that a day should come when he shall have to leave. Not only that, but what makes him most sad is to feel, "Once I am gone I will be nothing", for life does not wish to become death; life wants to live. But this means ignorance and a false conception of life which is gained by the senses, by experience through the senses. The one who has lived with the senses, who has realized life through the senses, things through the senses does not know life. Life can be very different from this.

The third inclination man shows is to gain power in any way whatever. Every person strives throughout life to gain power. The reason is that the soul strives to exist against the invasion of the condition of life, because life's conditions seem to sweep away everything that has no strength. When the leaf has lost its strength it falls from the tree; when the flower has lost its strength it is thrown away. Naturally the soul wishes to keep its strength; therefore every individual seeks for power. But the mistake lies in the fact that however much power a man may have, it is limited. With the increase of power there comes a moment when a person sees that there can be another power greater than the one he possesses. This limitation makes man suffer, he becomes disappointed. Besides, when we look at the power that man possesses, the power of the world, what is it? It did not take a moment for a powerful country like Russia to drop down, or the power of Germany to be crushed. If such enormous powers and strengths, built in hundreds of years, can be crushed in a very short time what is their power? If there is any power it is the hidden power, the almighty power. And by getting in touch with that power one begins to draw from it all the power that is necessary. The secret of all the miracles and phenomena of sages and masters is to be seen in the power that they are able to draw from within. There are fakirs and dervishes who practise jumping into the fire or cutting their body and healing it instantly. But there exists a power even greater than that. Those who can do great things do not show them; small things they show. At the same time there is this power which gives proof that spirit has power over matter. Spirit is buried under matter for some time - and that makes one powerless.

The fourth inclination man shows is to be happy. Man seeks happiness in pleasure, in joy, but these are only shadows of happiness. The real happiness is in the heart of man. But he does not look for it. In order to look for happiness, he seeks leasure. Anything that is passing and anything that results in unhappiness is not happiness. Happiness is the very being of man. Vedantists have called the human soul *Ananda*, happiness. The soul is happy, that is why it seeks happiness. And because the soul cannot find itself it is looking for something that will make it happy. But what it finds can never make it perfectly happy. Sin and virtue, good and bad, right and wrong can be distinguished and determined on this principle: What brings real happiness cannot be bad, it is virtue. What is called right is that which leads to happiness. What is good is good because it gives happiness; and if it does not do so it cannot be good, it cannot be virtue, it cannot be right. Whenever man has found virtue in unhappiness he has been mistaken, whenever he was wrong he has been unhappy, miserable. Happiness is the being of man. Therefore he craves for it.

The fifth inclination mans shows is for peace. It is not rest or comfort or solitude which can give peace. It is an art which must be learned, the art of the mystics by which one comes to experience peace. One may ask, "If it is natural for the soul to experience peace, why must one strive for peace by practice, by meditation, by contemplation"? The answer is that it is natural to experience peace, but life in this world is not natural. Animals and birds all experience peace, but not mankind, for man is the robber of his own peace. He has made his life so artificial that he is as moved away from what is called a natural life. He can never imagine how very far he is removed from what may be called a normal, natural life for mankind to live. It is for this reason that we need the art of discovering peace within us. It is not by making outside conditions better that we shall experience peace. Man has always longed for peace and he has always caused wars. It was not only in ancient times that people sought for wars. At the same time every individual says, "I am seeking for peace". Then where does war come from? It comes because the meaning of peace has not been fully understood. It is therefore that man lives in a continual turmoil, in a restless condition, and in order to seek for peace he seeks war; if this goes on for many more years we shall not have peace, for everybody must seek peace within himself first.

What is peace? Peace is the natural condition of the soul. The soul which has lost its natural condition which practically belongs to it, is restless and longs for peace. The normal condition of mind is tranquillity, and at the same time the mind is anything but tranquil, the soul experiences anything but peace.

The question which arises in the mind of every thoughtful person is, what was the reason, what was the purpose of the creation of this world, of this manifestation? The answer is, to break the monotony. Call it God, call it the Only Being, call it the source and goal of all; being all alone, He wished that there should be something for Him to know. The Hindus say that the creation is the dream of Brahma. One may call it a dream, but that is the main purpose. The Sufis explain it thus: that God, the Lover, wanted to know His nature; and therefore through manifestation the Beloved was created, in order that love might manifest. And when we look at it in this light, then all that we see is the Beloved. As Rumi, the great writer of Persia says, "The Beloved is all in all, the lover only veils Him; the Beloved is all that lives, the lover a dead thing".

Sufis have therefore called God the Beloved, but they have seen the Beloved in all beings. They did not think that God was in heaven, apart, away from all beings. In everything, in all forms they have seen the beauty of God. And in this realization the main purpose and the ultimate purpose of life is fulfilled. As it is said in the old scriptures when God asked Adam, "Who is thy Lord"? he said, "Thou art my Lord". Briefly explained, this means that the purpose of creation was that every soul might recognize his source and goal and surrender to it and attribute to that source and goal all the beauty, wisdom and power and by doing so may perfect himself. As the Bible says, "Be ye perfect as your Father in Heaven is perfect".

2

Every intelligent person sooner or later comes to a stage in his life where he begins to ask himself what purpose there is in life, in being on earth. "Why am I here? What am I to accomplish in life?" No doubt the moment this question has arisen in a person he has taken his first step in the path of wisdom. Before, whatever he did without being conscious of his life's purpose, he remained discontented. Whatever be his occupation, his condition in life, whether he be wise or foolish, learned or illiterate, there is always discontent. He may have success or failure, but that desire "my life's purpose should be accomplished" remains, and unless it is accomplished a person cannot be satisfied. It is because of this that many people who are successful in business, doing very well in their profession, comfortable in their domestic life and well-off in society, yet remain dissatisfied because they do not know the purpose of their life. After knowing the purpose of life one may be handicapped by many things, one may lack means and conditions favourable to go forward, but in spite of all that there is strength of conviction in the knowledge, "I am here for a particular purpose".

There is a story told of the Prophet Muhammad's life. At the time when the Prophet - who was born with his particular purpose in life - felt a kind of restlessness, a dissatisfaction with all things in his life, he thought he had better go into the forest, into the wilderness, into the mountains and sit there alone to get in touch with himself, to find out why there was that yearning which he did not understand. He asked his wife if she would allow him that solitude for which his soul longed, and she agreed. Then he went into the wilderness and sat there for many days. When the vibrations of the physical body and of the mind which are always upset and in turmoil in the midst of the world calmed down, and when his mind became quiet and his spirit was tranquil, when the heart of the Prophet became restful, he began to feel in touch with all of nature there: the space, the sky, the earth. Then it seemed as if everything was talking to the Prophet; the water which was running to him and the clouds, everything was talking to him. He was in communication with the whole world, with the whole of life. And then the word came to the Prophet, "Cry in the name of thy Lord". This meant the lesson of idealism: not only to be in touch with nature, but to idealize the Lord.

At the present time there is the great drawback that when people become very intellectual they lose idealism. If they want to find God they want to find Him in figures. There are many who would rather meditate than worship, than pray. In this way there has always been conflict between the intellectual and the idealist. The Prophet was taught as the first thing to idealize the Lord, and when this ideal he had made became his conception of God, then in that conception God awakened, and the Prophet began to hear the voice saying, "Now you must serve your people. You must awaken in your people the sense of religion, the ideal of God, the desire for spiritual attainment and the wish to live a better life". He then knew that all the prophets who had come before him had always been intended to accomplish the same thing which it was now his turn to accomplish.

Sa'di, the great poet of Persia, says that every soul is born with a certain purpose and the light of that purpose is kindled in that soul. So we are each born in this world to accomplish a certain purpose, and as long as we do not know the purpose we have to accomplish, we remain ignorant of life; comfortably situated or uncomfortably, we remain ignorant of the purpose of our life which is the first knowledge we must receive. It is a great pity that education as it is to-day gives very little attention to this question. Children, youths and grown-ups, all go through life toiling from morning till evening, studying or working and at the same time not knowing what purpose they have to accomplish. Among a thousand persons there may be one exception, but ninehundred and ninety-nine are placed in a situation, whether they desire it or not, where they are working just like a mechanism, a machine put in a place which is made for it, where it must work. Out of a hundred persons ninety-nine are discontented with the work they are doing. Either it is their life's condition that has placed them there, or it is because they have to live and therefore must work, or because they have the idea that they should first gather what they need. By the time they have gathered the means to be able to do something in life the desire of accomplishing it has gone.

In spite of progress it is a great drawback that individuals have no occasion to accomplish something they desire. Many youths and grown-ups never think about it; they think, "We must do that work and finish it", and they have no time to think of the purpose of their particular life. Therefore hundreds and thousands of lives are wasted. In spite of all the money they make their hearts are not satisfied, because it is not the wealth one gains that can give that satisfaction.

When we look at life with a philosopher's view we see that every person is as one note in this symphony of life, that we all make this symphony of life, each contributing the music which is needed in this symphony. But if we do not know our own part in the symphony of life, naturally it is as if one of the four strings on the violin is not tuned, and if it is not tuned the violin cannot give the music which it must produce. So we must each produce that part for which we are born; we must contribute the part that is meant for us by destiny. Be it a crude part, a higher pitch or a lower, it is only by playing that particular part which belongs to us that we shall get satisfaction.

Maybe many people will not think as I do: for instance those who believe in pacifism, those who believe so much in the idea of peace. They will say, "Is it not madness that anybody should make war!" But everything one does, whether it looks better or worse, belongs somewhere in the scheme of life and we have no right to condemn it. If only every individual becomes conscious of the duty for which he is born, that is the principal thing.

Now coming to the question of the purpose of life: there are two purposes, one is a minor purpose, the other a major purpose; one is preliminary and the other is the final purpose of life. The preliminary purpose of life is just like a stepping-stone to the final one. Therefore one must first think about the preliminary purpose of life. For instance, if a person wishes to collect wealth his whole thought is absorbed by it. You can tell him, "No, that is not a good thing. What is wealth after all? Is it not material? Is it not useless? You ought to be devotional, spiritual". But his mind is not there. He cannot be spiritual, his whole thought is concentrated on that wealth, and if he cannot collect the money he wants to have he is unhappy. If you force spirituality upon him, religion, devotion, prayer, these will not help him. Very often in the place of food people give water, and in the place of water they give food. That is not good. Spirituality comes in its time, but the preliminary purpose is what a man will contribute to the world as the first thing before awakening to spiritual perfection.

All the great teachers of humanity have taught this preliminary purpose of life in their religion, whatever teachings they have given. Muhammad, Moses, Christ, Krishna, Buddha in their teachings to their followers had the motive to help them to be able to accomplish that first purpose of life. For instance, when Christ called the fishermen he said, "Come hither, I will make you fishers of men". Christ did not say, "I will make you more spiritual". He wanted them to accomplish the first purpose of life; it was the first step. The next lesson was, "You will become more spiritual". The teachers of spiritual knowledge who look at it in this way consider it their first duty to show a person the first purpose of his life or to help him to accomplish it. When this is done then comes the second purpose.

As to the preliminary purpose of man's life, there are four different ways people can take. One way is the way of material benefit. By his profession, by his occupation, business, industry a person wants to make money. Something is to be said both for and against this ideal. Against it may be said that while working for money one very often loses the right track, thought and consideration; one overlooks the rights of others. And what is to be said for it is that it is after all those who possess wealth who can use wealth for better purposes. Charitable institutions, hospitals, schools, colleges, all are founded by charitable people who have given generously to such organizations. Therefore there is nothing wrong in earning money and in devoting one's time to it as long as the motive is right and good.

Another way is that of duty. One thinks that one has a duty to one's community, town, city or country; one does some social work, one tries to do good to others and considers this one's duty. It may be that one has a duty towards one's parents, one may be looking after one's mother and sacrificing one's life for her or for one's wife and children. There is great merit in this also. No doubt what is against it is that very often the lives of the dutiful ones are spoiled and they have no chance of doing something worthwhile in the world, but if it were not for them the world would be devoid of love and affection. If the wife had no sense of duty towards her husband, nor the neighbour towards his friend, then they would be living like creatures of the lower creation. It is the sense of duty that makes man greater than other beings; that is why we admire it. Heroes who give their lives for their country are not doing a small thing. It is something great when a person gives his life for the sake of duty. Another example is a wife who sacrifices her own ambition to care for her invalid husband. Duty, the sense of duty is a great virtue, and when it is valued and deepened in the heart of man it wakens him to a greater and higher consciousness. People have accomplished great things. The great heroes have lived a life of duty.

The third way one chooses in life is to make the best of the present. It is the point of view of Omar Khayyam who says in his *Rubayat* :

O my Beloved, fill the cup that clears
To-day of past regrets and future fears.
To-morrow? Why, to-morrow I may be
Myself with yesterday's sev'n thousand years !

It is the point of view of the person who says, "If I was a great person in the past, what does it matter? What matters is what I am just now. The past is forgotten, and the future - who knows what will come out of it ! No one knows his future. In order to strengthen myself for the future I have to make the best of this moment and make my life as happy as I can". It is not a bad point of view. It is a philosophical point of view. Those who adhere to it are happy and give happiness to others.

No doubt all these different points of view have a wrong side also, but when we look at their right side there is something in it to appreciate.

People nowadays use a phrase, "He is a jolly good fellow". In songs on different occasions this phrase is used; it expresses what everyone wishes and what he wants to be. It appreciates the tendency of mind which tries to make the present moment happy. It is difficult, very difficult, and not everyone can manage to do it, because life has so many conflicts, so many troubles. One has to face so many difficulties in life that to be able to keep on smiling is not everyone's work. Yes, in order to keep smiling a person must either be foolish and not feel or think about anything, just close his eyes and his heart to the world, or he must be as high as such souls as in the miracle of Christ walking upon the water.

There are some who sink, others who swim and some who walk over the water. Those who are drowned in life's misery are those who cannot come out of it; they are tied down in the depths of life, they cannot get out and are miserable there; they are the ones who sink. Then there are others who are swimming; they are those who want to strive through the conflicting conditions of life in order some day to reach the shore. And there are others who walk upon life. Theirs is the life which is symbolically expressed in the miracle of Christ walking upon the water. It is like living in the world and not being of the world, touching the world and not being touched by it. It needs a clear perception of life, keen intelligence and thorough understanding of life, great courage, strength and bravery.

Therefore I do not mean to say that the man who makes the best of the present moment is the same as the one whom we call happy-go-lucky, who is a simple man. He lives in another world, not aware of life's conditions, not awake to the conflicting influences of life. If he is happy it is not surprising; he is happiness itself. I mean to say that for those who are awakened to life's conditions, who are tender and sensitive to the thoughts and feelings of others, for them it is very difficult to go on living and at the same time to keep smiling. If a person can do it, it is no doubt a great thing.

The fourth way is that of those who think, "What is life on earth after all? Is it not just four days to pass somehow? The day ends, the months and years pass, and so time slips by. One comes to the end of life before one has expected it, and the past becomes only as a dream of one night". Ask a man who has lived a hundred years, "What do you think about life on earth?" he will say, "One night's dream, my child, it is no longer than that".

If this is all there is to it, then those who think about what may come after this life say, "We should think of the hereafter. While we are able to work we must strive in order to make provision for our old age that we may be more comfortable. In the same sense we should work for the hereafter. Life means a short stay, it is nothing but an opportunity to prepare something so that later we shall have the benefit of it". No doubt there will be some who have a proper understanding, while others make too much of it and have a wrong conception of the hereafter. But the wise ones who think, "We must use the time and opportunity which are given to us in this life to prepare for the next one", have accomplished a great deal. It is something to admire.

These are the four different ways people take in order to accomplish the purpose of their lives: gathering wealth, being conscientious in their duty, making the best of every moment of life, and preparing for the future. All these four ways have their good points, and once you know this there is no need to blame anyone for having taken a path different to the one you have taken for the accomplishment of your life's purpose. By understanding this we become tolerant.

Now we come to the ultimate purpose of life which is one and the same. Every person has in the end to accomplish the same purpose of life in whatever way he will. He comes to the purpose either consciously or unconsciously, easily or with difficulty, but he has to accomplish it. That is spiritual attainment. You may ask if a person who never thinks about it, who is so material that he refuses to consider the question, will attain to spiritual realization. The answer is : yes, everyone, consciously or unconsciously, is striving after spiritual attainment. Sometimes he does not take the same way as you do, sometimes his point of view and his method differ. And sometimes one person attains spiritual realization much sooner than another; it may be in a day. And another person may strive his whole life long and not have attained it yet. What determines it? It is the evolution of a particular soul.

There are stories told in India of how a person was awakened to spiritual consciousness after hearing one word from his guru. That one word inspired him instantly to touch the higher consciousness. Then again we hear stories in the East of people who went to the forest, to the mountains, who fasted for days and months, who were hanging by their feet, their head downwards or who stood for years and years. This shows how difficult it is for one person and how easy for another. We make a great mistake when to-day we take every man's evolution to be the same. We say, "They are all human beings". It is not so, there are great differences between people : one is creeping, one is walking, one is running and another is flying. Yet all live under the same sun.

It is the custom in the East that those who begin to seek for a spiritual purpose in their lives look for a spiritual teacher. They do not set forth on the spiritual journey by themselves, because in the East after thousands of years of experience they have found that in order to tread the spiritual path it is necessary to have a leader to whom one can give one's confidence and trust so as to follow him to the end. The difficulty in the West is that there is no doubt a general awakening - everybody wishes to know something about the spiritual path - but people do not stick to one and the same thing. There are many who go to one esoteric school and then to another and so on. In the end they have learned so much that they do not know what is true, which is right and which is wrong. It is just like visiting a restaurant and eating so much that one is not able to digest it. Besides when a person takes in all that is false and true there remains no discrimination between the two. The greatest merit that seekers after truth can show is their confidence and trust in their teacher. It is according to the confidence one gives to the teacher that the heart is able to receive the knowledge which leads one to higher consciousness.

Now one may ask, "How are we to realize the preliminary purpose of our life?" By coming to our natural rhythm. To-day people adopt wrong methods. They go to a clairvoyant and ask him about the purpose of their life. They do not know it themselves. Anybody else must tell them except their own spirit, their own soul which cannot tell them, because they do not tune themselves to that pitch where they can feel intuitively what they live for. If another person says, "You are here to become a carpenter or a lawyer or a barrister", that does not satisfy our need. It is our own spirit that must speak to us. We must be able to quieten our condition, to tune our spirit to the universal consciousness, that we may know the purpose of our life.

Once you know the purpose of your life the best thing is to pursue it in spite of all difficulties. Nothing must discourage you, nothing must keep you back. Once you know, "This is the purpose of my life", then go after it at the sacrifice of everything, for when the sacrifice is great the gain in the end gives a greater power, a greater inspiration. Rise or fall, success or failure do not matter as long as you know the purpose of your life. If ninety-nine times you fail, the hundredth time you will succeed.

The ultimate purpose for which our soul is seeking every moment of our life is our spiritual purpose. Therefore we must always keep on that path and nothing, duty or outside work, must keep us away from that purpose. Through all our striving and struggles in life we must keep steadily on the spiritual path which leads us to the purpose of life. This alone can give us satisfaction.

CHAPTER IV

The Art of Personality

FIRST OF all I shall explain why I call personality art. One may think of art as something inferior to nature, but I do not think so. I think art finishes nature, that in art there is something divine, that God Himself, through man, finishes this beauty which is called art. In other words, art is not only an imitation of nature, art is the improvement upon nature, be it painting, drawing, poetry, or music. But the best of all arts is the art of personality. This must be learned in order to use it in every walk of life. It is not necessary for everyone to become a painter, nor is it necessary to become a musician, to become a drawer or an architect, but it is necessary for everyone to learn the art of personality.

Once a person came to me and said with great contentment and satisfaction, "I was grown and brought up by my parents just like a plant in the forest, growing naturally". I answered, "It is a pity. If your parents wanted you to grow naturally they ought to have kept you in the forest. It is a pity that you are in the midst of the world. The world is made by art; in order to be in the world you ought to know the art of personality".

Very few of us distinguish between individuality and personality. Individuality is that which we have brought with our birth. We are born as a separate entity; that itself makes us individual. But personality is something that is acquired; it has not come with us, it is something we gain. Therefore in ancient times they did not consider anything else as education but learning and practising the art of personality. That was the culture of ancient times; to-day it is passing examinations. As long as a person has a degree he thinks he is safe: now he can go into the world and will get on. But that is not enough.

Besides, examination is becoming every day more difficult. The other day I met a man who had passed a sea-captain's examination. He told me, "Within ten years the examination has become so difficult, and when we look at what we have to study, there are unnecessary books and things we never use in the work we do. And why? In order to make as few captains as possible". I saw a man studying for doctor of philosophy. When I asked him what study he had to do, he said he had taken the mystical line and was reading some German philosophers. "But", said he, "at the same time there are so many books on language and grammar; so every year more and more are added and it is more and more difficult to pass the examination". By the time the student has passed the examinations his nerves are wrecked and he has lost the best time of life. Even when he has passed it is difficult to obtain a job. And if you ask him, "What have you learned?", he says, "I have read so many books". That central theme of culture, that something which alone can be called education - the art of personality - seems to be totally forgotten. That is why generally in the midst of the crowd there is lack of manner, of ideal. An external qualification is different. The inner qualification, the inner culture, these can only be obtained by development of personality.

Coming now to the idea of the use of personality, we see that in a business the salesman has success according to the power of his magnetism. His influence solely depends on his personality, it is his personality that attracts. Whether he goes to other offices or is in a shop, it is his personality which stands out, which gives you the thought of buying or selling or dealing with him, and the lack of it causes you to go away and never come back. A statesman, a politician, a teacher, a sollicitor, a barrister, a lawyer, all require personality. A physician may be a great physician, most qualified, and yet if his personality is not agreeable, if he is rude, crude, unsympathetic, however many patients he may have, his medicines make them feel bad and his personality makes them worse. Very often a doctor with a sympathetic personality, good manner and wisdom can cure a person by a word of consolation before his medicine reaches him. It is the same with a barrister, a lawyer who can dishearten a person in one visit.

When a person has lost courage and hope then naturally there is little hope for healing or success, because there is no power of mind. If the power of mind is strong then a doctor or lawyer can succeed. Therefore in all walks of life what counts is the personality. The one whose personality is against him the world is against him.

There are four categories of personality. The first is likened to a walnut, another is like a grape, yet another like a date and the fourth is like a pomegranate. The date-like personality is soft outside and hard inside. As soon as one puts a date in the mouth and the seed comes between the teeth one has a horror of it. Then there is another personality which is walnut-like. There is a hard shell, hard to penetrate; but when you know the person more it is like breaking the walnut and then comes a nut which is soft. Then there is a pomegranate personality, hard outside and hard inside. The pomegranate is hard, the cover is hard and the seed inside is hard too. And then there is the grape personality, soft outside and soft inside. You will always find these four classes of persons.

The personality of the one who is hard outside is repellent at first, but in the end you will become his friend. Therefore in the beginning he always loses friends. You understand him only when you come to the inner being of this man. The one whose personality is soft outside and hard inside will at once attract people, but they will not stay with him. They will stay for some time and then leave; when they know him they go away from him. The person whose personality is hard outside and hard inside is isolated in this world; this is not the place for him. Everyone will want to keep away from him, and after some time he will find himself in difficulty. The one whose personality is soft outside and soft inside naturally will be the most magnetic. The grape is the most attractive fruit.

But then there are stages in the evolution of man, and at every stage there is a different kind of magnetism. There are four different aspects of magnetism : physical magnetism, intellectual magnetism, sympathetic magnetism which is sometimes called personal magnetism, and spiritual magnetism.

Freshness, newness, good health, cleanliness, harmonious movements, regular form, all these help physical magnetism, but endure for a short time. Next is intellectual magnetism. Keen perception, ready conception, clear vision, wit and the art of expression, all these things create magnetism in man and that is intellectual magnetism. This lasts longer. Then comes the sympathetic or personal magnetism. Everyone who is loving, affectionate, kindly, gentle, who has developed a sympathetic nature, will always attract, without knowing it, because sympathy has the greatest power. This magnetism is lasting. Whatever your relationship may be to a person, if there is no link of sympathy, there is no attraction because there is no magnetism. Often a person may be very qualified, very intellectual, imposing in appearance and at the same time, without feeling, he greatly lacks magnetism. In many cases he fails to succeed because of his lack of sympathy.

The fourth kind of magnetism is spiritual magnetism. It can be recognized, it can be seen in the innocence of a man, in the purity of a person, in the simplicity of a being. One might think a spiritual person is most evolved, but in his appearance the spiritual person is the most simple one, the innocent one. If not ignorant he is less complicated, broader in outlook, keen in perception, with lofty ideals, with raised consciousness, and yet humble and democratic in the true sense of the word.

What many understand to-day as democracy is a wrong ideal. The principle "I am as good as you" is a wrong principle of democracy. It takes away humbleness, gentleness, the high ideal. Besides, to think that camphor and bone and chalk and sugar are all equal because they are white! It is a very sweet idea that everybody is equal, but when you tune the piano so that all notes are the same you need no more music. When a person has a wrong conception of democracy he tunes the whole piano to the same note. Thereby the music of his soul becomes dull. It is more obsession with democracy than democracy itself. Real democracy is raising oneself, raising oneself by appreciating the ideal one meets. In this way one rises to a high ideal; it is to be equal on a higher plane, instead of being ignorant. Pulling a high person down to earth and then to speak of democracy is wrong democracy.

The high ideal is not appreciated by many. They

appreciate the spirit of the revolutionary, of people who make revolutions, mad about one particular idea, regardless of anything else, as has been done in many places. For instance, when a revolt came against the Catholic Church, what happened? It was not only against the church, but against the ideas of the church. Every good thing about it was disregarded too, because the revolt was not only against what was not desirable but against everything to do with it. It is from that time that the sense and depth of religion which existed in the Western world seems to have been diminishing, and diminishing more and more every day. In spite of the many churches there is less ideal : it has been drowned - the ideal which in some form or other is necessary for every soul. It is being drowned because of the revolt against something, regardless of what is good about it.

When a person disregards the God-ideal the tendency is to disregard everything that belongs to it - not only that which is undesirable. But as soon as he goes against it he goes against everything about it. And so it is with the world to-day that the art of personality has been lost in the obsession of democracy, instead of having been realized in a higher spiritual evolution. It is spirituality alone, a spiritual outlook alone, that gives man real democratic feeling: for every person any other is his parent, be he brother, enemy or great friend. According to the spiritual outlook a person sees everyone as himself. He sees his own spirit, his soul reflected in the other one. That is the real democracy: when one sees oneself in a higher and in a lower person. That is the highest ideal of spiritual attainment, and it is that which makes man really democratic.

No doubt, by degrees one rises to such an ideal. The first degree towards this high ideal is gentleness. In the English language therefore the word gentleman is used. Why gentle? Because a gentle man has taken the first step towards accomplishment, towards the art of personality. It is not necessarily because he is rich or in a good position or occupying a high rank. That does not necessarily make a person gentle; with all the position and rank one may have one may not be gentle. Once a person has become thoughtful his first step is to become gentle. As soon as this one thing, thoughtfulness, is developed in a person, he takes his first step towards real evolution.

One might think that everyone tries to be thoughtful. And yet when we consider two things in our daily life, the necessity for silence and that for speech, we may find that we make a thousand mistakes. Often we speak more than we need to speak, or we give our confidence to someone to whom it had just as well not be given, or we spoke to someone while we should not have done so. But it is too late afterwards. Sometimes in a mood of haste, or opposition, or in a distressed condition a person might say something hurtful without meaning it; he says it and then he repents. By saying it he has not gained anything but has lost much. Very often there is no gain in speaking except that it is a pastime or has released a desire to say something. Afterwards this has a result. The heart of man, just like fragile glass, is so delicate that once broken it is very difficult to mend. It is never really mended; every hurt and harm once given is never mended . One can apologize and ask forgiveness, but what is done is done, what is said is said. The word is not lost. Every word we speak remains somewhere: in the heart of one listening, in space, in the ground. It stays and results in something.

Then very often a person makes a habit of being talkative. He loses his own time, his own thought and the time of others, and often it ends in confusion. One accomplishes nothing by useless arguments, and it is amusing to see that often a person argues because he does not know. He goes on arguing because he does not know and wants to learn from the other fellow what he knows. Besides, what you cannot understand by your own wisdom, by intuition within, how can you understand it by discussing, by arguing? It is very often a loss of time.

There are others for whom talking is a kind of fashion, a kind of amusement, a pastime. The end of it is that they exhaust themselves, they become nervous and nothing is gained. Silence sometimes seems very hard to keep, but at the same time it has its great benefit. Very often disagreement is avoided, inharmony is avoided. Silence is good for both the wise and the foolish. For the wise man it is good because it avoids unnecessary talk; he can keep his precious thought within himself well cherished, and so he rears the good thought as a plant. And the foolish one, as long as he keeps silence, covers his stupidity - and so much the better. Silence raises the dignity of the wise one and covers the stupidity of the foolish one.

Besides, the more you evolve the more you will see the different grades of persons, just like the different keys on the piano : one is lower, another is higher. So every person has a different grade of evolution. Then, the higher you evolve, the more you will find that you cannot drive everyone with the same whip; you have to talk to everyone differently. In other words, you have to speak to every person in his own language. If you speak in another language that he does not understand, it is gibberish, he will not understand you. If he is less evolved he will abuse the words you have spoken. If he is highly evolved and you say something which does not reach up to his evolution, it will make you small in his eyes. What is the use ? Besides, you will always find that inharmony is unnecessarily caused by words. There is no need for it. However inharmonious the atmosphere of other persons may be, if you have the word of wisdom you can dispel the clouds of inharmony.

I will tell you an amusing story of my own experience. Once when travelling I met a man of a very dense evolution, a soldier who had always lived in the military and who had his own ideas. A modern educated man in the East understands differently and is sometimes criticized by uncultured men. When we were talking together I happened to say, in order to harmonize, "Well, we are brothers !" He looked at me with great anger and said, "Brothers! How dare you say such a thing!" I said, "I forgot. I am your servant, Sir". He was very pleased. I could have argued which would have created disharmony without reason. The foolishness of the one arose just like fire. I put water on it and extinguished it. It did not make me small - we are all servants of one another - and it pleased and satisfied him.

There is also a story of a wise healer. A woman went to

him and said, "I have a difficult time with my husband. Can you tell me how this can be avoided? Every day there is a quarrel at home". He said, "That is very easy". "I would be so grateful", said she. "I give you these lozenges, these sweets, You keep them in the mouth when your husband comes home and all will be well. They are magnetized sweets". Every day she experienced that there was no quarrel any more. After ten days when the sweets were finished she went back to the healer and said, "I would give you anything if you could give me more sweets. They were wonderful". The teacher said, "My friend, now you must understand after ten days of having the sweets that your husband after toiling all day is nervous, tired and weary when he comes home. Naturally he is not in tune, and you made him worse by talking. By your keeping silent he had nothing to quarrel about and your home became more harmonious. This must teach you a lesson : that silence is the key to harmony".

Many of the sages in the East keep silence either for some hours or perhaps all day long. One might think that it is very difficult, but once a person gets into this habit then it is not so difficult. The atmosphere these sages create and the healing power they show and the harmony they spread all over is so wonderful that sometimes one sage in a whole village has his atmosphere of peace spread all over the village. He is just like a peacemaker of the whole village. Silence has silent power that spreads around and brings about wonderful phenomena. Besides this, everything odd, whether a movement, words, action or thought, takes away magnetism and hinders harmony. Therefore the wise always avoid all that is odd.

In order to understand the law of harmony one must compare it with the harmony in music. Sometimes there are two notes of the same kind which harmonize. And so the wise will harmonize with wise and foolish. The foolish could have harmony with the wicked, for it is the same note with the difference of an octave; there may be this difference of octave, yet it is the same note.

There is another law of harmony: a note may harmonize with another note. It is not the same note but it harmonizes with the other one, it responds to it. It is a question of positive and negative. If one is positive the negative will harmonize; if one is negative then the positive will harmonize. Two persons who are negative will not harmonize, and two persons who are positive will not harmonize.

Then there is a third law to be observed: there may be two notes of music which are quite different, but if you add a third note, they will make a chord. In this way two persons may not harmonize, but a third will create harmony between them. But at the same time when two persons are most harmonious together, a third will perhaps create inharmony.

And there is still another law : the wise will be in harmony with the foolish one, but he will not be in harmony with the semi-wise.

The law of attraction and repulsion depends upon the law of the harmonious blending of persons. If they do not blend harmoniously then there is repulsion; if they blend harmoniously there is attraction. It is just like different colours: used according to the law of harmony they harmonize, and if not they do not harmonize; it is not the colours that are not harmonious, it is the blending. All persons do not harmonize; whether they blend or do not blend is all according to the law of the notes in music. You will always find that this is similar to the law of notes.

In India the Brahmins believed that there are four kinds of persons: the angelic person whom they called *deva*, the human person, *manusha*, the animal person, *pashu* and *rakshasa*, a monstrous person. Whenever there was a marriage people used to consult the Brahmin, who said that he would make the horoscope and would advise them accordingly. But he did not always advise according to the horoscope but to a psychological idea. The Brahmin's intuition was more developed and he had insight into the law of harmony, the law of attraction and repulsion. He knew that if the boy was *rakshasa* and the girl angelic this would not do. Then he said that it was against the horoscope, but most often it was his own conception. The same thing applies to friendship and also in marriage: neither friendship nor marriage lasts if there is a difference of this kind.

In order to develop the art of personality no study nor any particular practice is required. If anything is most necessary it is first to acquire a right attitude of body and of mind: the body working regularly, rightly and steadily, the mind working steadily and rightly. Perhaps you know or have read in books that in the East adepts sit in a certain posture for hours on end in order to get the attitude of the body right, and then we hear that they concentrate for hours on end to get the mind right. When the attitude of body and mind is right, then naturally the personality becomes right. Right living, right thinking develops the personality, but the principal thing is the development of the heart quality. Many people develop intellectually, but the more sympathy is developed in a person, the keener is his perception. He develops in himself an outgoing nature so that his atmosphere embraces all those in his presence.

The spiritual magnetism which finishes the art of personality is gained by meditation, by realization of the oneness of all, by union with God, by having high ideals and high aspiration.

CHAPTER V

The Development of Personality

IT IS as important to think of the development of personality as it is to think of spirituality. A poet of Delhi says,

> If God had created man to offer prayers - there were many angels to do it.
> Man was created to become human.

Many ask, "Is nature not greater than art?" I say, "Art finishes nature". Someone proudly said to me, "I was brought up by my parents just like a plant", and I replied, "It is a pity". When people say that they leave their children alone to take the way they like, that means that while they live in a world which is art, they do not give their children the education in the art which is needed to live in this world. By this I do not mean that one must not be natural. I mean to say that one must develop naturally; if one remains undeveloped one loses a great deal. Even if one were a spiritual person and the personality was not developed, one would be missing a great deal in life. The personality must be developed. Parents think very little about this nowadays. They think that these are old-fashioned ideas; to be new-fashioned is to overlook all these things. But I say that it is not fashion at all. The fashion is to think about it; it is out of fashion not to think about it.

Individuality is one thing and personality is another. A soul is born as an individual, but without a personality. Personality is built after birth. What birth brings is hands and legs and a face, but not personality. Personality is made here on the earth. Very often people have taken the ascetic path, where they have kept away from the world. Because they did not care for the person, for the self, they kept themselves aloof from the crowd, they were allowed to be as they liked. If they want to be like a tree or plant or rock, they may. But when it comes to personality it is a different thing. You either have a manner or you do not have it, either you have an ideal or not, a principle or not, conventionality or not. All these things have or do not have their place.

Manner, conventionality, principle, ideal - all these things have their value in life, and the person who goes about in the world without consideration for them is just like a wild horse let loose in the city; it goes here and there, frightening everybody and causing a lot of harm. That is what an untrained personality is, and what is real culture is a matter of personality - not mathematics, history and grammar. All these different studies are practical studies; the real study is how to develop personality. If you are a business man, a professional man, a man of industry, or of politics, whatever be your occupation in life, you are forced, you are expected to have a personality in every walk of life. It is the personality of the salesman which sells, not always the goods. It is the personality of the doctor which can heal and cure a person much sooner than medicine can cure.

There are four different grades of evolution with four kinds of personality. A person is either born in one of these grades or evolves through it. The first grade, where a person is coarse and crude, thoughtless and ill-mannered, is called *ammarah* in the East. Ill manner is connected with ill luck. Whenever there is thoughtlessness failure is connected with it, whenever there is blindness there is always disaster. This is the first grade of personality.

With a little more evolution comes thoughtful consideration, a civilized manner, refinement, a choice of action. When a person has developed to the third stage, he is still further. It is not only that he is thoughtful, but he is sympathetic, it is not only that he is considerate, but he is kind; it is not only that he has a civilized manner, but he has a natural politeness; not only is he refined, but tender-hearted. And once a person goes still further there is a still greater charm of personality. There is calm, quietness, gentleness, mildness, tolerance, forgiveness, understanding of all beings. When this fourth personality is developed then a person is entitled to go on the spiritual path. Before that he is not entitled to do so.

To-day's thought, the modern thought of recognizing a

wrong equality, has taken away the ideal of the better personality. That respect and appreciation which were due to the higher personality is taken away by this madness of equality. If a person does not have any ideal before him to reach up to, then he has no means of progressing. When everybody thinks, "I am satisfied as I am. I earn so much money every day, is this not sufficient?", they are quite satisfied; there is nothing to reach up to. Besides this there is that ancient thought* that people of olden times held, in spite of all their faults and errors.

There is a little story of a dervish - a free-thinker who walks around in the world looking at it from a spiritual point of view, but not recognized as such; he may be a beggar or a wanderer, insignificant and yet distinguished in his heart. This dervish was standing in the middle of the street, and there came the procession of the king. First came the pages who ran before the procession. They pushed him and said, "Don't you see? The king is coming! Away!" The dervish smiled and said, "That is why". He went forward and stood in the same place. Then came the horse-riders, the body-guards. They said , "Get away, the procession is coming !". The dervish smiled and said, "That is why". Then the courtiers came and saw the dervish standing there. Instead of telling the dervish to get away they moved their horses a little aside, and so the dervish said, "That is why". Then came the king. When the king saw a dervish standing there he greeted first, and the dervish in answer said, "That is why". An intelligent young man asked the dervish, "What is it?" The dervish said, "You can see that is why he is what he is".

This ideal we have wiped from our minds. Where is democracy? The kingliness of greeting the dervish - that is democracy. But when a man who is not evolved pulls the more evolved down to his level - that is wrong democracy; it is going downwards instead of going upwards. If lack of manner and thoughtlessness can be democracy this takes away its real ideal and true spirit. Democracy is the result of aristocracy. When the spirit of aristocracy has evolved enough it becomes democracy. Then a person thinks, "I can be equal to any person in the world; no one is lower than me". But if

* the thought of the ideal of the better personality.

he says, "No person is higher than me" - that is not democracy.

I will tell you about a democratic religious feeling that I found near India, in Burma. The people of Burma are Buddhists of a very wonderful type. Here one finds the one race which for centuries believed that there is no religion inferior to theirs. Imagine this! To-day the one who follows a certain religion looks down upon another religion, but these people say, "Whatever be the religion, Christian, Muslim or Jewish, it is no worse than ours. Perhaps it is better". Each person there had that belief; even to-day they believe this. That is democracy. But when a person says, "No one is better than I am", it is not democracy; it is going downwards, because it means closing one's eyes to what is greater, higher and better. If one cannot appreciate, cannot see it, one cannot rise up to it. We can only rise towards that which we value and that to which we aspire.

If I were to speak before the world to-day about occult power, psychic power, spirit communication, breathing practices, people would be glad to hear. If I say simple things like this it is nothing to them. But suppose one did not develop personality, what then about spirituality? First one must be a person and then spiritual. If one is not a person what use is being spiritual? It is just like going back instead of going forwards. Man is born to fulfil the purpose of his life. He is made to be a man, to prove to be a human being, someone who can be relied upon, whose word can have authority, who uses thought and consideration, to whom you can entrust your secret, who under no conditions will humiliate himself, who will lose his life rather than humble his life, who will not deceive or cheat anybody, who will never go back on his word, who will carry through what once he undertakes. All these qualities make one a human being.

To-day our condition is such that we cannot believe in one another's word; we have to have a stamp on a contract. Why are we in such a condition? Because we are not evolving towards that ideal which ancient people had, that great ideal of personality. We cannot trust one another individually, nations cannot trust each other, because human beings live just in order to live from day to day, to strive and work for the loaf of bread, and that is all. But is that all? To earn a loaf of bread? Then we do not do any better than the dogs and cats, than the beasts in the forest - and they appear better than us. Rich and poor, all are wretched; in every walk of life, be it business or politics, there is nothing but competition between individuals, nations, parties and communities. We have made our life wretched.

What are we here for? If we were only born to meditate and to be spiritual, then we had better live in the forest and in the caves of the mountains; it would not be necessary to be in the world. If we only had to live as animals do - and as generally the worldly person is doing to-day - we would accomplish nothing, besides competing and even wrecking life. Therefore it is the first necessity for those who are seeking after truth to develop the spirit of personality. I remember a quotation: "If one has gold and if one has jewels it is nothing. If one's personality is not valuable, nothing is valuable". Personality can be more valuable than wealth. How strange it is that there is such a large population in this world and so few personalities. It reminds me of that Greek philosopher who went about with a lantern in the daylight. When people asked what he was looking for he said, "For a human being".

The reason is that this subject of developing the personality has been overlooked, it is not that man is not capable of it. He is more capable of it than ever before, because he has much to suffer. This life to-day is a most painful life; it crushes and grinds him - and makes him a better man. If he gave his thought to it he would profit by it and would become a better person. In ancient times people went through different sufferings, trials and tests. We to-day do not need to do this. We have other trials to-day, we do not need to seek them. If only we knew how to profit by them! If not, our suffering is lost. To-day every little skin , every bone, every nail of any animal is used, yet we do not use our own life's experience which is more precious than anything else. If people hear of an oil-well, of a gold-mine they are all interested, but they are not interested in this gold- and silver-mine, this mine of jewels and gems, the cultivation of which will bring all that can be produced. That which is most valuable, people do not think about!

Nevertheless the great gurus and teachers of all times have put great emphasis on this one subject: that for those who wish to seek truth the greatest necessity is to give thought and mind to the development of personality.

Question: What are the forces in nature which cause one's personality to be different from another?

Answer: The law of variety comes from the nature of the manifestation : every current taking a different path becomes different and manifests differently.

Difference is also caused by time and space; every personality is different because of time and space. A person born in one year will be different from a person born in another year; a person born in one month, on one day, will be different from a person born in another month or on another day. And so every moment, every distance makes a difference; their breath is different also.

But there is not only this, the difference of personality is in the direction of one's thought; in which direction one's thought goes makes the personality different. Also action, motive, expression - all these cause difference in personality.

Personality has all elements in it : spirit and mind and thought and body, all together. A self-conscious person is not necessarily a person who develops personality. That sometimes gives a tendency to vanity. The one who develops his personality is he who enriches and ennobles himself in manner, principle and ideal.

Question: Would you please speak of poverty? The rich are always held in scorn.

Answer: There is no need to hold the rich in scorn. Sometimes the rich man is poorer than the poor. Because he has some money in the bank sometimes his condition is much worse than that of the poor man. They are mistaken who say a person is rich because he has money in the bank, or because he has a high rank. Therefore the question whether a person is poor or rich has nothing to do with personality. You can develop personality being rich or poor just the same. Besides, if only you know the secret of it, poverty does not draw you back from spiritual progress, nor does riches, for all that is in the world is for your use. If you have it, so much the better; if you do not have it, it is better still.

Question: How to treat mind, body and feeling in unison, all at once?

Answer: It is by meditation. One should learn meditation: how to tune body with mind and spirit. The one who has tuned these, naturally becomes a personality.

Question: In this material world we need abundance. How to attain it?

Answer: Not only in the material world, in all worlds it is our continual striving. If we have ten we want hundred and thousand, and we do not stop at thousand.

But I do not say that in order to attain a great height one must lose the thought of abundance. You are after all training for perfection; either with open eyes or with closed eyes, it is all striving for perfection. I do not see why we should not desire abundance. Only we should not drown ourselves in it: to live in the world and not to be of the world.

Question: There is a difference between annihilation of the self and development of the personality?

Answer: Very often when I say, "Develop personality", people ask, "What about annihilation?" But you do annihilate. You can only be a spendthrift when you have wealth. You cannot annihilate when you have nothing. So when an individual is not a person he has nothing to annihilate; there must be something first. If a person began in his life with self-effacement he would never become a self. What has he to efface? Effacing comes afterwards. First he must be a self, a real self that is worth being.

Now you may ask, "Should we then be proud to be better than others? Is that not conceit?" My answer is that there are many thorns and few flowers. You must not try to become a flower to feel that you are better than a thorn, but you should only do so for others. There are many thorns. You may suffer much trouble and pain and difficulty for others. If among so many thorns you turn out to be a flower, it is for others. That must be the idea. The idea must not be "I must be a flower to be better than thorns". No, you should be so for the others, for all have many thorns and very few flowers. Besides, to become a flower is not an easy task, but it is easier than anything else to be a thorn, because one is naturally born a thorn. One has to become a flower. It is easy to say, "You have hurt me, insulted me, troubled me, disturbed me", but one never considers for one moment if one has harmed or disturbed someone else. One never thinks about it.

Therefore to develop personality one learns self-effacement. It is an annihilation, continual unconscious annihilation, which turns self from thorn into flower.

CHAPTER VI

The Attitude

IT IS the attitude of mind that very often makes right and wrong and it is the attitude of mind which draws friends to you, or gives you a repulsive influence. Also it is the attitude of mind which brings happiness or unhappiness. It is true that there is an influence of time; there is a certain time in your life which has an influence for good or bad, for rise or fall, for happiness or unhappiness. But at the same time your attitude either controls it or is controlled by it. And if the attitude is controlled by it then the situation at that time conquers you, but if your attitude is in your hands then there is a chance of conquering the situation.

There is a phrase in Hindi, "If your attitude is right, life becomes easy". Most often one's failures, one's unhappiness and one's disagreement with friends come from a wrong attitude. When a person takes up an enterprise, and is not sure about it, does not think about its success or doubts whether he will have success or not, whether the partners in business will help him or not, in that situation his attitude will create all that he imagines. The partners in business will act wrongly towards him, unjustly towards him, and the situation will follow the attitude, because the attitude is the current which is moulding the situation. Therefore, however promising a business, a work may be, if one's attitude is not right, it must go wrong. It cannot come right. It is a hidden influence, and yet a most powerful influence under all circumstances of life.

It is the same with your attitude towards friends. Whether you feel, "This friend will prove to be kind and nice and faithful and constant", or "This friend will change, I doubt if I can hold him, I feel this friend will one day deceive me, I think he will disappoint me one day", then in either case you are creating that, you are inspiring the friend, and the friend, without knowing it, will act in the same way as your attitude was. I repeat again the Hindi saying, "If your attitude is right, life becomes easy". In any enterprise, in anything you wish to accomplish, what is mostly wanted is the attitude.

Besides the attitude about right and wrong, if a person thinks "everything I touch, and everything I do, and every where I look, it is all wrong", certainly, it is wrong, there is no doubt about it. It is his attitude that is wrong, and therefore whatever he does is wrong. It is just like taking a red lantern, and throwing its light upon everything; every object that appears in that light will appear red. You will be frightened and will see there is danger everywhere. But the danger is in your hand. It is the red lantern.

Sometimes a person gets into a wrong attitude out of humbleness. By correcting oneself one grows to correct too much, and then one calls oneself wrong; with every move he makes this person thinks, "I have done something wrong, something dangerous, what a terrible thing I have done". He only has made a turn, nothing else. And it results in a great danger too. When people do not progress in their lives, it is very often because of their attitude towards life. They are enemies to themselves, and they themselves are the hindrance to their progress. They might think this is the reason or that is the reason, lack of money, unkindness of friends, and lack of acquaintances, a thousand things. They may say, "The planets are against me". But what is most against them is themselves; they cannot progress. When one's attitude is analysed and understood, and one has controlled oneself to take any attitude one wishes, then the latent influence in man naturally begins to manifest.

There are three gifts of God given to some in this world. These gifts are greater than jewels and gems and wealth, or anything in the world, and nothing can buy these three gifts of God. They are born with the person, and very often the person does not know it. One gift is the influence to progress, another gift is an influence to attract, and another gift is the influence to make difficult situations easy.

As to the first gift: a soul who has the gift to progress, in other words to flourish, to prosper, to come out, nothing in the world can keep him back. There is a well known story that a poor man, who was selling empty bottles in Bombay, came to a merchant and asked a salary to do this work for him. From the day he came, gradually the merchant became prosperous. So one day he thought, "I have worked for twenty years in this shop, and it is since this young man has come that I have prospered." He did not tell this to the young man, but he thought "Now let us see what will happen". Next he made this young man his partner in his business. From that day his business began to flourish and after six months he was prospering in every way. This young man was the secret, but the merchant did not tell him. In the end, as he had no son, no children, he gave his business to this young man, who in thirty years time became the wealthiest man in the whole country.

I do not mean to say that it is a spiritual influence, and yet it is the influence of spirit, there is no doubt about it. It is not a material influence. Influence cannot be material. An influence that works from within, and works towards a perfection, in whatever form, is a wonderful influence. And there are some who are born with that influence, whether they will act alone, or with someone else, whatever they will do, there is progress, it cannot be helped, whatever they will touch, it flourishes.

The second gift of God is the influence to attract; and that influence is that the person will never be without friends. If he left the whole humanity, and went among lions, tigers, bears and rhinoceroses, they would be his friends. Let him go among the educated, illiterate, wise, foolish, wherever this person will go, he will attract friends. This person will never be alone, in riches, in poverty, in health, in sickness, every time and at all times, he will attract friends from all sides. That person is born with that gift. People have perhaps relations or friends, three or four, or five or six. But when it comes to this influence, every person is his friend, and very often his friends will prove greater than relations. I think of this when some of my collaborators come and tell me that in the particular place where they are asked to work for the Cause, people do not respond to it, that the place is such, the people are such, that they do not respond to it.

Human beings apart, even animals, cats and dogs, wolves, foxes, they will all come to him. It is an influence. Very often, wanderers, dervishes, without one penny, wandering here and there had influence. If they sat in a place somewhere in the desert or in a forest or somewhere in the country, people were attracted to them. May be that six months or one year or two years had passed that only the animals of the country knew him, only the birds recognised him. But then the time comes when human beings begin to come, and they are attracted.

Very often people say that the place has an attraction, beautiful nature, nice mountains, beautiful riverbanks, sea shores, desert, forest, but man has a greater influence than all these places. Imagine, the Prophet Muhammad was born in Mekkah, a place in Hejaz, without anything interesting. For industry there were no gold mines, there were no coal mines, there was no oil. As nature nothing beautiful, nothing to take from that country, nothing interesting. No art, no science, no literature, no interest, there was nothing. There was only one soul who was interesting. The soul who was a magnet, and attracted the people of the whole world. And after the Prophet had passed, then the tomb of the prophet attracted. It attracted millions. In his lifetime thousands were attracted. After his death millions were attracted to this same spot without any interest.

Then there is a third influence, and through this influence, however difficult a situation may be, when a certain person handles it, it becomes easy. It is just like different miners and workmen striking, thousands and millions; everyone tries to make peace, and no one can. And there comes a person with some influence given to him by God. It is not intellect, not knowledge, not psychology, it is influence. With that influence the person goes among them, and makes everything right.

When there is a disagreement between nations, and a person of that influence comes along after or during the war, by merely going there and touching the condition that person will make it easier. If one wanted to develop this influence, one could not develop it. It is God's gift. It is therefore that they call him the man of the day. That man may be in politics, or in industry, or business, whatever form of work, it does not matter. The influence is there. But no doubt, any of these three great gifts may be in a person, and yet if his attitude is not right, it is just like a lantern which is dimly burning. It could burn much better, if the attitude was right.

There are many examples of those who are born with this. There is this gift; anyone who sees it, can find out that they have it. And yet they never use it, they do not know it. The reason is perhaps that their attitude is wrong. A person may have the greatest occasion and chance in his life to progress, to flourish to make things easy, and in spite of this, and in spite of having all the power to make things easy for oneself, one may fail because of one's wrong attitude.

And now one might ask, what do I mean by the right attitude? And how can one have the right attitude? One can have the right attitude by right thinking and by keeping one's mind focused on what is just and true. Wrong always attracts wrong, and right always attracts right. And one might ask, what is right, and what is wrong? What you think at this moment right is right for you, and what you think at this moment wrong, is wrong for you. It does not mean that what another person says is wrong for you *is* wrong, or what another person says is right for you *is* right. The first basis of right and wrong is what you are thinking at this moment. And never for one moment think that those who do wrong, think it to be right. It is not true; they do not believe it. They think it is wrong, and yet they do it, either out of weakness, or out of lack of power, or lack of discrimination, something. They are not clear in their mind. It is not true that there are many who do wrong thinking that it is right. It is not so. They think that it is wrong. But the one who thinks that it is right for him, maybe tomorrow will think that what he thought right, is wrong. Well, then tomorrow it will be wrong, but to-day it is right.

Besides that, all one says, does, and thinks, comes out of an impulse, the one end of it is in one's own mind, and the other end is in the mind of God. And therefore whatever people think about it, whether they think it right or whether they think it wrong, one end of every impulse that comes, is in the heart of God. It is a spark that first manifests in the heart of God, then it manifests outwardly.

One might say, God cannot guide a person wrongly, because God is just and good and perfect. The answer is that God's justice and goodness and perfection cannot be compared with what we consider just and good and right. Maybe that God's justice and what is considered right and perfect by God is considered quite imperfect and unjust by man. Because the horizon of man's vision is very narrow, he cannot think, and he cannot imagine what is meant by God in every action that takes place. In the Qur'an it is said that there is not one atom that moves without the command of God.

Then one might say: "How about perfect and imperfect things, all things wrong and right?" Yes, they are wrong and right, they are perfect and they are imperfect from our point of view. What is our point of view? Our point of view is a narrow, small, a limited point of view, we cannot see further than we can see. We see and hear according to our eyes and ears. Our ears cannot hear more than they can, our eyes cannot see further than they can. So is our limited view. If from our limited view we judge God's right and wrong, it is the greatest pity. Then can one say, "We must let everything be done as it is done, because everything is done from the right point of view of God"? No, as individuals we have a certain responsibility towards ourselves and towards others. And the moment that the idea of just and wrong and right is given to us, we are responsible to act according to that idea. Maybe that tomorrow there will be a greater light put upon us, and that we shall act still better. In this way, by acting every day, we shall prove a better instrument for the work of God.

CHAPTER VII

The Secret of Life

MAN'S ATTITUDE is the secret of life, for upon man's attitude depend success and failure; man's rise and fall both have behind them his attitude. One may ask: what do I mean by the word attitude? Attitude is that impulse which is as a battery behind the mechanism of thought. It is not man's thought which is man's attitude, it is something behind man's thought pushing it outward; and according to the strength of that impulse that thought becomes realized. In the beginning of every work it is the attitude which is the most important factor in bringing it to a successful accomplishment.

There are three different sides connected with this subject that one could observe. One side of it is one's attitude to oneself, whether one treats oneself as a friend or as an enemy, whether one is harmonious with oneself or inharmonious. And remember, it is not everyone who is harmonious with himself and it is not everyone who treats himself as a friend, although a person may think so. For man generally is his own enemy; he does not know it, but he proves it in his doings. We read in the Qur'an, "Verily, man is foolish and cruel". Foolish because he does not even know his own interest, and cruel because he very often proves to be his own enemy. Being cruel to others apart, man begins his cruelty on himself; but that cruelty has as its cause foolishness. That foolishness is imprudence; imprudence means ignorance.

The best explanation of ignorance could be found in the example that Buddha has given. Someone asked Buddha, "What is ignorance, what is it like?" Buddha said, "A person was clinging to a branch of a tree, his feet not touching the ground. All night he was hanging in the air, and was every moment afraid lest he might fall and hurt himself. Neither did he know that there was ground, nor did he think that there was water, he was only afraid for his life, he only felt his own body. And in order to protect his body he was clinging to the tree all night. But with the breaking of the dawn he saw that he was but two feet's distance from the earth. He could have just let go the hold he had upon the little branch if only he had had trust, and faith that the ground was just beneath his feet. And this is the ignorance of man". Man may consider himself very practical and very clever, but at the same time he very often proves to be his own enemy.

As Sa'di, the great writer of Persia, says, "My cleverness, very often thou provest to be my worst enemy". Very often worldly cleverness without that faith and strength and trust is nothing but a delusion. It is the development of trust in the heart, the development of faith that gives man a friendly attitude first to himself. But how must one become one's own friend first? By bringing one's external being into harmony with one's inner being, for when the inner being seeks something and the external being does something else there is inharmony in oneself. When one's good self, one's higher self desires one way and the lower self strikes another way, then there is inharmony. And what is the result of this inharmony? The result is like a volcanic eruption. The two parts of one's own being, which should unite together in love, strike each other, and fire comes out of it.

What causes people to commit suicide? What brings that illness and depression and despair? Very often that conflict which exists within oneself. Therefore the attitude towards oneself must be first friendly, must be first kindly and harmonious. Even in such things as spirituality one must not go against oneself. I remember that when beginning my interest along spiritual lines, I once asked my Teacher, "Murshid, do you approve of my staying up most part of the night for my night vigils?" "Whom could you torture?" said my Murshid, "Yourself. Is God pleased with it?" I had no word to say more. I thought, "If I go further, he will say, 'Do not do it'; then I shall not be free to do or not to do it".

When one thinks about one's dealings with one's friends, with one's relatives, with those with whom one comes into contact in one's everyday life one finds one attracts them or repels them according to one's attitude. Whether a person is in business, in commerce, in whatever walk of life, he either repels or attracts them; and on that depends his success or failure in life. That is the secret of magnetism, whether you consider yourself a friend or an enemy, whether a stranger or a friend. And to the one who considers anyone else a stranger, to him even the friend is a stranger, and the one who considers anyone a friend, to him even a stranger is a friend. If you are afraid of someone who will, you think, harm you, then you inspire that person to harm you; if you distrust someone and think that one day he will deceive you, certainly you will inspire that person to deceive you; but if you have trust even in the enemy, the power of your trust may some day turn him from your enemy into your friend.

In everything one does honesty and dishonesty are reflected in the same way. If the attitude is not right, whatever work one does, whomever one sees, that wrong attitude is reflected upon that person; and that person will answer in the same way. Therefore rightdoing and wrongdoing are not only teachings of a religion, some virtue which is forced upon people; they are a scientific, a logical truth; for with the wrong attitude nothing right can be accomplished, and with the right attitude nothing can go wrong, even if there are difficulties.

I was so interested in the story a young friend of mine told me about his own experience. He was a jeweller, and he used to take jewelry to the houses of people who liked to buy, and in this way he did his business. One day I asked him, "What is the psychology of your business, will you explain?" "Every day more and more I am convinced of spiritual truth while doing this business", he said. "In the business of jewelry there is a very great scope for dishonesty". "But", he said, "the day I take some jewels and people see them, and I honestly tell them the right price, mostly I see that they are sold, and I profit by it. But", he said, "you cannot be always a saint in business. Sometimes I have felt that a person had really seen something which he wanted to take, and seeing this I added a little more to the price, and it seemed that I was robbed of some power, and all day I experienced nothing but the loss of the day". He said, "It is not just once, but many times. I thought it might be an accident, but whenever that temptation robbed that sacred power which is in me, then that day I was not successful in my business".

What does this show us? It shows us that there is hidden in our heart a wonderful power, a power which can be called Divine Power, a sacred power, a power which can be developed and cherished by keeping our attitude right. But then it is not always easy to keep the attitude right. The influence of this life on earth that one has, this life full of changes, full of temptations, full of falsehood, continually upsets that steadiness of attitude. Nevertheless, strength lies in the steadiness of the attitude, and any lack in that steadiness is the cause of every failure and disappointment. There is a Hindustani saying, "A steady attitude secures success".

And when we come to the spiritual region the same rule applies. It is not the prayer that man says, it is not the house where the man prays, it is not the faith that man claims, it is the attitude that counts in religion. It is just like a ticket wanted at the gate of the railway station. They do not ask what position you have, what property you have, what ancestor. No, they ask, "Ticket"; and you are admitted. That ticket is man's attitude. In order to enter the spiritual spheres, that right attitude is needed; and that shortens the path.

Now the question is how to know the right attitude from the wrong. To know the right attitude from the wrong is as easy as seeing all things when the eyes are open. When one does not see the wrong attitude it means that at that time man closes his eyes. His eyes do not fail him, he closes them. He does not want to admit to himself his wrong attitude, he is afraid of his own fault. But he who looks at his own error, face to face, is the man who criticizes himself; he has no time to criticize others. It is that man who will prove to be wise. But mostly human nature seems to be doing quite another thing, everyone seems to be most interested in criticizing another. If one would criticize oneself, there are endless faults; however saintly or sagely, there is no end of faults in a soul. And it is only conscientiousness in correcting one's faults, in making oneself better, in taking hold of that right attitude which is the secret of success, by which one attains to that goal which is the object of every soul.

Now, adding to this subject what the Sufi Movement,

especially the Esoteric School, has to teach in this direction, according to the Sufi point of view there is only one Teacher, and that Teacher is God Himself. No man can teach another. Only what one can do to another is to give one's experience to another to make him successful. For instance, if a person happens to know a road, a way, he can tell another, "That is the road that leads to the place you wish to find". The work of the spiritual teacher is like the work of Cupid. The work of Cupid is to bring two souls together, and so the work of the spiritual teacher is to bring together the soul and God. But what is taught to man who seeks after Truth? Nothing is taught; what is taught is only how he should learn from God. For it is not man who teaches spirituality, it is God alone who teaches it.

And how is it learned? These ears which are open outwardly, when they are closed to the outside and when they are focused on the heart within, then instead of hearing all that comes from the outer life one begins to hear the words within. Therefore, in a few words, if one were to say what is meditation, it is also an attitude, the right attitude to God. Right attitude to God is a direct response to God, for the voice continually comes as an answer to every call. It is the ears of the heart which should be open and focused on that source from where the voice is coming. And once that is done, then the teacher within is found, and there is a continual guidance. And then there only remains the question to what extent one keeps close to that guidance; to that extent one is guided. It is true that one needs no other guidance than the inner guidance, but in order to come nearer to the inner guidance, if there is any guidance to come to that, that is necessary. The Esoteric School therefore presents the way to that inner guidance. Once a person has come into contact with it, then he can go alone through life.

Attitude builds a channel for an effort. A right attitude builds a channel for a right effort. The world is a place of tests and trials. If one does not live in the world, one has no chance of doing good or ill, and if one lived a very spiritual life in the wilderness it is no good to anybody, not even to oneself, because one has not gone through the tests and trials of the world. Neither can one praise the life of a hermit, nor can one condemn it. If he is happy, it is good; each knows his own life. When he is happy he will give happiness to others also. For instance, a man is born to live a hermit's life; living a hermit's life he does not find any torture or trouble. Let him live that life. In it he will prove to be his own friend; in a second step he will be the friend of another. If my friends ask me, "Is the hermit's life ideal?" I will say, "It may be ideal for him, you need not follow it".

Question: Is it not that the life of a hermit is selfish?

Answer: If we observe life, it is very difficult to say who is not selfish. But at the same time the life of a hermit is not a life for which one should make all sacrifices in order to follow it. I would be the last person to recommend it to anyone. But if one followed it for one's own pleasure and found happiness in it, I would not prevent it. For a Sufi maintains from the first to the last the freedom of the soul.

Question: What must be the attitude to come near to that direct communication with God?

Answer: The attitude must be first to seek God within. And after seeking God within, then to see God without. The story of Aladdin that we hear in the "Arabian Nights" is that Aladdin went to find a lantern. That lantern is the divine light within. And that lantern is very difficult to find. Once a person has found that lantern, the next thing to do is to throw its light on the outer life, in order to find God both within and without. For instance, a prayer, a night vigil, a form of worship, all these things are helpful. But if man is not inclined to make peace with his brother, to harmonize with his fellowman, to seek the pleasure of those around him, then he has not performed the religious duties. For what can man give to God who is perfect? His goodness? Man's goodness is very little. His prayers? How many times will he pray? The whole day he spends for himself. If he prays two times, three times, it is nothing. If man can do something in order to please God, it is only to please His creatures, to seek their pleasure. There cannot be a better prayer and a greater religion than being conscientious of the feeling of man, being ready to serve him, to please him in every way, to forgive him, to tolerate him. And if in doing wrong he thinks that he is doing wrong to God, and if in doing right he thinks, "I am doing right to God" his attitude is right.

All mysticism and philosophy and meditation, and everything that we learn and develop, the end and the sum total of the whole thing is to be a better servant to humanity. The whole thing, from the beginning to the end in the spiritual path is a drilling, is a training to be better able to serve mankind. And if one does not do it with that intention, one will find in the end that one has accomplished nothing. There are many who seek wonderworking, or great power to accomplish things. Yes, they may try and gain perhaps this or that power. But the soul will never be satisfied. The true satisfaction of the soul is in an honest and humble service to another. If there were two people before me: one with great power of wonderworking, who could perform phenomena; another, humble and kind, gentle and willing to do all he could for his fellowmen, I would prefer this last man. I would say he is wonderful, and the other is a sage.

The soul of man is goodness itself. If only man begins to love goodness; it is not something that is acquired, it springs from itself.

CHAPTER VIII

What is Wanted in Life

IF SEVERAL people were asked this question each would perhaps make out a list of not less than one thousand things that he wants in life. And at the same time perhaps after writing a thousand things that he wants in life, one rarely knows what one really wants. What one apparently wants in life is not what one really wants, because the nature of outer life is illusion. As soon as one feels, "I want this in life", then the world of illusion answers, "Yes, you want me in life. This is the particular thing you want". Because when a person finds a lack in life he only finds the outer lack, he does not find the lack which is within himself.

If there is anything with which we can all agree: what we lack in life, is to be tuned to the infinite, and to be in rhythm with the finite. In simple words, to be in rhythm with the conditions of life, and to be in tune with the source of our existence. What do I mean by being in rhythm with conditions of life? Our perpetual complaint against all things in life comes from our not being in rhythm with the diverse conditions that we have to face. And then we think that if these conditions will change into something that we wish it will make our life easier. But that is an unexperienced expectation. If we were placed in the same condition that we just desired, we would not say, "We are quite satisfied", we would then find the lack in that condition also. With all the errors and mistakes and shortcomings which we find in our external life we see a perfect hand working behind it all. And if we look at life a little further than we look at it generally, we will certainly find that all the lacks and errors and mistakes and faults add up to something, making life as complete as the wise hands which are working behind it wish it to be.

There is a Persian saying "the Gardener of this garden of the world knows best which plant to rear and which to remove". One might say that it is going too much towards what they call fatality. No, I do not wish to take you further into fatality, I want to bring you into the sphere of action. What I wanted to do was to touch the boundaries of fatality, and now to come to the sphere of action. No doubt, there is a great deal man can do to improve his life's condition, if only he does not lose patience before a desirable condition is brought about, if his courage has not been exhausted, and if his hope is kept alive.

And now the question is: how can one become at one with the rhythm of life, in other words, with the conditions of life? A condition of life and one's own desire, these are usually two conflicting things. If the desire gives in to the condition then the condition gets the upper hand. And if the condition is mastered then no doubt, desire has the upper hand. But the condition is not always mastered by a conflict, by a struggle. A precaution is always needed in fighting with a condition in life. If by peace harmony can be established it is better to avoid battling. If one can harmonize with a condition in life without struggling it is better than to harmonize with it by struggling. Do not be surprised if I say that those who complain most about life and those who are very disappointed and very much troubled with life, are the ones who struggle most with life's conditions. Therefore in becoming at one with the conditions of life one need not always use a weapon; one must try to harmonize with a particular condition of life. And the great heroes who really fought through life and gained life's victory in the real sense of the word, were not those who fought conditions. It is they who made peace with the conditions. The secret in the life of the great saints, in whatever part of the world they were, was that they met conditions, whether favourable or unfavourable, with a view to harmonizing, with a view to becoming at one with the rhythm of life.

A desire is sometimes our friend, and sometimes our own enemy. Sometimes in unfavourable conditions desire becomes agitated, desire loses its patience, and wishes to break the conditions; and instead of breaking the conditions it breaks itself. The great souls extended their hand first to their worst enemy; because the one who makes his enemy his friend will make his friend his own self. A condition as bitter as poison will be turned into nectar if you will get into rhythm with that condition, if you will understand that condition, if you will sustain that condition with patience, with courage, with hope. When there is a favourable condition, a person is very often afraid that this might pass. But when there is an adverse condition one does not generally say that it will pass. One thinks that it will last forever. Where does this come from? It comes from fear of the condition. It comes from the agitation, from the desire to get out of it; thus one even loses hope, the only source that keeps us alive. When we see the nature of life, that from morning till evening everything in life changes, why should we not hope that an unfavourable condition will change, and a favourable condition will come? A person gets into a habit of expecting the worst. A person who has had some bad experiences in life always thinks, "Whatever will come to me cannot be good. Nothing good will come to me, because I have gone through bad circumstances". He thinks, "Anybody else can have a better time than me, because I am born under that dreadful star; that unfortunate condition will be with me throughout my life".

Just as there are many imaginative and intelligent people who day after day read newspapers, and draw from them the conclusion that there will be a war. Every little struggle they read about, the only idea it gives them is that the world must go to pieces. There are other people, interested in astrology, who have gone further than ordinary astrology, who are expecting the end of the world, year after year, month after month. This gives people a topic to speak about at the dinner table, and at the same time it gives a shock to those who wish to live a little longer, beyond the end of the world. Many such warnings of the world's destruction have passed, but the prophecy and expectation still remain, and will continue. The best thing is to go through every condition that life presents with patience, with understanding, with open eyes, and one should try to rise above it with every little effort one can make.

Coming to the other side of the subject: how can one be in tune with the infinite? The nature of being in tune with the infinite is this: comparing our souls to a string of an instrument. It is tied at both sides; one to the infinite, and the other to the finite. When a person is conscious all the time of the finite, then he is tuned to the finite. And the one who is conscious of the infinite is tuned to the infinite. Being in tune with the former makes us limited, weak, hopeless, and powerless. By being in tune with the infinite we obtain that power and that strength to pull us through life under all adverse conditions. The work that the Sufi considers as his sacred work, has nothing to do with any particular creed, nor has it to do with any particular religion. It is only this simple thing: to be in rhythm with life's conditions, and to be in tune with the infinite.

Question: How can we arrive at being in tune with life?

Answer: Instead of being frightened by life's conditions, meet them and observe them keenly and then try to harmonize for a time with these conditions; and the next effort is to rise above them, if they are adverse.

For instance, a young Arab was sleeping in the field, and a snake happened to crawl over his palm, and he in his sleep did not know and held the snake with all his might. So the serpent was helpless and could not bite, but as soon as he awoke from his sleep the young man was frightened at the sight of the snake in his hand, and he let it go at once. As soon as the serpent was out of his hand, the first thing it did was to bite. One can manage a condition better when it is in one's hand than when the condition has been lost; then the situation is out of one's hand. For instance, if a person is cross, if a person has lost his temper, the natural tendency is to pay him back in the same coin. The outcome is a struggle. It culminates in disappointment. But when the person is cross and has lost his temper, he is the weak one, and that is the time that you can manage him. Then the situation is in your hand, you have not lost your temper. That person is weak, you are strong.

Question: If one wishes to improve one's position in life, and everything depends upon other people, does one not run the risk of creating by that same action a worse situation for those who are near one, particularly for those for whom one has an affection? For instance: someone wishes to become very rich, and if he becomes extremely rich and everyone is in a sort of slavery towards him, this slavery will be heavy to him and his surroundings.

Answer: Our lives in this world are dependent upon one another. And wealth, however powerful it seems to be, in the end of the examination is not so powerful as it appears to be. Its power is limited, and it does not always take away that dependence that a person has upon another. The whole thing is to meet one's condition with understanding, not with complete resignation, "I shall not improve my condition". No, the first thing is to meet the condition as it is and the second thing is to better the condition. The more one can avoid conflict the better it is. For instance, you are travelling through the wilderness, and there you meet a robber who says, "I am going to take your life or you give me your purse". I say that in order to meet this situation the first thing you could do is to reason with him, and get out of the danger without having to kill him. What I mean is that we cannot always avoid conflict, and we must not turn our back if it comes to a conflict. After all life is a struggle, and we must be ready to struggle. Only, struggle must not make us drunk so that we lose the way of peace, which is the first way to consider. We must not be like a boxer who is always looking for another person to box with him: "I would like to box, it is my great pleasure".

Question: What is the other way?

Answer: The way of tuning oneself to the infinite. It is by the way of silence, by the way of meditation, by the way of thinking of something which is beyond and above all things of this mortal world, by giving some moments of our life to that which is the source and goal of all of us, in the thought of coming to be in tune with that source. In that source alone is the secret of our happiness and peace.[1]

CHAPTER IX

Life, a Continual Battle

1

NO ONE in this world, whatever be his position or experience, will deny that life means a continual battle. Therefore one's success, failure, happiness or unhappiness mostly depend upon one's knowledge about this battle. Whatever be one's occupation, whatever be one's knowledge, if one lacks the knowledge of the battle of life, one lacks the main knowledge which is most important in life.

Now the question arises what this knowledge of life's battle contains. It contains the knowledge of warfare: how to battle and how to make peace. Human nature usually or very often makes the mistake of taking one side, either the side of war or the side of peace. If you study the history of nations and races you will find that it is this mistake which has caused their failure. There have been times when nations and races developed in their character the knowledge of peace - for instance people such as the Hindus of the most ancient civilization - but it could not bring the satisfaction which was necessary, for the reason that one side of human nature was neglected and not understood.

In this present age it seems that the knowledge of battle has developed, but on the other hand the knowledge of peace is absent. The full knowledge of warfare is both the knowledge of battle and the knowledge of peace. This can be learned according to the idea of the mystics by battling with oneself and by bringing about peace with one's own soul. The life of an individual being is not much different from the life of the world. An individual person's home is not different from the world. An individual's body and mind and spirit make the whole universe. An individual life can fill the gap between the dawn of creation and the last day. Man does not realize how important is his own life, his self, and it is the study of his own life and his self which is of the greatest importance.

A healthy person has waiting at his door several illnesses, several diseases, waiting for an opportunity to attack him. A person with wealth has many waiting at his door for the occasion to take from him what he possesses. When good is said about a person, how many there are awaiting a chance, a moment when something bad may be said about him! A person who has power or position, how many are not waiting for the opportunity to pull him down and to see him slide down from the place where he stands! What does it show? Often one may ask why this is so. You may give a thousand reasons and you cannot give one proper reason. The best explanation you can give is that life is one continual battle.

The process of creation began like this. According to science light comes from friction: one power against another power, fighting. By two different forces striking each other comes an effect, and that effect, really speaking, may be called life. In this lies the secret of both love and hate. One sees therefore in the animal creation that the instinct and the first tendency of animals is to fight one another. This tendency becomes modified, and it is its modification and its reduced force that produces in animals what we call virtues. It is said in the Qur'an that the world was created out of darkness, and so one can see that wisdom comes out of ignorance.

The best knowledge is not only the knowledge of all that is good and beautiful, all that is harmonious and peaceful, but knowledge of the causes that are behind all the conflicts and battles one has to face in life. The reason why man generally lacks this knowledge is because, when facing a battle, he wants to fight instead of wanting to find the cause behind it. The one who goes into life's battle without having attained the knowledge of warfare loses in the end; but the one who learns this warfare of life, who first learns its reason, its cause - he becomes more capable of fighting the battle of his life.

It was pointing to this secret that Christ said, "Resist not evil". This means that, if you resist or fight your battle every time something appears to you wrong or unjust in another person, you will always lose your power. The competent general is not the one who always attacks, the competent general is he who stands firm in defence. His success is more secure than that of the one who continually attacks. Very often in everyday life one sees that by losing one's temper with someone who has already lost his, one does not gain anything, one only takes the path of stupidity. The one who has enough self-control to stand firm when another person is in a temper, wins the battle in the end. It is not the one who has spoken a hundred words aloud who has won, it is perhaps the one who has spoken one word.

Now for this battle in life the first thing that is necessary is to keep the army in order. What is this army? It is one's nervous power. Whatever be one's occupation, profession, or walk in life, if one has no control over one's own nerves one will be unable to control one's walk in life. To-day people study political economy and different other kinds of economics, but the most essential economy is economizing the forces which make one healthy and strong through life.

This army must be drilled and made to work at command, and one will find the proof of this when one can sleep at will, when one can rest and eat and work at will. Then this army is really at one's command.

There are officers in this army and these are the faculties of the mind. These faculties are five: the faculty of retaining thought, the faculty of thinking, the faculty of feeling, the faculty of reasoning and judging, and that faculty in man which is the principal one, the feeling of "I" or the ego. Even in a body with strong nerves, when these five faculties which work as generals of the army are not in working order, if they are not clear, one cannot expect success in life's warfare. And there is much to study and to practise in the art of training these generals of the army in one's own body.

Even with an army and with competent generals one must have the knowledge of what one is battling against, for often a man is fighting against his own real interest. During the battle there is intoxication: he is battling and does not know where he is going. But at the end of the battle, even if he is victorious, he finds in his victory his loss.

To-day there seems to be much seeking and enthusiasm everywhere. A new interest seems to be aroused in humanity to understand life and truth more. A very large number of people are looking for the best way of gaining power in order to battle through life, and a small number are looking for some way of bringing peace to themselves and to others. But both of these in their pursuit lack that balance which can only be brought about by understanding, by studying and by practising the knowledge of both war and peace together. Without knowing about war one cannot thoroughly know about peace, without understanding peace one cannot thoroughly know about war.

What is necessary at present is the study of life in general, and in this study the knowledge of such questions as the purpose of life, what is really beneficial in life, what is nature and where is the goal? It is no use trying to practise something before studying it. What does world-wise mean? It means expert in this warfare of life, knowing how to battle, how to make peace, why to battle and what aim is accomplished by peace.

This must be understood: battle with oneself is peace and battle with another is war. As long as a person has not practised this with himself he cannot very well be competent to battle with others.

When one finds out the secret hidden in this whole creation, it is perhaps only that out of one life - the origin and the goal of all - this life of variety has come. The nature of that life from which this world of variety has come is peace, and the nature of this life of variety is war. Therefore we can neither be without war nor can we be without peace, and to say that war in life must end - one may say it but it has no meaning. One might just as well say that the world of variety should not exist. Where there is plurality there must be conflict, and although conflict seems tragedy, the true tragedy is ignorance. Therefore instead of wanting to end the battle of life or instead of opposing peace, one should acquire the knowledge of life and attain to that wisdom which is the purpose of life.

2*

In this continual battle of life the one who stands firm through it all comes out victorious in the end. But if with all power and understanding one gives up through lack of hope and courage, one has failed.

What brings bad luck in this life, in this battle? A pessimistic attitude. And what helps to conquer in the battle of life, however difficult? An optimistic attitude. There are some in this world who look at life with a pessimistic view thinking that it is clever to see the dark side of things. So far as it makes one see also the difficult side it is beneficial, but the psychological law is such that once the spirit is impressed with the difficulty of a situation it loses hope and courage. Once a person asked me if I looked at life with a pessimistic attitude or if I was an optimist. I said, "An optimist with open eyes". Optimism is good as long as the eyes are open, but once the eyes are closed optimism can be dangerous.

In this battle drill is necessary, and that drill is control of one's physical organs and control of the faculties of the mind, for the one who is not prepared for this battle, however courageous and optimistic he may be, cannot succeed.

Another thing is to know something about this warfare: to know to retreat and to advance. If one does not know how to retreat and always wishes to advance, one will always be in danger and will become a victim in life's battle. Many people who in the intoxication of life's battle go on battling, go on fighting, in the end will meet with failure. People, young, strong and hopeful in life, who have had few difficulties, think of nothing but battling against all that stands before them. They do not know that it is not always wise to advance. What is necessary is first to fortify the position and then to advance. We can see the same thing in friendship, in business, in our profession: a person who does not understand the secret of the law of warfare cannot succeed.

Besides this, one must protect one's own from all sides. Very often what a person does in the intoxication of the battle is to go forward and forward without protecting what belongs to him. How many people in the courts of law go on

* This lecture was given to a smaller audience and took place a week after the preceding one.

spending a lot of money for perhaps a very little thing! In the end their loss is greater than their success. Again, how many in this world will perhaps lose more than they gain only because of their fancy or pride! There are times when one must give in, there are times when one must let things go a little bit, and there are times when one must hold fast the reins of life. There are moments when one must be persistent and there are moments when one must be easy.

Life is such an intoxication that although everybody thinks he is working for his interest, yet you will find hardly one among a thousand who really does so. The reason is that people become so absorbed in what they are trying to get that they become intoxicated by it and, so to speak, lose the track that leads to real success. Very often in order to get one particular benefit people sacrifice many other benefits because they do not think of them. The thing to do is to look all around, not only in one direction. It is easy to be powerful, it is easy to be good, but it is most difficult to be wise - and it is the wise one who is truly victorious in life. The success of those who have power and of those who perhaps have goodness has its limitation. If I were to tell you how many people bring about their failure themselves you would be surprised. There is hardly one person in a hundred who really works for his real benefit, although everyone thinks that he is working for it, but most people do not realize where their real interest is.

The nature of life is illusive. Under a gain a loss is hidden, under a loss a gain is hidden. Under this illusion it is first very difficult for man to realize what is really good for him. Even of a wise person much of his wisdom is demanded by life and its battle: you cannot be gentle enough, you cannot be sufficiently kind. The more you give to life, the more life asks of you - there again is a battle. No doubt, the gain of the wise one is greater in the end although he has many apparent losses. Where an ordinary person will not give in, the wise will give in a thousand times. This shows that the success of the wise is very often hidden in apparent failure, but when one compares this success with that of an ordinary person the success of the wise is much greater.

In this battle a battery is needed, and that battery is the power of the will. In this battle of life arms are needed, and these arms are the thoughts and actions which work psychologically towards one's success. For instance, there is a person who says to himself every morning, "Everybody is against me, nobody likes me, everything is wrong, everywhere is injustice, all is failure, for me there is no hope". When he goes out he takes that influence with him. Before he arrives anywhere, at his business, his profession, or whatever he does, he has sent his influence before him and he meets with all wrongs and failures, nothing seems worthwhile, he finds coldness everywhere.

There is another person who knows what human nature is, who knows that one has to meet with selfishness and inconsideration everywhere. But what does he think of all this? He thinks it is a lot of drunken people, all falling upon each other, fighting each other, offending each other, and naturally a sober person with some thought will not trouble with those who are drunk. He will help them, he will not take seriously what they say or do. Therefore naturally in this world of drunkenness a person who is drunk has a greater fight than he who is sober, for the latter will always avoid it. He will tolerate, he will give in, he will understand, for he knows that these people are drunk, he cannot expect better from them.

Besides this, the wise one knows a secret of human nature, and that secret is that it is imitative. For instance, a proud person will always revive the tendency of pride in his surroundings; before a humble person even a proud one will become humble, because the humble one vivifies the humbleness in that person. So you can see that in this life's battle you can fight the proud with pride, and you can fight pride with humility and sometimes gain.

Seen from a wise point of view human nature is childish. If one stands in the crowd and looks at it as a spectator, one will see a lot of children playing together. They are playing and they are fighting and they are snatching things from each other's hands; they are bothering about very unimportant things. One finds their thoughts small and of little importance and so is their pursuit through life. And the reason for life's battle is often very small when it is looked at in the light of wisdom. This shows that the knowledge of life does not always come by battling; it comes by throwing light upon it. He is not a warrior who becomes impatient in one moment, who loses his temper in one moment, who has no control over his impulses, who is ready to give up hope and courage. The true warrior is he who can endure, who has a great capacity to tolerate, who has depth enough in his heart to assimilate all things, whose mind reaches far enough to understand all things, whose every desire is to understand others and to make them understand.

Sensitiveness is no doubt a human development, but if it is not used rightly it has a great many disadvantages. A sensitive person can lose courage and hope much sooner than another. A sensitive person can make friends quickly, and quickly runs away from his friends. A sensitive person is ready to take offense, ready to take all things that come to him, and life can become unbearable for him. Yet if a person is not sensitive he is not fully living. Therefore the idea is to be sensitive and not to abuse it. Abusing sensitiveness is yielding to every impression and every impulse that attacks one. There must be a balance between sensitiveness and will-power. Will-power must enable one to endure all influences, all conditions, all attacks that one meets with from morning till evening, and sensitiveness must enable one to feel life, to appreciate it, and to live in the beauty of life.

What is most advisable in life is to be sensitive enough to feel life and its beauty, to appreciate it, but at the same time to consider that your soul is divine and that all else is foreign to it. All the things that belong to the earth are foreign to your soul; they must not touch your soul. All things come before the eyes and when they are before them, they come into the eyes; when they are gone the eyes are clear. Therefore your mind must retain nothing but beauty, all that is beautiful, for you can search for God in His beauty. All else must be forgotten. By practising this every day, forgetting all that is disagreeble and ugly, and remembering only all that is beautiful and gives happiness, you will attract to yourself all happiness that is in store.

Question: By the cultivation of will-power does one not sometimes persuade oneself wrongly? One is not infallible!

Answer: Yes, there is that danger, but there is danger in everything. There is even danger in being healthy, but that does not mean that one must be ill.

What I have said is that we must acquire balance between power and wisdom. If power is working without the light of wisdom behind it, it will always fail because power will prove to be blind in the end. But what is the use of a wise person without the use of his hands and feet, a person who has no power of action, no power of thought? This shows that wisdom directs - but by power one accomplishes. Therefore for the battle of life both are necessary.

Question: Does not sensitiveness bring us surprises which come upon us too fast to avoid the evil they may cause?

Answer: What is sensitiveness? Sensitiveness is life itself, and as life has its good and evil so sensitiveness has its good and evil. And if one expects to have all life's experiences, so all these experiences must come from sensitiveness. However, sensitiveness must be kept in order, if one wants to know and understand and appreciate all that is beautiful, and does not want to attract all the depression, sorrow, sadness and woes of the earth.

Once a person has become so sensitive as to be offended by everybody and to feel that everybody is against him, trying to wrong him, then he is abusing his sensitiveness. He must be wise together with being sensitive. Before being sensitive he must realize that in this world he is among children, among drunken people, and as he would take the actions of children and of the drunk, so he must take all that comes to him from all sides. Then sensitiveness can be beneficial. If together with sensitiveness one has not developed will-power, it is certainly dangerous. No doubt spirituality is seen in a person who is sensitive to others. No one can develop spiritually without being sensitive.

Question: How can we distinguish between the wisdom of the warrior and his lack of courage in the battle of life?

Answer: Everything is distinguished by its result. There is a very well-known saying in English, "All is well that ends well". If at the end of the battle the one who was apparently defeated has really conquered, of course that shows wisdom, not lack of courage. Very often apparent courage leads to nothing but disappointment in the end. Bravery is one thing, knowledge of warfare another. Brave is brave, but not always victorious. The one who is victorious knows and understands; he knows the law of life.

Question: In what measure can free will counteract a condition of *karma* such as ill health?

Answer: I must tell you that the difference between human and divine is the difference between two ends of the same line. One point represents limitation, the other point the unlimited. One point represents imperfection, the other perfection. If we take all human beings of this world, they do not all stand near the same point, they fill the gap between the one extreme and the other. Just now the world is going through a phase of what they call equality, where the nobility of the soul, even its divinity, is ignored. The whole arrangement of life is like this: when there is one vote for everybody in the state then it is the same at home and everywhere. But when we come to understand the spiritual life of things, we shall always realize that just like on the piano all notes are not the same, so all souls are not the same.

Man starts his life as a mechanism, a machine, and he can develop to a state where he is the engineer. The restriction of *karma* is for the machine. Every soul has to be a machine first in order to become an engineer later. A man does not turn at once into an engineer, but he gradually changes from machine into engineer. Therefore the influence of *karma* is not the same on every soul. At the same time one must realize that it is the ignorance of the divine part of one's soul that keeps one away from God - not only from God, but from the birthright of one's power. When one becomes conscious of the divine power, then one rises above being a machine, then one becomes the engineer.

CHAPTER X

The Struggle of Life

1

LIFE IN the world is one continual struggle, and the one who does not know the struggle of life is either an immature soul or a soul who has risen above the life of this world. The object of the human being in this world is to attain to the perfection of humanity, and therefore it is necessary that man must go through what we call the struggle of life.

There are two different attitudes that people show while going through this struggle of life. One struggles along bravely, the other becomes disappointed, heart-broken, before arriving at his destination. No sooner does man give up the courage to go through the struggle of life than the burden of the whole world falls upon his head. But he who goes along struggling through life he alone makes his way. The one whose patience is exhausted, the one who has fallen in this struggle, is trodden upon by those who walk through life. Even bravery and courage are not sufficient to go through the struggle of life, something else must be studied and understood: one must study the nature of life, one must understand the psychology of this struggle.

In order to understand this struggle one must see how many sides there are to it. There are three sides: struggle with oneself, struggle with others and struggle with circumstances. One person is perhaps capable of struggling with himself, but that is not sufficient. Another person is able to struggle with others, but that is not sufficient either. A third person answers the demands of circumstances, but even that is not sufficient. All these three sides must be studied and known, and one must be able to manage the struggle in all three directions.

Now the question is: where should we begin and where should we end? Generally a person starts by struggling with others; he struggles along all his life and it never comes to an end. If the person is wise he struggles with conditions and perhaps he improves things a little. But the one who first struggles with himself is the wisest, for once he has struggled with himself, which is the most difficult struggle, the other struggles will become easy for him. Struggling with oneself is like singing without accompaniment. Struggling with others is the definition of war; struggling with oneself is the definition of peace. In the beginning and in its outer appearance it might seem cruel to have to struggle with oneself, especially when one is in the right, but the one who has reached deeper into life will find that the struggle with oneself is the most profitable in the end.

Now coming to the question of the nature of the struggle with oneself: this has three aspects. The first is to make our thought, speech and action answer the demand of our ideal, while at the same time giving expression to all the impulses and desires which are there as our natural being. The next aspect of the struggle with oneself is to fit in with others, with their various ideas, their various demands. To fit in with them we have to make ourselves as narrow and as wide as their accommodation demands us to be - which is a delicate matter, difficult for everybody to comprehend and to practise. The third aspect of the struggle with oneself is to give accommodation - big or small as the demand may be - to others in our own life, in our own heart.

When we consider the question of the struggle with others, there are also three things to think about. The first is how to control and to govern people and activities which happen to be our duty, our responsibility. Another aspect is to what extent to allow ourselves to be used by others under different situations and positions in life, where do we set the limit beyond which we should not allow others to make use of our time, our energy, our work, our patience, and where to draw the line. And the third aspect is to fit in with the different conceptions that other personalities have who are at various stages of evolution.

As to the third aspect of the struggle, that with conditions, there are conditions which can be changed and there are conditions which cannot be changed, before which one is helpless. Again there are conditions that can be changed and yet one does not find in oneself the capability, the power and the means to change them. If one studies these questions of life, thinks about them and meditates for inspiration and light to fall upon them, that one may understand how to struggle through life, one certainly will find help. Certainly one can arrive at a state where one would find life easier.

In addition to what I have said I should like to say how a Sufi would look at this and how a Sufi would set to work. The Sufi looks at the struggle as unavoidable, as a struggle which must be gone through. He sees from his mystical point of view that the more he takes notice of the struggle the more the struggle will expand, and the less he makes of it the better he will be able to pass through it. When he looks at the world, what does he see? He sees everybody, hand on forehead, looking only at his own struggle which is as big as his own palm. He thinks, "Shall I also sit like this looking at my own struggle? That will not answer the question". His work therefore is to engage in the struggle of others, to console them, to strengthen them, to give them a hand. By doing so he makes less of his own struggle; this frees him to go forward.

Now the question is: how does the Sufi struggle? He struggles with power, with understanding, with open eyes and with patience. He does not look at loss; what is lost is lost. He does not think of the pain of yesterday; yesterday is gone for him. Yes, if there is a pleasant remembrance he keeps it before him, for it is helpful on his way. He takes both admiration and hatred coming from around him with smiles; he only thinks that both form a rhythm within the rhythm of a certain time of music. There is 'one and two', a strong accent and a weak. Praise cannot be without blame, nor can blame be without praise.

He does not allow his power to lead him blindfold, but he keeps the torch of wisdom before him, because he believes that the present is the re-echo of the past and that the future will be the reflection of the present. It will not do to think only of the moment, but one should think where it comes from and where it will go. Every thought that comes to his mind, every impulse, every word he speaks is to him like a seed - a seed which falls in this soil of life and takes root. In this way he finds that nothing is lost; every little good deed, every little act of kindness, of love done to anybody will some day rise as a plant and bear fruit.

The Sufi does not consider life any different from business, but he sees how real business can best be achieved. The symbol of the mystics of China was that they held a branch with fruit in their hand. What does it mean? It means that the purpose of life is to arrive at that stage where every moment becomes fruitful. And what does fruitful mean? Does it mean bearing fruit for oneself? No, trees do not bear fruit for themselves but for others. True profit is not that which one makes for oneself; true profit is that which one makes for others. The attainment of all one wants to attain, be it earthly or heavenly, what is the result of it all? The result is only this: that one can place before others all one has attained, all one has acquired whether earthly or heavenly. *Propkar*, which in the language of the Vedanta means working for the benefit of others, is the only fruit of life.

2

As long as the infant is innocent he is happy, he knows nothing of the struggle of life. I remember these lines written by the late Nizam of Hyderabad, a great mystic:

> What were those days when my eyes had not seen sorrow,
> my heart had no desire, and life no misery!

This is the first stage. From this we come to the maturity of the intelligence. Then a person sees that no one can be trusted, not the friend nor the relation; none can stand the time of trial, all are false, none is true. At first he thinks that this is all directed especially against him. A dervish once wrote these lines on the wall of the mosque where he had spent the night:

> The world believes in the ideal of God,
> yet not knowing whether He is friend or foe.
> The waves of the sea go up and down.
> The atom thinks that they rise and fall for it.

It thinks, "The wave raises me, it is favourable to me; the wave falls, it is unfavourable to me". A man thinks, "My friend is favourable or he is unfavourable to me", but then he realizes that this is the nature of the world. In all of us there is the *nafs*, the ego, and every ego fights against the other. There is a sword in every hand, in that of the friend as well as in that of the enemy. The friend strikes after kissing - there is no other difference.

Then one realizes that nothing else can be expected from the world. The great Indian poet Tulsidas said, "Each one does and says as much as he has understood". Why should we blame another for what he could not understand? If he had no more understanding, from where could the poor man borrow it? As much as he understands, that he does. Then a person understands that whatever comes he should take it calmly. If an insult comes he takes it calmly, if a good word comes he takes it with much thanks; if a bad word comes he takes it quietly and he is thankful. If it is a bad word only he is thankful that it is not a blow. If it is a blow he is thankful that it is not worse. He is ready to give his time, his service to all, to the deserving and the undeserving alike, because he sees in all the manifestation of God. He sees God in every form, in the highest, in the lowest, in the most beautiful, in the most worthless.

The Sufi says, "If God is separate from the universe then I would rather worship that God who can be seen, who can be heard, who can be tasted, who can be felt by the heart and perceived by the soul". He worships the God who is before him, he sees the God who is in everything.

Christ said, "Ye shall see me that I am as He who sent me". This does not mean that Christ laid claim to Godhood for his own person. It is what the dervishes call *hamin ost* - all is He and He is all. There is not one atom of the universe that He is not. We must recognize Him, we must respect Him in every face, even in the face of our enemy, even in the most worthless. Our piety, our spirituality are worthless if we do not do this.

To read a few books on philosophy and know that all is God is not enough. To read a religious book and feel that we are pious is not enough. To go to some religious place and be pleased that we are religious is not enough. To give to charity and be conceited that we have done something great is not enough. We must give our services and our time to the deserving and the undeserving alike, because this is the only opportunity we have of giving. This life lasts a few days and we shall never again have the opportunity of giving, of serving another, of doing something for another. We must be thankful to God that He has made us able to give, able to serve others.

CHAPTER XI

Spiritual Attainment and the Continual Struggle of Life

LIFE PROVES to be a continual struggle; the only difference between the struggle for spiritual attainment and that of worldly life lies in the direction. In worldly life, be it business, politics, industry, or whatever be your life's path, if you prove to be lacking the power that enables you to struggle along, you will meet nothing but failure. You may be a very good person, a saintly person, a spiritual person - that does not count. For this reason many in the world lose faith in goodness, in spirituality, because they see that it does not mean anything in worldly life. It is absurd for a spiritual person to say, "By your goodness, spirituality and piety your worldly struggle will be helped". No, these alone cannot help; you must have the inspiration and power to answer life's demands in life's struggle.

By this I want to tell my friends who seek the spiritual path not to forget that floating in the air is no good; standing on the earth is the first thing that is necessary. There are many who dream, who live in the air, but that does not answer our purpose. They may say, "We are doing spiritual work, yet we are in bad circumstances". But the language of this path is different, the law of this path is different. It is for this reason that I distinguish between the spiritual path and worldly life, in order to realize that the one has little to do with the other. This does not mean that the wicked person succeeds, that success is gained by evil or by an evil character; if it were so, it would only be a mortal success. Nevertheless, we must not blame spirituality for failure in worldly things, for worldly things are of another inspiration; if this were not so all great sages would have been millionaires.

The worldly struggle is an outer struggle, the struggle on the spiritual path is an inner struggle. No sooner does one take the spiritual direction than the first enemy one meets is one's little self. What does the little self do? It is most mischievous. When you say, "I want to fight", it says, "I am yourself. Do you want to fight me?" When it brings failure it is clever enough to blame someone else. All those who have failed in life, do they accuse themselves? No, they always accuse the next person. When they have gained, then they say, "I have done it". When they love something and cannot get it, they say, "Someone got in my way". In little and big things it is all the same: the little self does not admit a fault but always finds it in another, and its vanity, its pride, its smallness, its egoistical tendency, its contentment keeps one blind.

The little self does not hinder the worldly path as it hinders the spiritual path. I remember a Persian verse of my *murshid* which relates to the little self, "Whenever I feel that I can make peace with my little self, it finds time to prepare another attack." That is our condition. We think that our little faults are of little consequence; we do not even think of them at all. But every little fault is a flag for the little self, for its own dominion. In this way of battling the little self deprives man, who is the sovereign, of the kingdom of God. Very few realize the great power that lies in battling with the little self and conquering it. But what does man generally do? He says, "My poor self! It already has to withstand such conflicts in the world! Must I also battle with this self?" So he gives the little self its kingdom, thus depriving himself of the divine power that is hidden in the heart of man.

There is in man a false self and a real self. The real self has eternal life in it, the false self has mortal life in it. The real self is wisdom, the false self is ignorance. The real self can rise to perfection, the false self is limitation. The real self is all good, the false self is productive of all evil. We can see in ourselves both God and the other one. By conquering the other one, we realize God. The other power has been called Satan, but is it a power? In reality it is not. It is and it is not. It is a shadow; we see it and yet it is nothing. If we realize this we see that the false self has no existence of its own. As soon as the soul has risen above the false self it begins to realize its nobility.

Now coming to the practical aspect of this false self, how does it show itself? In what form? It rises up in support of its own interest. It defends itself from the attacks of others. It feels exclusive towards everyone. It knows itself as an entity separate from friend and foe. It concerns itself with all that is right now, blind to the future and ignorant of the past. It manifests in the form of self-pity, it expresses itself in the form of vengeance. It lives feeding upon bitterness and it always lives in obscurity. Its condition is restlessness and discontentment. It has a continual appetite to have all that is there and is never contented. It has no trust in anyone, no thought for anyone, no consideration for anyone. It lacks conscientiousness and therefore manner. The little self only considers its own benefit, its own comfort. Giving to others, to those around it, is something dreadful for the little self, for it knows no sacrifice; renunciation is dreadful for it, worse than death.

That is the little self. When we see it in somebody else we blame that person, we dislike him, but we overlook the same element in ourselves. No one in the world can say, "I don't have this in me". If only one were just one would see it, for often it is the unjust person who blames another. The more just you become, the more quiet you will be in all circumstances. Outwardly you will see faults in others, inwardly you will see the sum total within yourself. For instance, a little child cannot help loving. There may be a thief, a robber - the child wants to love him and smiles at him because the child is sinless. Why is this? Because the thief is not awakened in him. The child comes from heaven, the thief from the earth; there is no accommodation for the thief in the child, and therefore to the child there is no thief.

We accept things because we have them in us. If we consider our knowledge, the thousand things we have experienced, most of what we know we have been told by others, and we have believed them at once. As soon as a person tells us about someone wicked, we think, "Now we know, we can be quite sure of it". But if a person comes along and says, "I have seen something most wonderful: this person is so good!", then everyone thinks, "Is it really true? Do we know all about him? Is it possible to be good? Is there not something bad in him?" Good would seem to be unnatural.

Now the question arises if it is necessary to struggle. Why should we take the spiritual path? Is it tyranny over ourselves? It is by struggling that we mould our character, form our personality. Herein resides all religion. When a person begins to think, "I must not harm or hurt anyone I meet, worthy or unworthy, friend or foe", only then he begins his work in the spiritual direction. Spirituality is not in wonder working. Spirituality is attained by good manner, right manner.

Where is the shrine of God? It is in the heart of man. As soon as man begins to consider the feeling of another, he begins to worship God. That feeling does not bring profit, but what other way is there of worshipping God? One might say that it is difficult to please everyone. No doubt it is difficult, and it becomes more difficult still if one has the inclination to please everyone.

There is a story of a *murshid* who went with his *mureeds* to visit a village. He was fasting and the *mureeds* had also taken a vow to fast. They arrived at the home of a peasant who with enthusiasm and happiness arranged a dinner for them. When it was brought to the table the *murshid* went and sat down, but the pupils did not dare because of their vow. Yet they did not mention it, as spiritual persons never mention such things. As to their *murshid* they thought, "*Murshid* has forgotten the vow". *Murshids* are forgetful sometimes! After dinner was over and they went out the pupils asked, "Did you not forget the vow to fast?" "No", was the *murshid's* answer, "I had not forgotten, but I preferred breaking my fast to breaking the heart of that man who with all his enthusiasm had prepared the food".

If only we would think of our everyday life, of all the little things which, when overlooked, make us lose an opportunity of doing some good! Every moment of life is an opportunity to be conscious of human feeling, in prosperity, in adversity, in all conditions. It costs little; only a little thought is necessary. A person may be good within, but he may not be conscientious about little things. There is no greater religion than love. God is love. The best form of love is to be conscientious about the feelings of those with whom we are in contact in everyday life.

As we go further more difficulties come; we see greater faults as we advance in the spiritual path. It is not the number of faults that increases but the sense that becomes so keen - otherwise we would not have found them. It is the same with a musician: the more he knows and the better he plays, the more faults he hears. The one who does not find faults is in reality becoming worse. There is no end to faults. To think of this makes one humble.

If one has not yet realized this truth, there is an aspect of metaphysics which does not make one humble: the profane thought, "God is in me". Yes, God is in the depth of the heart, but the intellect is of no use if the doors of the heart are not open. It is the realization of our numberless faults which makes us humble and effaces the little self from the consciousness. It is in this effacement of the little self that lies real spiritual consciousness, spiritual attainment.

One may ask, "What is real spiritual consciousness?" Spiritual consciousness is being conscious of the spirit. Before that consciousness the little self was covering the spirit. When the little self is moved aside, then what is there? There is spirit - call it whatever you may, it is what it is.

CHAPTER XII

Reaction

EVERY CONDITION, favourable or unfavourable, in which a person finds himself, and every person, whether agreeable or disagreeable in whose presence a person is, causes man to react. Upon this reaction depends man's happiness and man's spiritual progress. If he has control over this reaction it means that he is progressing. If he has no control over it it shows that he is going backwards. When you take two persons, wise and foolish, the wise person reacts more intensely than the foolish one. If you take a dense person and a fine person, the fine person naturally reacts more than the dense one. If you take a just person or an unjust person, naturally the just person reacts more than the unjust one. If you take a spiritual person and a material person, naturally a spiritual person reacts more than the material one. And yet it is against mastery when one has no control over this reaction. A person, fine, spiritual, sensitive, wise, and just, and yet without control over reaction, is incomplete. And this shows that even to become fine and just and spiritual is not sufficient, for all these things make one fine, more sensitive, and at the same time weak against disturbing influences of the crowd. This shows that a person, just, wise, spiritual and fine, and yet weak, is not perfect.

The balance in life is to be as fine as a thread and to be as strong as a wire of steel. If one does not show that durability and strength to stand the opposing and disturbing influences among which one always has to be in life, one certainly shows a weakness, a lack of development. In the first place this reaction gives us a certain amount of vanity. We feel, "I am better than the other who disturbs me". But we certainly cannot say, "I am stronger than the other who disturbs me". When we cannot stand conditions around us we may think that we are superior, we cannot stand conditions; but in reality the conditions are stronger when we cannot stand them. If we are born on earth, if we are destined to walk on the earth, we cannot dream of paradise, when we have to stand firm in all the conditions that the earth brings before us. When a person progresses towards spirituality he must bear in mind that together with his spiritual progress he must strengthen himself against disturbing influences. If not, he must know that with every desire of making progress he will be pulled back against his will by conditions, by circumstances.

There are four different ways in which a person reacts: in deed, in speech, in thought, in feeling.

A deed produces a definite result, speech produces effect, thought produces atmosphere, feeling produces conditions. And therefore no way in which a person will react will be without effect. A reaction will be perceived quickly or slowly, but it must be perceived. And very often a reaction is not only agreeable to oneself, but to another also. A person who answers by insulting another stands on the same level; the one who does not answer stands above it. And in this way we can rise above things, against which we can react, if we only know how to fly. It is flying above things instead of standing as a material person would stand against them. How can one call oneself spiritual if one cannot fly? That is the first condition to be spiritual.

The whole mechanism of this world is an action and reaction, in the objective world as well as in the world of persons. Only in a person there is a possibility of developing that spirit which is called the spirit of mastery. And that spirit is easily developed and best developed by trying to get control over that spirit of reaction. Life offers us abundant occasions from morning till evening to practice this lesson. Every move, every turn we make, we are faced with something agreeable or disagreeable, harmonious or inharmonious, either a condition or a person. If we react automatically we are no better than a machine, and no different from thousands and millions of people who act automatically. But if we can trace in ourselves a divine heritage, a heritage which is called mastery, it is in finding control of reaction against influences. In theory it is simple, it is easy; in practice it is the most difficult thing there is to master, to conquer. And when we think of the usefulness of this development we shall find that there is nothing in the world that is more necessary and more important than this development. If there is any strength to be found in the world, it is that strength within oneself. And the proof of having that strength is when one is able to control one's reaction. This preserves dignity, this maintains honour. It is this which sustains respect, and it is this which keeps man wise. For it is easy to be wise, but it is difficult to continue to be wise. It is easy to think, but it is difficult to continue to be a thoughtful person.

Very often people have asked me if there is any practice, if there is any study, if there is anything which one can do in order to develop willpower. And I have answered: "Yes, there are many practices and many ways" but this is the simplest and best practice which one can do without being taught: to always have one's reaction in hand. The words: "I cannot endure, I cannot stand, I cannot sustain, I cannot have patience", all these mean to me: "I am weak". By saying this we only admit in other words, in better words, that we are weak. And can there be any person in the world who is a worse enemy than our own weakness? If the whole world were our friend, this one enemy would be enough to ruin our life: our weakness. Once this enemy is conquered we can stand against all who will come into conflict with us.

Now the question is how one must set to work in this direction. One must also take into consideration one's physical condition. The nervous system must be in its proper condition. It is by nervousness that man goes from bad to worse. And even a good person with good intentions may prove to be otherwise, for he may have good intentions, but he cannot carry them out because his nerves are weak. He needs the habit of silence, of concentration, of meditation. A person who goes on talking continually or doing things, and does not meditate a while, who does not take a rest, cannot control his nervous system, cannot keep it in order. If there is anything that can control the nervous system it is right breathing; and when the right breathing is done with a concentration, a thought connected with it, then a great fortification is made in the nervous system. All the strength of the mystics, of the Yogis, has come from these practices which keep the nervous system in hand. Besides, there are many things which cause unhappiness, and by holding the nervous system in hand these can be avoided.

When we look at it from a higher point of view it is done by denying to oneself at times the impulses which arise suddenly, and which want their answer. What is called self-denial is really this, that one must control one's thoughts and wishes and desires and passions. But that does not mean retirement from the life of the world. It only means to take oneself in hand.

Question: Can one begin with that control in advanced age of life, or must it be done when one is young?

Answer: It is never too soon to begin, and it is never too late to improve.

Question: Ought not the proper control over oneself be a part of good education given to children?

Answer: Of course; I think that if from childhood that education is given, wonderful results can be brought about. There was a time in India, one sees very little of it just now, but in ancient times youths were trained in *Asana*, a certain way of sitting, of walking, and of standing. By that they first achieved control over their muscles and nerves. It would be of immense value if education to-day adopted two things. One thing is the study of controlling the reaction; and the other the practice of it in sports or gymnastics.

Question: Is it not much more difficult to control one's reaction, when one suffers unjustly from someone whom one loves than from someone to whom one is indifferent?

Answer: The control of the reaction will always give a certain amount of pain. But at the same time, by suffering, by that pain one will gain a certain power of rising above it. But if it is not understood rightly, of course one might endanger oneself. But the danger is in both cases. On one side there is a pit, on the other side there is water. For instance, there is a person who, by being afraid to hurt or by being oppressed by someone, is always keeping his thought or feeling suppressed. If he had expressed them he would have become worse, but if he had not expressed, but suppressed them he would be ruined. Therefore a discrimination, a thought, must be developed in order to analyse, to understand, before the reaction is expressed. Because one must know, "Something which is in my hand now, if I throw it away, shall I do something wrong? Where shall I throw it? Shall I throw it on my head? What will become of it?" He must know what he has in his hand. If in order to avoid breaking another person's head he has broken his own head, he has done wrong too.

Question: Then what to do?

Answer: He must first weigh and measure the impulse that comes to him instead of throwing it out automatically. He must first weigh it, analyse it, measure it and utilize it to the best advantage in life. A stone is not only used to break another person's head, or to break one's own head, but it is also used to build houses, to utilize it. Use everything where it will be useful, where it will be of some advantage. All such things as passion and anger and irritation, one looks upon as very bad, as evil. But if that evil were kept in hand it could be used to good purpose; because it is a power, it is an energy. In other words, evil better utilized becomes a virtue, and virtue wrongly used becomes an evil.

Question: Can you give an instance of the way in which an impulse of anger can be utilized?

Answer: For instance, when a person is in a rage and when he really feels like being angry, if he has controlled that thought and not expressed it in words, that has given him a great power. Otherwise the expression would have had a bad effect upon his nerves. By controlling it it has given him a strength; it remains with him. I prefer a person who has anger and control, to the person who does not have it at all.

A person came to me and said he thought that I would be very pleased with it , "I have been a vegetarian for twenty years". I said, "What made you be a vegetarian?" He said, "It takes away the anger and passion, and all the evils that make man go wrong". I said, "That is a wrong way of becoming a vegetarian". If by being ill a person becomes virtuous that virtue is worth nothing.

Question: Does self-control not take away spontaneity?

Answer: Selfcontrol gives a greater power of spontaneity. It only develops thoughtpower, it only makes one think with every impulse which otherwise manifests automatically.

Question: Must he not feel first?

Answer: He must know about it. At every impulse he must be awake so that he holds that impulse in hand and knows what it is. In other words, to hold the word between the lips before it drops out.

Question: The impulse in itself, before it is controlled, is it wrong in itself?

Answer: When we think about the origin of impulse we go in quite a different direction of thought. Then we have to think of what direction it is facing. Also the direction of mind: whether it is in illumination or in darkness. The mind is sometimes illuminated, sometimes in darkness. One should think about the condition of mind at the time. There is another thing to be considered in this connection. A person may have good intentions and his mind focused to good ideals. There is another person who with evil intentions and wrong ideas has said or done something and has automatically turned the mind of the other person to the wrong, against his own will. There is a word of the Bible: "Resist not evil". Sometimes evil comes as a fire thrown by a person in the mind of another, a mind which did not have a fire; that fire started there. And in reaction that mind then expressed that fire. To resist evil is to send fire in answer to fire. In other words, to partake of the fire that comes from another. And by not partaking of fire, one has thrown the fire away. The fire has fallen on the same person who has thrown it.

CHAPTER XIII

The deeper Side of Life

WHEN WE consider life deeply, we can divide it into two parts and call one the lighter and the other the deeper Side of Life. The importance of both these sides may seem at moments equally great. When a person is thinking of the lighter side of life, at that moment that side is more important, while the other side, of which the person is not conscious, seems to have no great importance. But then there are other moments which come in life, perhaps after suffering, or after a loss or some other experience, that a person suddenly awakens to a quite different realization of life; and when one is awakened to that, at that time the deeper side of life seems to have more importance than the lighter side. No one, neither clergyman nor mystic nor any authority can say which side is more important. It depends upon how we look at it. If we raise its value, though it may be a small thing, yet we shall attach a greater value to it. If we do not look at it, it can be a shallow thing. There is nothing in this world which has a common value attached to it. If there seems to be such a thing, it does not always stay in the same position.If something like money is subject to change, then what is there in this world which does not change in importance?

When we picture these two parts of life, the lighter and the deeper side, we see that we picture them in our present experience. We are travelling together*, some from one country, some from another, coming from different parts of the world. Yet we are gathered together. By what? By destiny, or still clearer, because of a common destination where we all wish to go and which brings us together for a few days on this ship. It is our happy disposition, our favourable attitude to one another, our desire to be kind, friendly, sociable and serviceable which alone makes us understand one another and will help us to make one another happy. It brings us far closer together than destiny did. This is a little picture of life. When we consider the life of a

* Hazrat Inayat Khan gave this lecture on board the S.S. Volendam en route between New York and Rotterdam on December 22nd, 1925

community, a nation, a race, even of the whole world, what is it? Is it not a large ship on which all are travelling, whether knowingly or unknowingly, all moving, all changing? Therefore it is only travelling.

There are two aspects to a traveller. There are travellers who do not know from where they come and where they are going. Only when they open their eyes, they realize that they are on this ship, that they come from somewhere and that they are on a ship which is moving, travelling. And it is like this that many people live in the world to-day. They are so absorbed in their everyday occupation that they are ignorant of where they come from and where they are going. Imagine the difference between these travellers and the one who knows from where he comes and who must also know or will know one day why he has come, why he is travelling, and sooner or later he will prepare for the place where he is going. But the one who does not know from where he comes only knows where he is and what his occupation is; he knows about things in his immediate surroundings. The one who does not know where he is going is not prepared to arrange and to face his destination. He does not know what is in store for him, and therefore he is not prepared for it.

Buddha, great Master of the East, was asked one day by his disciples what he meant by ignorance. And he gave an example in this story: once there was a person clinging in distress to the branch of a tree in the utter darkness of the night, not knowing whether there was earth or a ditch or water beneath his feet. All night long he trembled and wept and held fast to that branch. And with the break of dawn he found he was not one foot away from the earth beneath his feet.

Ignorance can be defined as fear, doubt, passion, confusion. Where do all these come from? They all come from our ignorance of one side of life and that is the deeper side. We may be clever in making the best of what we call the lighter side, profession, art, industry, business, but that is one side of life, it is not all. With all our efforts from morning till evening we do not know what we shall arrive at, what we gain by it. If we consider wealth, position, fame, name, or anything else, it only confuses us, for life is moving; it is all moving. We cannot hold it. A person may have riches one day and the other day be poor; he may be successful one day and it is possible that sooner or later he will meet with failure. Who could have thought that such powerful nations as Russia and Germany would fall down in a moment's time; nations which took hundreds of years to become strong and to build themselves up? But when their time came their downfall did not take long. If such great powers, with manpower, wealth, qualifications, politicians, statesmen are subject to falling in a moment, if such construction built in hundreds of years can be broken, if that is the nature and character of life, no thoughtful person will deny the fact that there must be some mystery behind it, some secret to which he would like to find the key. At least he would want to know what life is, what is behind it.

Those who have studied life and thought long enough about this subject, have arrived at the same point as other thinkers who lived perhaps eight thousand years ago. Buddha said and realized the same things that a wise man would realize to-day. This throws a light on life for us to see that wisdom is the same in all ages. We may be glad when evolving and sorry when going backwards, but wisdom never changes and will always be the same. The same realization will come to those who will think deeply and try to realize what life is. I do not mean that in order to realize life it would be necessary for a person to follow a certain religion, or to be so great or so good, so pious or so spiritual. The first and most necessary thing is that we become observant. We should look at life more keenly than we do instead of living superficially. It would cost us nothing. It only takes us away from our everyday occupation for a few minutes. Life always gives an opportunity of thinking, however busy we may be, if we care to know its secret.

It is not necessary to leave our occupation, our work, and go into the forest and sit in silence and meditate upon life. We can meditate upon life in the midst of life if only we want to. What happens is that man begins his life with action, and the more he is ignorant in action the less he thinks. Then his action becomes his thought. But if one thought beyond one's actions and one's thoughts connected with everyday action, one would also give a thought to the deeper side of life.

We fight, discuss, argue and dispute very often. Over what? Over a reason. When two persons are disputing, each of them has a reason and each thinks his reason is the right one. They may dispute for years and yet will arrive nowhere because the reason of each is different. Therefore to think more is to see behind the reason. The moment we have begun to see behind the reason, we will look at life quite differently. Then we find that where we put a blame there is perhaps behind that blame something to praise; and where there is something to praise there is perhaps a reason for blame. We shall begin to see what is behind all things and this will give us the proof that the whole of life is a kind of unfoldment. The deeper we look into life the more it unfolds itself, allowing us to see more keenly. It would not be an exaggeration to say that life is revealing. It is not only human beings who speak, but even plants and trees and all nature speak; if only the ears can hear. "Speak" in the sense that life reveals itself, reveals its secret nature. In this way we communicate with the whole of life. Then we are never alone, then life in the world becomes worth living.

The thoughtful of all ages have considered the source of creation to be one and the same. A great scientist will go so far to-day as to tell us that the cause behind creation is motion, vibration. But if from motion or vibration this manifestation has come before our view then that motion is not lifeless. If that motion is life itself, then it is intelligent, although it is not intelligent in the sense we understand this word. We know the most limited sense of it, we call the limited brain intelligence. Words such as things and beings have come into existence by our thinking that one thing is intelligent because it is living and another thing where we do not see life, we call unintelligent. We say intelligent being, unintelligent thing. In this way duality comes by our experience of defining what we call intelligent. An Indian scientist, visiting the West, has pointed out that even trees breathe. If that is true then the trees are living. And if to-day it is proved that trees are living, it will also be found that stones are living, that all we see is living. Then it all comes from one source which is the very life of all things; life is not only life but intelligence also. That which is life, religion calls God. Whatever we call it, it is the same. The difference is only in name.

Once when I was travelling to America I met an Italian young man who was travelling on the same ship. Looking at my priestly robe and thinking that I was a priest, he said, "What is your religion?" I answered, "It is your belief, it is all religion." He repeated, "But what is your belief?" I said, "One's belief cannot be told, everyone's piety is in himself, he knows it best." He answered, "But I do not believe, I believe in eternal matter." At my answer, "My belief is not very far from yours" he was very surprised that a priestly man would say such a thing, "Then what is your belief?" I said, "What you call eternal matter I call eternal spirit, it is just the same; what I call spirit, you call matter. I do not mind calling it so for your convenience, it is only a difference of words."

Differences between religious faiths, where do they come from? From looking superficially. If our ideas are material we discuss things which in essence are the same. The difference is only in words. A keen observation of life will in time awaken in us the view that, once the light is thrown upon life, life begins to reveal itself. As the great poet of Persia, Sa'di, has said, "Even the leaves of the tree become as pages of the sacred book once the eyes of the heart are open."

Question: What do you think is the best means to bring about better understanding and tolerance between those of different beliefs?

Answer: I think that the efforts which are made by missionaries of different faiths to convert those who do not belong to their faith are of no great importance to-day. The efforts we can make to-day must bring about an understanding among the followers of different religions by way of writing or speaking or preaching *the* religion instead of *a* religion, which means by trying to explain the truth of Christianity to the Buddhists in the realm of Buddhism; to

Christians Buddhism in the realm of Christianity, to compare with their own teachings not in order to show differences but to make them understand that it is all the same. The effort of every great teacher was to make humanity come to this understanding, but it has resulted in dividing people in communities. One said, "My church is the only one which will save you", the other said, "Only my temple or pagoda is worthwhile." The great teachers had no desire to further the cause of any particular religion, community or church. They wanted to bring about that religion which is the religion of humanity, which stands above all divisions. That service which takes nothing away from religion is of greater importance, it puts a new light on a person's religion and makes one more tolerant through the understanding of the ideal of others.

Question: There are some who consider the lighter side of life more important, others the deeper side of life. Would there be a possibility for those who consider the lighter side of life more important to develop into a situation where they may realize the deeper side of life more and more by practical thought? Not by words or dogmas which are not well understood by people, but by practical thought which leads to a proper understanding of the deeper side of life?

Answer: As it is necessary to have repose after action, so it is necessary to have a glimpse of the deeper side of life after having done one's everyday duties. That is why religions have taught prayers. There were also churches where people used to go every day to be in a right atmosphere and to be silent. Now religion has become a secondary thing and the life of man has developed more struggles to-day, greater struggles than yesterday; naturally a man has hardly time to go to a solitary place or into a church to sit down in silence. Those few who have some time and who care to continue with religion, go once a week to a service. Therefore, if I would suggest a way at the present time, it is the way of esotericism, the esoteric way, which means studying on one hand, practising on the other hand, and meditating besides, doing these three things.

You will ask, "What do we have to study?" There are two kinds of studies, one kind is by reading the teachings of the great thinkers and to keep them in mind, to study metaphysics, psychology, and mysticism. And the other kind of study is the study of life. Every day we have an opportunity for studying, but it should be a correct study. When a person travels in a tramcar, in the train, with a newspaper in his hand, he wants to read the sensational news which is worth nothing. He could read human nature which is before him, people coming and going. If he would continue to do this, he would begin to read human beings as letters written by the divine pen, which speak of their past and future. To look deeply at heavens and nature and at all the things we see in everyday life, and to reflect upon it, wanting to understand it, is a kind of study much greater, incomparably greater than the study of books.

Then there is practice, the practice which the Yogis and Sufis in the East have experienced for many, many years. They have given their thousands of years of experience as a tradition from teacher to pupil. Ways of sitting, ways of standing, of breathing properly, of being in silence, a way of relaxing, of concentrating, of feeling easy, inspirational, joyful, more peaceful. Of course for such practices the help of a teacher is necessary.

The third thing is the practice in every day life, to practise the principles one has esteemed in life, to uphold the ideal one has always held in one's heart. These things and many others besides, such as one's attitude to others, one's manner with others, everything one does from morning till evening, all these things help one's development, till one arrives at a stage when one can see the deeper side of life naturally. There are numberless people, unhappy, depressed, in great despair, wanting to commit suicide, who having done this practice, after three, four, six months say, "After all life is worth living."

Question: What do you think is the ideal life for the average person?

Answer: The ideal life is at least to try to live up to one's ideal. But in order to have an ideal one must awaken to an ideal. Not everyone possesses an ideal; many people capable of having one do not know of it. It is no exaggeration to say that the wars and disasters we have gone through, the unrest that all feel, and the disagreement among people which is sometimes seen and sometimes not seen, are all caused by one thing: the lack of an ideal. We are progressing commercially, industrially, but in all walks of life progress will be hindered one day or another if the ideal is destroyed. If there is anything which can be said to be the means of saving the world and the spirit of idealism it is the awakening of the ideal. This is the first task that is worth considering. Besides this, for the average man to consider living a life of balance would be of great importance, and not very difficult. When a person is busy at work he must know that recreation is also necessary. When a person tires himself it is necessary to take repose; when a person thinks too much it is necessary to rest the mind at certain times, not to think. But life is an intoxication, it is like drink; whatever be man's motive, whether he is compelled and put into it or not; it is all intoxicating, all drinking, going for his object with all his might and thought and feeling, till either he has accomplished what he wants, or he is destroyed. If we use balance in everything we do, we shall get the key to a life of greater happiness.

CHAPTER XIV

Life, an Opportunity

WHEN WE look at the world to-day and at its condition as it is just now, we begin to wonder if we understand the idea of "life an opportunity" any better than those who lived before us. In spite of the stage of evolution which we experience and of the scientific advancement of the world, the war, which humanity went through not long ago, shows to us that never in the history of the world such bloodshed, such a great catastrophe was caused by mankind. It seems as if the whole evolution of humanity intended to prepare, to create such means of destruction that the greater part of humanity has been ruined by it. And when we think of the distrust as it exists to-day among nations and how one nation has allowed another nation to be ruined, we begin to feel that we understand this idea of "life an opportunity" much less than those who lived before us.

Regarding education, the study in the schools and colleges is becoming hard and difficult; year after year it is so difficult for students to pass their examinations that it seems that by the time they have got a degree their nerves are shattered, their finer forces scattered and that they are less capable of making use of their qualifications.

When we look at the political world we see the same, each political party is striving for its own welfare just as each individual is trying to get the best of the other; and nations follow the same principle. Each nation again forms several parties running after the object which they profess to accomplish.

Domestic life seems to be reduced every day. Life is becoming more and more a hotel-life. Very few in the world to-day experience and enjoy what is called home-life or are even capable of appreciating it, because they do not know it. Those who lived before us were much happier, they knew the simplicity and affection of home-life and the joy and the pleasure of a home. The pleasures to-day are not like the enjoyments of the more intelligent and wise in ancient times. They used to enjoy poetry and higher music. To-day jazz has become most popular, there is a jazzband in every hotel, in every place. It is the same with all other entertainments. When we go to the theatre we find the plays more and more limited in pitch; there is no depth, no height, they are without ideal. They have the realism to show life as it is but that does not inspire or uplift mankind. What is needed is to show life better than it is so that man may follow that example. Besides that, the tendency of the writer, the poet, the artist, the musician is to appeal to the most ordinary person, to the man of the lowest evolution, "the man in the street". If all these different things which educate man: theatre, books, poetry and art, pull him down to his lowest evolution, it means going downward instead of going upward. When a person writes good music or poetry with higher subjects there is no market for it. Whenever a person comes with something higher he is told, "It is not wanted, it will not take". It seems that education, high ideals, everything is becoming commercialized, and by being commercialized is coming downward. At the same time, if we stood in the midst of the crowd and looked at the people hurrying by and carrying loads, we would think that never before have people tried so hard to make the best of life's opportunity.

The opportunity of life should be considered from a different point of view. The wiser we become the more our outlook changes, the more we look upon things differently. There are four different stages in life: childhood, youth, middle age and advanced age; and each of these four stages shows a great opportunity. For instance, in childhood the consciousness is in paradise. The child living in the same world of woe, treachery and wickedness is happy because it is not yet awakened to the other aspect of life. It only knows the better side of it, the beauty of life. And therefore the same world is the Garden of Eden for the child till it grows older and is exiled from the Garden of Eden. Before that it enjoys paradise on earth; it is unaware of the wickedness and of the evil and ugliness of human nature. It still maintains in itself the heavenly air and angelic innocence and the tendency to appreciate all beauty and to love every being.

As the child grows it gets away from that tendency; nevertheless by its words and actions and by every tendency it shows the angelic essence in its soul. This is the opportunity for every child to experience kingliness in life, and it is taken away by parents who send the child to school too early and place on it a burden of studies. We need not have this anxiety of preparing studies for the child so that it will be able to answer in school. This naturally takes away that kingliness that God has given to it, that joy and beauty for which it is born and which it longs to have. This period of its life should be made free to be without anxiety and worry, without hurt. The parents burden the child with studies and after all, what do these studies do? They take away strength and intelligence. Before the mind is developed it is burdened with unnecessary studies and this is increasing to such an extent!

Now people say, "We also must teach a child concentration", but they have forgotten that a child is born with concentration. It is the grown-up whose concentration is not right. Every soul is born with concentration; it loses this faculty as it grows up.

Once I was travelling in England and someone invited me to see a school where concentration was taught. They brought before me ten or fifteen children, and each child was asked to look at a blank curtain and say what was there. One child looked and looked and said, "A lily". Another child said, "A rose". The teacher asked a third child to tell her what was there. The child answered, "I don't see anything!" I thought, "That is much better, he says what he sees". And so the teacher asked ten or twelve children questions about what they saw. It was a lesson in hypocrisy, in becoming imaginative; unnecessary and too much. It could never help a child, for the child's concentration is already there; if the child is kept a child that is enough. We make a child into a grown-up person, but it is happy when left with its own tendencies of running about, of being cheerful. The child need not have this burden. We have made it for ourselves. We are not made to take this burden which makes life miserable for ourselves and others.

If life were not so complex there would have been no need of war and difficulties such as we have to-day. Because we have spoiled ourselves we want more and yet we make it so difficult for ourselves to get what we want that in the end we cannot get it at all. At the same time by wanting more than is necessary we make life miserable, and the life of others also.

The amount of study with which a youth is loaded, is the greatest wrong done to him to-day. The culture of youth seems to have disappeared. We have not thought about what is necessary for young people; they are not inspired with lofty ideals, with those impressions which make them do great things.

There is a kind of uniformity in all youths. They wish to become a hero, a most wonderful or inspired person, a great poet or musician. But because of this uniform education each child does not get that nourishment for his soul to make him that for which it was born.

Besides that, youth is an opportunity when a beautiful manner, high aspiration and lofty ideals can be taught. It is the youth who has the enthusiasm to take everything that comes, to assimilate and express it in return. But when the time of a youth is spent only in working hard all day long trying to pass examinations, and what little time is left is given to recreation and other things, that does not suffice for his life's purpose.

Those who understand this idea realize that youth is the greatest opportunity that comes in life; it never comes again. Life's spring never returns. It comes only once, and when that opportunity is taken away and the youth has not been inspired as he ought to have been, it is just like keeping a plant without watering it; for that is the time for the plant to be watered, that is the time for it to be reared; and that time should not be neglected.

There are thousands and millions of young people in the colleges without any good manners taught to them and without inspiration given to them. When they are grownup they show that they have passed examinations, that they have gained great knowledge, but the time of youth is the good ground for that knowledge which ennobles the soul, at that time the mind is receptive. The child with all its enthusiasm and concentration grasps everything good and beautiful.

The inspiration of the musicians and poets who have done great work in the world was created during their youth. Either they saw a living example which impressed them, or they were told or they read or studied something which was just like sowing the seed in their heart.

Youth is the only time which destines the child to become great in life; and if this time is past it will never come again. Whether a person wants to be a businessman or a politician, a professional man, a scientist, or a musician, it is in youth that it must be started and that he must be inspired with it. At that time the ground is fertile, and when that time is gone the chance does not easily come again.

Besides the training for all different professions and works and occupations, there remains another cultivation which is neglected in youth: the cultivation of the heart-quality. To-day every effort is made to train a youth to become intellectual, to learn. But there is a difference between intellect and wisdom; they are not necessarily the same. As we confuse pleasure and happiness so we confuse clever and wise, but the clever person is not necessarily wise, wisdom is different from cleverness. Intellect is that which one learns by impressions, by studies, and which one gathers in the form of knowledge of names and forms. Wisdom is something which is gathered like honey from a flower, like butter from milk. Wisdom is gained from within and from without. This combination makes it wisdom.

To-day there is hardly one percent among people who have cultivated this heart-quality. Instinctively the heart-quality is there, but every effort is made to blunt it, because what we learn to-day is intellectual. What do I mean by the heart-quality? There is intuition, there is inspiration and there is revelation. All these come from the culture of the heart, from the heart-quality. A person may be most cultivated, may have studied much, and at the same time not be intuitive. A person may learn all the technique of music and poetry without having the heart-quality. Heart-quality is something which must be developed within oneself; when no attention is given at the time of youth to developing that particular quality, what happens when a person is grown-up? He will be selfish, proud, mannerless and not ready to sacrifice. These qualities best guard his interest, and one calls such a person a man of common sense, a practical man. Just imagine! If everybody was like this, what else could one expect from life except constant conflict such as there is to-day? Religion or the devotional side of man's nature is also dying out for the reason that people do not need it because they have no heart-quality. Even if people go to church or to another place of worship their piety is lived intellectually. People can only enjoy something intellectual. If there is a mathematical explanation of something it is wonderful; but when it comes to feeling blessed, uplifted, to feeling the raising of the consciousness towards higher spheres, they cannot experience it for they live in their intellect.

There are two principal experiences of life: one experience is called sensation and the other exaltation. What is generally known and experienced by the average man to-day is what is called sensation: all the beauty that one sees of line, of colour, all that one sees with the eyes, that one hears, tastes and touches. It is living in sensation that makes man material, and after some time he becomes ignorant of the spirit.

Exaltation, which is a greater bliss, a higher pleasure, and which makes man independent of life outside in order to become happy, does not seem to be known by the majority. What do I mean by exaltation? The soul can have four different experiences which are all in reality the longing of the soul. And yet, by mistake man does not have those four experiences, and instead he experiences something else. For instance, it is a constant yearning of the soul to experience happiness and instead of that it becomes connected with what one calls pleasure, but pleasure belongs to sensation and happiness to exaltation. Pleasure is the suggestion, happiness is reality.

Then comes knowledge. Every soul yearns for that knowledge which will give exaltation. But the soul cannot be satisfied by the knowledge one gathers from books, by learning or by the study of outside things. For instance, the knowledge of science, the knowledge of art are outside knowledge. All these different studies give one a kind of strength, a kind of satisfaction, but this does not last. It is another knowledge that is the real seeking of the soul. The soul cannot be satisfied unless it finds that knowledge, and that knowledge does not come by learning names and forms. On the contrary it comes from unlearning. Do not be surprised therefore if you read in some books of the East that Masters, Mahatmas went into the mountains and sat there for many years. I will not say that we should follow their example, but we can appreciate what they have brought from there. They went there to explore life and that aspect of life which is unseen and remains unexplored. They sat there for years in meditation. They lived on vegetables, on leaves and food from trees, on what they could find in the forest. They contemplated. What they have gathered is not a knowledge learned from this world, but a greater knowledge which can be learned from within. One can see the picture of Buddha, eyes closed, sitting cross-legged. What does this symbol explain to us? That there is a knowledge that can be learned by closing not only the eyes but also the mind from the outside world. What we do is to go as far as closing the eyes, but we do not go further. If the eyes are closed and the mind is pondering over things, that is not concentration.

There is an amusing story from the time of Aurangzeb about a leader of prayers. Aurangzeb made it compulsory even for saints to go to the mosque for prayer. There was a dervish who was compelled by the police to go to the mosque and so he went there. The prayer began but before it was finished the dervish ran away. So the police went after him because running away was a great insult to the congregation and the leader of prayer. The dervish was brought to justice and was asked why he left the mosque during the prayers. He said, "What is meant by the leader of prayers?" They answered, "You have to be in thought with him, with his prayers". The dervish answered: "The thought of the leader of prayers went to his house because he had lost his keys. So I could not pray in the mosque and went to his house". They called the leader of prayers and asked him about it. He said, "Honestly, my thought went with my keys".

If the mind is going from one thing to another there is no concentration. Closing the eyes does not make the concentration any better. Those who can concentrate can do it without having to close the eyes. Once when travelling in the East I saw a person working in a telegraphoffice. Busy as he was, his concentration continued. I said, "It is very wonderful, that with all this work you can go on concentrating". He smiled and said, "That is the way of concentration". If one goes to church once a week and then closes the eyes for two minutes it cannot suffice one's purpose of life.

There is a well known story about a village girl in Punjab who passed a field where a religious man was offering his prayers. The religious law does not allow anyone to cross such a place. When this village girl came back the religious man said, "How rude you were, o girl, it is a sin to cross a place where a person is offering his prayers". She stopped and asked, "What do you mean by prayers?" He answered, "Prayers? Do you not know what they mean? Offering one's prayers means thinking of God". The girl asked, "How did you see me while thinking of God? When going my way I was thinking of my young man and I did not see you". Her concentration was greater than that of the man concentrating on God.

Besides concentration there must also be faith. It is by faith that concentration becomes strong and living. When faith lives then concentration is also alive, because faith in other words is will. When a thought is not held by the power of will it goes away, it must be held by will, and that will is faith. In a story explaining this a great preacher was telling people to have faith and there were many who heard him. A peasant was very impressed by his words that with faith one could walk on water. He came to the preacher and asked him, "Would you like to come and dine with me?" "I am much privileged", the preacher said, "Yes, I will come with you". Next day the peasant came to fetch the preacher. They had to cross a river and the preacher asked, "Where is the boat?"

"You have taught me the other day," answered the peasant, "that if we have faith in the name of God we can walk on water". "Have you done it?", asked the preacher. "Since you told me I never used the boat again", and the preacher answered, "I cannot walk on water". That is the result, one may preach and say such a thing but as long as there is no faith and will at the back of it one cannot do it. Wonders can be accomplished by thought if there is faith.

Another thing one experiences in life and for which the soul yearns is happiness. That can also be gained by getting in touch within oneself.

And the last thing is peace. It cannot be gained by outer means, by outer comfort and rest only. It can be gained when the mind is at rest.

After youth comes the stage of middle age, the time when one has gathered knowledge and experience of life, when one has gone through life's joy and sorrow, when one has learned a lesson from one's profession, from one's occupation, from one's home, from every side of life. It is the opportunity to make the best use of what one has gathered by experience. But what generally happens is what Sa'di, the Persian poet says, "O my self, you have come to middle age, and yet you are no better than a child!" If a person has not learned by that time all he ought to learn, he has indeed lost life's opportunity, because it is during that age that he has not only earned money, but gained experience and knowledge. And the more he has learned and the richer he is at that time, the better he knows how to make use of what powers he has and the more successful and fruitful he becomes.

Besides, that is the age when one begins to know life's obligations, and if one does not know them even then, one has not learned anything. To know one's obligation towards those who look up to one, who surround one, who expect some help, some advice, some service from one, that is the time when one must be conscious of these things. It is the beautiful age when the tree comes to full blossom, beginning to give fruit to the world. Not only for the singer whose voice is in full blossom, for the artist, for the thinker who expresses his thoughts fully, but for every person that age is the promise of the ripened mind expressing itself to the best advantage. And if that opportunity is not taken man has missed a great deal in life.

Then again advanced age has its own blessings. People do not appreciate the blessings of every period they live in this world, and so they appreciate one thing and dislike another. In the East, especially in India, great respect is given to age. There is every reason that this ideal should be known. That age is the time when man is the record of his whole life; whether he has been sympathetic, kind, wise, or foolish, whatever he has been, advanced age brings the record of it. One can read it in his face, in his features, in his atmosphere, one can read what he has done. He has a greater opportunity to inspire, to bless, and to serve those who want his service or who want to be directed. He shows a better manner, a better way of looking at life. It is the age when man can accomplish. But when he does not know his opportunity, in middle age he acts like a child, in childhood he works like an older person, and in youth he is burdened like someone in middle age.

If we only knew that every moment in life, every day, every month, and every year has its particular blessing! If we only knew life's opportunity! But the greatest opportunity that one can realize in life is to accomplish that purpose for which man was sent on earth. And if he has lost that opportunity, then whatever he may have accomplished in the world, whether he has gathered wealth, possesses great property, name, it does not matter, he will not be satisfied. He will have to live here without having fulfilled the purpose of life. Once man's eyes are opened and he begins to look at the world, he finds there is a greater opportunity in life than he had ever thought before.

If one knew what thought can do! Man is as poor as he is, as limited as he is, as troubled as he is, yet there is nothing in this world which could not be accomplished by man if he only knew what thought can do. Imagine the opportunity man has in life! It is ignorance which keeps him from what he ought to accomplish. If man only knew how to operate his thought, how to accomplish certain things, how to put his mind to the object that must be accomplished! If he does not know, then he has not made use of his mind and has lived like a machine. If man knew the power of feeling, that the power of feeling can reach anywhere and penetrate anything, he could achieve anything he might wish.

There is a Persian story of Shirin and Farhad. Once Shirin, the girl whom Farhad admired, in order to test his love said, "Farhad, do you love me? If you love me, you will have to make a way through the mountains". Farhad said, "Yes, I was waiting for that test". He went to the mountains full of the feeling of love he had for her. Every time he broke the rock with his hammer, he said the name of Shirin, and the strength of his hammer became a thousand times greater because of the feeling of his heart.

To-day man has forgotten the great power there is in feeling. It can break rocks. There is nothing that cannot be accomplished by the power of feeling. But generally there is no feeling; feeling has become drowned, it no longer exists. Life's greatest opportunity is to realize the power of feeling and to express it; but a still greater opportunity of life is to free oneself from the captivity of limitations. Every man is in some form or other a captive in his limitation; his life is limited. One could get above it by realizing the latent power and inspiration of the soul.

Kabir, the great poet of India, says, "Life is a field and you are born to cultivate it. If you know how to cultivate this field you can produce anything you like. All the need of your life is to be produced in this field. All that your soul yearns after, all you need is to be had from this field if you know how to cultivate it and how to reap the fruit". But if this opportunity is only studied in order to make the best of life by taking all one can take and by being more comfortable, that is not so satisfying. We must enrich ourselves with thought, with that happiness which is spiritual happiness, with that peace which belongs to our soul, with that liberty, that freedom, for which our soul longs; and attain to that higher knowledge which breaks all the fetters of life and raises our consciousness to look at life from a different point of view. Once a person has realized this opportunity he has fulfilled the purpose of life.

CHAPTER XV

Our Life

CONSCIOUSLY OR unconsciously we call to us the element which makes us what we are. What we experience in life therefore has come either from what we have already called to us in the past or from what we call at present. It is very difficult for a person to hear this for the first time and to accept it immediately, for no person in the world is desirous of calling something that he does not wish to have. But the philosopher Emerson said, "Think beforehand what you want". The principle of the whole creation is based on this.

Even the fruits and flowers, the plants and trees, in order to be what they are, call for the element that makes them so. If fragrance belonged to the flower then every flower would have fragrance. It is a certain flower which has fragrance: that flower has fragrance which calls for it. Each flower has a different colour. Why? Because each flower calls for it. Every seed or herb with medicinal value shows that its peculiarity belongs to it: it calls for it. The life of little insects will also show us the proof of the same fact. Their green or blue or red colour, their beautiful or ugly form is based, is constructed on what they have called to themselves. Little insects moving among beautiful flowers which are to be found in the green show beauty in their colour, in their construction, for they live in beauty, they call for beauty. Insects living in the mud show a different quality again. Why ? Because they call for it. The more we study science, be it natural science or chemistry, we shall find that each being and each object shows with its peculiarity that it is what it is, because it has called for a particular element to become so.

Man who is the finished specimen of the creation shows this doctrine in its fulness. His success, his failure, his sorrows, his joys all depend upon what he calls and what he has called to himself. Many will say, "Is it not that he is experiencing what he was meant to experience ?" That is the idealistic point of view - and a good point of view to take. It is consoling also. But at the same time when we come to the study of metaphysics we shall find that the secret behind creation is, as the Hindus say, that it is the dream of Brahma. Since each being represents Brahma, the Creator, so each being for his part is a creator of his own life. It is ignorance of this fact which keeps man back from progressing towards perfection, and it is the knowledge of this which alone can be called divine knowledge, for if anyone has arrived at a higher realization it is by this knowledge.

There is another side to this question to be considered. You may say, "There are many undesirable things which I could never have desired". And the answer is, "Yes, you did not desire them as you see them now, but as you saw them before. It was in another form that you desired them". Very often happiness shows itself in the guise of unhappiness; very often pain shows itself in the guise of pleasure. The one who does not seek after pain will seek after pleasure, but does not know that perhaps behind that pleasure the pain was hiding. A seeker after success may not see failure hiding behind it. At the same time the very seeking of that success would lead that person to failure, for it was success in appearance; in reality it was failure.

Life is a comedy, and the more you look at it the more you can smile at it; not smile at all persons, but smile at yourself. Life is always different from what one thinks it to be. Look at pain, look at pleasure, look at happiness, look at success and failure! Look at everything!

There are two ways of calling that which makes one's self. One way is by calling that which stands outside of one's life in order to make one's life complete, be it wealth, power, position or anything else. And there is another way of calling, which is to call the very self. By calling one's real self one naturally harmonizes one's spirit, and it may become so harmonized that with friend and foe both one would feel harmony.

Once we have communicated with our self, once we have called our self, our real self, naturally we become harmonized with pain and pleasure and we become contented with success and failure; for in spite of all diverse experiences of our external life there rise from the bottom of our heart a harmony and a peace and a power which keep us centralized. In order not to get wet in the rain we cannot stop the rain; all that we can do is to have an umbrella which is waterproof. We cannot by developing ourselves materially or spiritually stop natural consequences of life. When we are in the midst of the world we are exposed to all agreeable and disagreeable experiences which life gives us. If there is a way of making life easy for ourselves it is only this way : by harmonizing within ourselves so that we harmonize with all the different conditions and experiences of life.

If we complain there is no end to our complaining. In order to have no complaints we must not complain. Only we must be conscious of the fact that all we experience is called by us and that all we shall experience will be called by us also. At each step in our life we must be wise in order to distinguish in all things desired by us what we must call for ourselves and what we must not call for ourselves. If we mourn over the past - it is passed, it is no use mourning over it. It is just as well to forget the past, except beautiful impressions, good memories. It is the present for which we are responsible, for it is the present which will build our future. The most essential thing therefore is that by centralizing our thought within ourselves, by finding our real self we must so harmonize that the future may become harmonized. There is a prayer of Eastern people, "We give thanks for all we have experienced; only what we ask for is to make our end best".

Question: What is the exact relation of the present to the past and to the future?

Answer: The present is the reflection of the past and the future is the re-echo of the present.

Question: You were saying that the flowers and plants call the element that makes their colour. How does it happen that there is little difference sometimes in the colour of flowers and leaves, and that all roses have more or less the same scent?

Answer: There is the past of the rose which is behind it,

and since the seed of the rose had conceived those properties which the rose shows, it has maintained as its heritage that fragrance and colour. But at the same time as sustenance it takes from the air and the sun that which makes it the perfect rose.

In other words there is perhaps in the same garden another plant, a flower which is without fragrance. It has the same sun, the same air, it is in the same space, but it is the rose which calls for the properties which make it a rose. The other flower being in the same place does not call for them; it only calls for those properties which keep it as it is. Is it not said symbolically that one person creeps on the earth, another walks gently, a third runs and a fourth flies? And they are all on the same earth, under the same sun.

Question: Those are the inner qualities?

Answer: No quality can exist without being maintained by what it attracts every moment of the day. As our physical body depends for its existence upon physical sustenance and as our mind depends on the sustenance of its own sphere, so each quality has its food - a food which it calls, a food on which it lives. As the body would cease to exist if its sustenance were not given to it, so every quality, however great it may appear to be in a person, would cease to exist if there were no sustenance within reach. If we observe keenly the life around us we will find a thousand proofs of this. How many are born with genius, how many with a tendency to write poetry, with an inclination to sing, how many with a desire to do some good! Their qualities vanish, they themselves cannot find their qualities once they are starved of the food on which they live.

CHAPTER XVI

Communicating with Life

FROM THE point of view of the mystic, life in all its aspects is communicative if one only knows the secret of communicating with life. As long as one is ignorant of this secret one is deaf with ears and blind with eyes. There are stories of sages and saints who spoke with trees and plants, rocks and mountains and with seas. People take these to be legends, but they are as true as anything else in this world of variety. This is not only true of the past, it can always be, it is always possible, if one knows how to communicate with life.

In the lower creation we recognize a faculty which we call instinct: the tendency that makes the bird fly and the fish swim without learning. This instinct appears in the form of intuition among the lower creation. Many scientists to-day say that animals have no mind but in reality all creatures have a mind, even trees and plants. Those who live close to nature, those whose lifework is agriculture, always living in the solitude among animals, know the fact that animals often give a warning of illness, of death, of a storm or a flood. They have intuition. The mechanism of man's body and mind is finer still, and man is capable of a greater intuition; yet it seems that even before man knows, animals perceive. The reason is that man is so absorbed in his outer life, in his object in life, that it is very difficult for him to believe in intuition, and therefore his intuitive faculty becomes blunted and he proves to be less intuitive than the lower creation.

Those living close to nature in the solitude, peasants living a countrylife, have greater intuition than intellectual people who live in the midst of worldly life. This shows that the life we live to-day in large towns is an unnatural life, lived in an artificial atmosphere, eating artificial food, adopting artificial ways of living. So one loses that heavenly quality, the divine heritage of man which is shown in the intuitive qualities. Fine persons seem to have more intuition than gross ones, woman seems to have greater intuition than man. The reason is that woman is by nature responsive. It is the receptivity of her nature that makes her more intuitive. Sometimes man reasons and argues, and woman says, "Yes, but I feel it, I feel it is to be so"; and her feeling proves to be right. She cannot give a reason for it, she says, "I feel it".

In every person there is more or less a faculty of perceiving impressions, and that is the first step towards intuition. The finer the person the greater his perception. But everyone at times feels, as an impression, the conditions of a place, the character of the people he meets, their tendencies, their motives, their desire, their grade of evolution. When we ask, "Why do you feel like this", one cannot always give an explanation. Sometimes one will say, "It is from the features", or "from the atmosphere", or "from what he has said". But in reality it is a feeling which is beyond description. A fine, sensitive, intelligent person always gets an impression on seeing someone.

The next stage is intuition. By intuition one feels the warning of a coming danger, the promise of success, the warning of a failure; if any change is to take place in life one feels it. But very often by not having selfconfidence one loses that intuitive faculty. One fears that one's intuition is wrong; and in this way one loses selfconfidence. If one thinks, "Maybe my intuition is not right and by following my intuition I will fail", one takes another way, the way of reasoning, of logic. But naturally one's intuition becomes blunted after some time. If one does not make use of that faculty it disappears, and someone who is capable of perceiving intuitively then loses that faculty.

Another wonderful thing about intuition is that one is blessed with intuition according to one's sincerity. If a person is earnest, sincere, sympathetic, kind, he will be blessed with intuition; but if these qualities are lacking, intuition will be lacking too. Those who have no intuition have also difficulty in attaining to the spiritual ideal, because spiritual belief does not come from outer experience, by reason and logic, it is a belief that springs from within in the form of intuition. And if the intuitive faculty is not developed, that person's belief is not strong. In the first place a person who lacks intuition lacks belief too; and if he has belief, that belief will not be strong enough, because it is not built on a sound foundation.

The next step along the path of intuition is inspiration. Poets, writers, musicians, thinkers, philosophers, can make use of this faculty. Others have it but they do not know how to use it. That which one cannot create in ten years in the form of art, poetry, or music, one can create in a few moments by inspiration. It is a natural flow; one has no difficulty in working it out. Inspiration comes already arranged and there is very little to be done by the brain and by the mind. Besides, everything that comes through inspiration is living and is most beautiful, most harmonious compared with the art or poetry or music that is the outcome of the brain. Music of the past, such as the works of Wagner or Beethoven, is still living. And no matter how often you hear them you always thirst for them. Modern music has not that appeal.

It is the same thing with ancient art. There is something living in that art and to-day - with all the progress made in art - that something living is missing. It is the same with poetry. In Persia there were great poets such as Hafiz, Rumi, and Sa'di, whose works are still studied to-day and highly esteemed by millions of people in the East; they consider that without their works there would be no humane culture. Their work was the foundation of humane culture in the East; many later poets have tried to write such works as the works of Rumi and Hafiz, but they have not yet succeeded after many centuries; it seems that the inspiration is lost. Inspiration, whenever it comes, is living and lifegiving; and it will always last and one will never get tired of it.

What is the theory of inspiration? Where does one find it? Where does it come from? There is one treasurehouse where all knowledge collected, experienced, learned, and discovered by human beings is stored. And that treasurehouse is the divine Mind, a mind with which all minds are linked. There is no experience we go through that does not remain or that is not recorded in that treasurehouse. Every good or bad experience we have, every new thing we learn, every discovery we make, it is all stored in that treasurehouse. But one might ask, "How does one find it? If we have a large store, perhaps hundreds and thousands of things, it is difficult to find anything we want at a moment's notice". The power of the mind, the power of the will is such that if one has sufficient power of will one can find anything one wants to find. There is a story about a person of powerful will who wanted to buy a certain piece of furniture. In the first street he went to after leaving his house he saw that very piece of furniture exhibited in a showroom. In other words he was guided towards it. What you really want is attracted by you, and you are attracted by what you want. It is the same with the poet, the musician, the thinker, when he is deeply interested in what he is doing, then he has only to wish; and by the automatic action of the desire his wish becomes a light. This light is thrown on the divine storehouse, and it is projected on the object he wants to find. Such is the phenomenon of will and inspiration, that no sooner an inspired person is moved by the beauty and harmony of life and wishes to express his soul, than the light of his soul shines on that particular object or on that particular knowledge. It comes instantly to his mind, expressing itself outwardly through his mind. All that is brought from within in this way is perfect, harmonious, beautiful, and has a wonderful effect.

In ancient times the Shah of Persia expressed the desire to have a history written of the past of Persia. But he was told that the records were lost and that it would be very difficult to trace the accounts of the kings who had lived before. But there was a poet, Firdausi, who said, "I will write the history of Persia". He was a man of inspiration. People were amazed; they said, "How will he do it"? But Firdausi sent his soul, so to speak, into the past and his soul became a receptacle of the knowledge of the past which he expressed in the form of poetry. This book is called The Shah-Nameh of Persia.

Many people think that science is based upon the knowledge of facts proved by reason and logic, and very few know that its beginning was intuition. All scientific discoveries spring from intuition; then reason finds their place, and logic helps them. They are analysed and as such made intelligible to others, but in the beginning they come from intuition just the same. If the great inventors of America, such as Edison and others had been only great mechanics it would not have been sufficient; behind this there was intuition.

To-day there is a tendency not to admit that side of life. People believe it is not solid enough to rely upon intuition or inspiration. Once in Paris, I was surprised at hearing a great writer say, "Is there such a thing as inspiration"? I thought, "Here is a great writer who has made a name, and still he does not know if there is such a thing as inspiration". By continual material strife, and by continually ignoring the Godspirit, people have become so material that they do not think that such a thing as inspiration exists. This man became famous without believing in inspiration, and that was all he wanted. When I began to know more about the work of this person I found that his works were nothing but superficial. There was no depth to them and no height; a very narrow pitch. And that is what takes these days.

When one goes to see modern plays one finds the same thing. There is hardly a play with depth. And if you ask why it is so, the answer is: in order to please the man in the street. That means, we must keep everybody back in order to please the man in the street. One day a newspaper reporter, to whom I spoke about philosophy, said, "How very interesting! But say, how shall I put it before the man in the street"? So the general education is to keep every man on the level of the street. In stagemagazines all is at a narrow pitch, it does not touch depth. Then where is the hope of progress if inspiration is ignored and intuition blunted? To-day the trend of mind is towards facts void of truth.

The step after inspiration is what is called vision. It is more than inspiration. One need not see a vision in a dream; one can have a vision in wakeful condition. There is nothing to be frightened about. It is only clearness of the inner sight. Knowledge comes in a flash and a problem is solved; a philosophical problem or a certain hidden law of life or nature has become manifest in a very clear form. Or one has got in touch with something or with someone at an unimaginable distance. People have very often misunderstood the meaning of vision and have pretended to be visionary. But in reality the development of the inner vision is a great progress of the soul.

When one goes still further on the path of intuition one comes to what we call revelation, which means that everything and every being reveals to one its secret. Such a one finds that every leaf has a tongue to tell its legend. He finds that every soul is a living book which reads its own story. He finds that every condition of life brings his inside out before him once he begins to look at it. He feels that he is at home on earth and in heaven, that the here and the hereafter all become manifest to his soul. As Sa'di, the great Persian poet, has said, "Once a person begins to read, every leaf of a tree becomes a page of the Holy Book".

How does it happen that one experiences or perceives intuition, inspiration and that one sees visions and gets revelations? There is a story of the apostles who instantly knew many languages. This does not mean that they knew French, English, German, and Spanish. It means they knew the language of every soul, that every soul began to speak to them, that they began to communicate with every person. The meaning of revelation is the understanding of the language of the soul. Every soul is always speaking if one can hear it. It is not only from the noise of the world or the voice of man that one hears, but even the silent trees and the still mountains speak to us when we are able to hear them. It is a language of vibrations, an imperceptible language, and yet a fine mind can grasp it. The only explanation of it is that it is a music. For a musician music is a language, it tells him something. The high and the low note, the flat and the sharp, all are expressing and telling him something; it all has a meaning. A person who is not a student of music does not know that language. He will enjoy music but he does not know the language.

Then there is the language of life, because life is music also. Each person is a note in that music, and that makes the symphony of life. One person is in tune, the other person is out of tune, one soul is sounding the right note, the other a false one. In this way every person makes or mars the music.

Revelation comes from the understanding of this music. You cannot learn it; you cannot teach it, but you can tune your heart to such a pitch that it begins to live and to enjoy the music of life.

In this way revelation is perceived, when the heart has become wakeful, living, so that it can perceive the vibrations coming from every soul, every condition which convey a certain meaning.

The great prophets and teachers who have given religion to humanity, who have inspired humanity to a higher ideal, who have guided mankind towards spiritual attainment, they were the revealed souls. And what they gave to the world was their interpretation of the revelation they had. But no sooner does a composer put his music on paper than much of it is lost. And when the prophet gives his teachings in the form of words much is lost too.

There are some who say, "This is something sacred, it is my belief", and they keep to those words. But there are others who want to know the spirit of it. The words that have come down are only interpretations of the revelations the prophets had.

If all the people in the world knew the spirit then there would not be so many different religions and so many different creeds. They would all agree to that one truth. That there are so many creeds, so many different religions, is because they do not understand religion. If one understood it then there would only be one religion, interpreted differently by the different teachers of humanity. And their revelation comes from the music of life which is interpreted in human tongue.

CHAPTER XVII

The Intoxication of Life

1

THERE ARE many different things in life which are intoxicating, but if we were to consider the nature of life we would realize that there is nothing more intoxicating than our life itself. We can see the truth of this idea by thinking of what we were yesterday and comparing it with our condition of to-day. Our unhappiness or happiness, our riches or poverty of yesterday are a dream to us, only our condition of to-day counts.

This life of continual rise and fall and of continual changes is like running water, and with the running of this water man thinks, "I am this water"; in reality he does not know what he is. For instance, if a man goes from poverty to riches and if those riches are taken away from him he laments, and he laments because he does not remember that before having those riches he was poor and from that poverty he came to riches. If one can consider one's fancies through life one will find that at every stage of one's development in life one had a particular fancy; sometimes one longed for certain things and at other times one did not care for them. If one can look at one's own life as a spectator, one will find that it was nothing but an intoxication. What at one time gives man a great satisfaction and pride at another time humiliates him, what at one time a person enjoys at another time troubles him, what at one time he values extremely at another time he does not value at all.

If man can observe his actions in everyday life and if he has an awakened sense of justice and understanding he will find himself doing something which he had not intended to do or saying something that he would not like to have said, or behaving so that he says, "Why was I such a fool!" Sometimes he allows himself to love someone, to admire someone; it goes on for days, for weeks, for months, years (although "years" is very long); then he feels, "Oh, I was wrong," or there comes something that is more attractive; then he is on another road, he does not know where he is nor whom he loves. In the action and reaction of his life sometimes man does things on impulse, not considering what he is doing, and at other times, so to speak, he gets a spell of goodness and he goes on doing what he thinks is good; at other times a reaction comes and all this goodness is gone. Then in business and in professions and commerce man gets an impulse, "I must do this," "I must do that," and he seems to have all strength and courage, and sometimes he goes on and sometimes it lasts only a day or two and then he forgets what he was doing and he does something else.

This shows that man in his life in the activity of the world is just like a little piece of wood raised by the waves of the sea when they are rising and cast down when the waves are going down. Therefore the Hindus have called the life of the world *Bhavasagara*, an ocean, an everrising ocean. And the life of man is floating in this ocean of the activity of the world, not knowing what he is doing, not knowing where he is going. What seems to him of importance is only the moment which he calls the present; the past is a dream, the future is in a mist, and the only thing clear to him is the present.

The attachment and love and the affection of man in the world's life is not very different from the attachment of birds and animals. There is a time when the sparrow looks after its young and brings grains in its beak and puts them into the beak of its young ones, and they anxiously await the coming of the mother who puts grain in their beak. And this goes on until their wings are grown, and once the young ones have known the branches of the tree and they have flown around in the forests under the protection of the kind mother they no longer know the mother who was so kind to them.

There are moments of emotion, there are impulses of love, of attachment, of affection, but there comes a time when they pass, they become pale and they fade away. And there comes a time when a person thinks that there is something else he desires and something else he would like to love. The more one thinks of man's life in the world the more one comes to understand that it is not very different from the life of a child. The child takes a fancy to a doll and then it gets tired of the doll and takes a fancy to another toy. And when it takes a fancy to the doll or the toy it thinks it the most valuable thing in the world; and then there comes a time when it tears up the doll and destroys the toy. And so it is with man; his scope is perhaps a little different, but his action is the same. All that man considers important in life, such as the collection of wealth, the possession of property, the attainment of fame and the rising to a position that he thinks ideal, any of these objects before him have no other than an intoxicating effect, but after attaining the object he is not satisfied. He thinks, "There is perhaps something else I want, it is not this I wanted." Whatever he wants he feels to be the most important thing, but after attaining it he thinks that it is not important at all, he wants something else. In everything that pleases him and makes him happy, his amusements, his theatre, his moving pictures, golf, polo, tennis, it seems that it amuses him to be in a maze and not to know where he is going, it seems that he only desires to fill his time and he does not know where he is going or what he is doing. And what man calls pleasure is what he feels at the moment when he is more intoxicated with the activity of life. Anything that covers his eyes from reality, anything that makes him feel a kind of sensation of life, anything that he can indulge in and that makes him conscious of some activity, this is what he calls pleasure.

The nature of man is such that whatever he becomes accustomed to, that is his pleasure, in eating, in drinking, in any activity. If he becomes accustomed to what is bitter that bitterness is his pleasure, if to what is sour then sourness is his pleasure, if he becomes accustomed to eat sweets he likes sweets. One man gets into a habit of complaining about his life and if he has nothing to complain about then he looks for something to complain of. Another wants the sympathy of others, to complain that he is badly treated by others, he looks for some treatment to complain of. It is an intoxication.

Then there is a person in a habit of theft, he is pleased by it, he gets into this habit; if there is another source of income before him he is not pleased, he does not want to have it. In this way people become accustomed to certain things in life, these things become a pleasure, an intoxication. There are many with whom it becomes a habit to worry about things. The least little thing worries them very much. They can cherish a least little sorrow they have; it is a plant they water and nourish. And so many, directly of indirectly, consciously or unconsciously, become accustomed to illness, and the illness is more an intoxication than a reality. And as long as man holds the thought of that illness he so to speak sustains it, and the illness settles in his body and no doctor can take it away. And the sorrow and illness are also an intoxication.

Then man's condition in life, every individual's environment and condition of life create before him an illusion and give him an intoxication so that he does not know the condition of the people around him, the people of the city and country in which he lives. And the intoxication not only remains with him in his wakeful state but it continues in his dreams, as the drunken man will also dream of the things that have to do with his drunkenness. If he has joy, if he has sorrow, if he has a worry or if he has a pleasure, the same will be his condition in his dream. And day and night the dream continues to exist, and the continuation of the dream with some lasts the whole life, with others it lasts only a certain time.

Man loves this intoxication as much as the drunken man loves the intoxication of wine. When a person sees something interesting in his dream and somebody tries to wake him, even on waking he feels for a moment that he should go to sleep and finish that interesting dream. Knowing that it was a dream and that someone is waking him he wishes to sleep and to finish that interesting dream.

This intoxication can be seen in all different aspects of life, manifests even in the religious, philosophical, and mystical aspects. Man seeks after subtlety, man wishes to know something that he cannot understand, he is very pleased to be told something that his reason cannot understand. Give him the simple truth, he will not like it, he wants to find before him something that he cannot understand. When the teachers like Jesus Christ came on earth and gave the message of truth in simple words the people at that time said, "This is in our book, we know it already." But whenever there is an attempt made to mystify people to tell them of the fairies and the ghosts and spirits they are very pleased, they desire to understand what they cannot understand.

What man has called spiritual or religious truth has always been the key to that ultimate truth which man cannot see because of his intoxication. This truth nobody can give to another person. It is in every soul, for the human soul itself is this truth. And if anything can be given, it is only the means by which the truth can be known. The religions, in different forms, have been methods. By these methods man has been taught by the inspired souls to know this truth, and to be benefited by this truth which is in the soul of man. But, instead of being benefited by a religion in this way man has taken only its external part to be his religion, and has fought with others, saying, "My religion is the only right one, your religion is false".

However, there have always existed some wise ones; it is said in the Bible that the wise of the East came when Jesus Christ was born, to see the child. What does it mean? It means that the wise have existed at different times, and it has been their life's mission to keep themselves sober in spite of this intoxication from all around and to help their brothers and sisters to gain this soberness. Among those who were wise by their soberness there have been some who had great inspiration and great power and control over themselves and over life within and without. And such wise men have been called saints or sages or prophets or masters.

Man, in the world, through his intoxication, even when following or accepting these wise men has monopolized one of them as his prophet or teacher and has fought with others, saying, "My teacher is the only true one," and in this way he has shown his intoxication and drunkenness. And as a drunken man will, without any thought, hit or hurt another person who may be different from him, who thinks or feels or acts differently, so many great people of the world who came to help humanity have been killed, crucified, hurt or tortured. But they have not complained about it, they have taken it as a natural consequence. They have understood that they were in a world of intoxication or drunkenness, and that it is natural that a drunken man will hurt or harm. That has been the history of the world in whatever part of the world the message of God has been given.

In reality the message comes from one source and that is God, and under whatever name the wise man gave that message it was not his message, it was the message of God. Those whose hearts had eyes to see and ears to hear, they have known and seen the same messenger, because they have received the message. And those whose hearts have no eyes or ears, they have taken the messenger to be important and not the message. Yet at whatever period that message came and in whatever form the message was garbed it was only that one message, the message of wisdom.

And it seems that the drunkenness of the world has increased and increased to such an extent that the great bloodshed and disaster have come about that the world has gone through recently, the like of which cannot be found in the history of the world. That shows that the drunkenness of the world has reached its summit. And no-one can deny that even now the world is not in a sober condition, but even now the traces of that drunkenness can be found in the unrest of the time, even if the great bloodshed, for the moment, is over.

The Sufi Movement[2] originates from *sophia*, wisdom, the message of wisdom. Its aim is the same that was at all periods of the world's history the aim of the message, to bring about that soberness in humanity, to bring about that love for one's neighbour. No doubt, politics or education or business are the means of bringing people of different races or nations in contact with one another, but spiritual truth and the understanding of life are the only means of bringing about that brotherly feeling in the world, which nothing else can bring.

This message does not work to form an exclusive community, as there are already so many communities, fighting against one another, but the object of the message is to bring about a better understanding between different communities in the knowledge of truth. It is not a new religion, and how can this be a new religion when Jesus Christ has said, "I am not come to give a new law, I am come to fulfil the religion." It is the combination of the religions.

The chief aim of this Movement is to revivify the religions of the world, in this way bringing together the followers of the different religions in friendly understanding and in tolerance. All are received with open arms in the Order of the Sufis; whatever be their religion, to whatever church they belong, whatever faith they have, there is no interference with it. There is personal help and guidance of the methods of meditation. There is a course of study to consider the problems of life. and the chief aim of every member of the Order is to do the best in his power to bring about that understanding, that the whole humanity may become one single brotherhood in the Fatherhood of God.

2

It is not only what man eats or drinks that gives him a certain amount of stimulus, but also what he smells, sees or hears, even that has an influence and effect on man's being. A stimulus that one experiences through food and drink in the real sense of the word is a small intoxication. But it is not only the food that one eats, and the water that one drinks, and all that one sees, hears and touches which gives man intoxication, even breathing the air from morning to evening, continually gives man a stimulus and intoxication. And if this is true, then is there one moment when man is not intoxicated? He is always intoxicated, only sometimes more than other times.

But this is not the only intoxication. A man's absorption in the affairs of his life also keeps him intoxicated. Besides that second intoxication of the work and affair in which one's mind is absorbed there is a third intoxication. And that third intoxication is the attachment that man has to himself, the sympathy that man has with himself. It is this intoxication which makes him selfish, which makes him greedy and very often unjust towards his fellowmen. The effect of this intoxication is that man is continually busy feeling, thinking, and acting: what would be to my interest, what could bring me a certain interest and profit. And in that his whole time and life become fully involved. It is through this intoxication that he says, "This is my friend, and that is my enemy; this one is my wellwisher, and that one is against me". It is by this intoxication that the ego, the false ego of man, is made. So it is this third intoxication which keeps man continually in the thought of attaining that which is for the profit of himself.

But as an intoxicated man does not really know what is profitable to him, so a selfish man, in his selfishness never knows, he does not understand what really is to his benefit. And at moments of soberness man wonders: "If this is intoxication, then what is the reality? I would like to know what reality is". But for the reality it is not only the eyes and ears that are necessary. It is the soberness besides it which is needed to hear and see better. One might ask, "How could we call this intoxication, if this seems to be a normal state, to be the state of every person?" Yes, it may be called normal only because it is the condition of everyone. But intoxication is intoxication. Intoxication is not satisfaction.

And then there is an innate longing for a certain satisfaction which man does not know, and that satisfaction man seeks, the satisfaction which is the continual longing of his soul. No active person with some wisdom will deny the fact that every effort he makes for happiness always seems to bring out a disappointing result. This shows that the effort is always made in the wrong direction. But apart from making an effort to find reality, the first thing is to realise what this intoxication is; and the first step in the path of truth is to know that there exists such a thing as intoxication.

There is the intoxication of childhood. If one could only imagine what attention, what service, what care the child demands! At the same time it does not know who takes the trouble, who takes care of it. It plays with its toys, it plays with its playmates, it knows not what is awaiting it in the future. What it wants, what it is pleased with is what is immediately around it; it does not see far. Nobody has ever known in his childhood what value is his mother or his father or those who care for him, until he arrives at that stage when he begins to see for himself. And when we see the condition of youth, that again is another intoxication, it is the time of blossoming, the time of the fullness of energy. The soul in that time of spring never thinks that there can be anything else. The soul never thinks that this is a passing stage. The soul only thinks that at that time it is full of intoxication; it knows nothing else but itself. How many errors, how many follies, many thoughtless things, and many inconsiderate things a youth has done of which he afterwards repents! But at the same time the soul never thinks about it. It is not the fault of the soul; it is the time, it is that intoxication. The person who is intoxicated is not responsible for what he does; he is intoxicated. Neither is a child to be blamed for his not being responsible or appreciative enough, nor the youth for being blind in his energy. It is natural.

This intoxication goes on as a person goes on in life. It is only the change of wine. The wine of childhood is different from the wine of youth. And when the wine of youth is finished, then some other wine is taken. Then according to the different walks of life that man goes along he drinks that wine which absorbs his life, either collecting wealth or requiring power, or seeking a position, all these things are fuel which intoxicates man. Even if one goes further in life intoxication still pursues one. It may be joy in music, or fondness of poetry, it may be love of art, or delight in learning. It is all intoxication.

If all these different occupations and things of interest are like different wines, then what is there in the world that can be called a state of soberness? It is wine no doubt, from beginning to end. Even those who are good and advanced spiritually and morally, they also have a certain wine. Wine one has to take all along, but it is a different wine. A highly advanced artist, a great poet, an inspired musician, will admit that there are moments of intoxication which come to him as a joy, often as an upliftment, from his art, music, poetry, and it makes him exalted; it is as if he is not living in this world.

The higher intoxication cannot be compared with the lower intoxication of this world; but it is intoxication. What is joy, what is fear, what is anger, what is passion, what is the feeling of attachment, and what is the feeling of detachment? All these have the feeling of wine, all have their intoxications. Understanding this mystery, the Sufis have founded their culture upon this principle of intoxication. The Sufis call it *Hál*. And *Hál* means in its verbal meaning: condition, state. And there is a saying of the Sufis, "Man says and does according to his condition".

One cannot say differently, and cannot do differently from the wine one has had. The one who has had the wine of anger, what he says or does is irritable, it is irritation. The one who has drunk the wine of detachment, in his thought, speech, action you will find nothing but detachment. With the one who drinks the wine of attachment, you will feel in his presence that all are drawn to him, and that he is drawn to all. A person does and says all that he does and says according to the wine he has taken. And if that is true, then the Sufi says, "Heaven and hell is in the hand of man if he only knew its mystery". The world therefore, for a Sufi, is a winepress, a store in which all sorts of wine are collected. He has only to choose what wine he will enjoy, and what wine will bring him that delight which is the longing of his soul.

I once had an experience in India which was my first impression, and deep impression indeed, in this direction of life. When walking in the district of dervishes, where they have their solitude, I found ten or twelve dervishes, sitting together under the shade of a tree in their ragged clothes, talking with one another. As I was curious to hear and see the path of different thoughts and ideas, I stood there watching this assembly and what was going on there. These thinking souls sitting on the ground without a carpet, made first the impression as if they were poor people, helpless ones, who have nothing perhaps in their possession, sitting in disappointment. But as they began to speak to one another I could not keep that impression any longer, for when they addressed one another they said, "O King of Kings, O Emperor of Emperors". All that was to be said was said afterwards, but that was the address. I was taken aback at first on hearing these words. But after giving a little thought to it,

I thought: what is an emperor, what is a king? Is the real king and emperor within or without? And the emperor who is the emperor of the environment without is dependent on all that is without. The moment he is separated from the environment he is no longer an emperor. But these emperors sitting on the bare ground were real emperors. No one could take away their empire, for their empire, their kingdom was not an illusion; their kingdom was a real kingdom. It seemed as if an emperor had a bottle of wine before him; but these emperors had drunk that wine, and had become real emperors.

Do we not see in our everyday life a person who says, "I am ill, I am sorry, I am miserable, I am wretched"? Put him in a palace, and put a thousand doctors and nurses around him, he will still be wretched. And another may have a great suffering and pain, and at the same time he says, "No, I am well, I am happy". All is well, all goes right, for that person is right. Does it not show to us that we are, we become that wine which we drink? The man who is drunk with the wine of success, he knows no failure. And if circumstances make him fail nine times, the tenth time he will succeed. The one who has drunk the wine of failure, you may give him all the possibility of success, but he has drunk the wine of failure, he cannot succeed.

But with all this, there is one subtle feeling every soul has, a feeling which cannot be explained in words, a feeling which makes man more comfortable in his armchair at home than perhaps with ten thousand people standing before him paying him homage. A person may be loaded with wealth but the moment when he sets aside all the pearls and jewels and he sits without anyone and takes a rest, that is the time when he breathes a free breath. And what does this teach us? It teaches us that man may have all else in the world, which may have the greatest value in his eyes, but yet there is something hidden which he is seeking. When he has that then he is happy.

One might explain it with perhaps more examples; it is the same idea: one does not want to have a person, however beloved, around one all the time; one wants to have one moment away from even the dearest person in the world. However proud a person is of his thoughts, the thoughts may be great, deep, and good, yet his greatest joy is the moment when he is not thinking. He may have the best feelings of love, tenderness and goodness, but there are moments when there are no feelings. Such moments are more exalting.

What does it show? This shows that the whole life is interesting because it is all intoxicating. But what is desired by the soul is one thing, and that is a glimpse of soberness. How does one experience this glimpse of soberness which is the continual longing of the soul? One experiences it by the way of meditation, by the way of concentration. But if it is a natural thing, why has one to make an effort for it? The reason is that one enjoys this intoxication so much that afterwards one becomes addicted to drink; that is the condition of every soul in this world. Every soul becomes addicted to drink the wine of life. At the same time there comes a moment, if not in the early part of life then later, if not when a person is happy then when he is unhappy, when he begins to look for that soberness which is the continual longing of his soul. The Sufi culture therefore is a culture in order to experience that soberness.

It is no doubt very difficult to explain how this soberness is attained. And yet after having explained this subject of intoxication it is not so very difficult. For it is as simple as saying that how to get rid of a drink is to keep away the drink for a time, and let one be without a drink. There are three principal wines, three principal intoxications: the intoxication of oneself, the intoxication of the occupation, and the third intoxication which is what the senses feel every moment. Now these three wines cannot be taken away at once. It is just like taking away his life's sustenance from a person who lives on wine. But one can give a person a certain time, that during that time he may keep sober, he may take two wines, not three. Another time try only one, not two; and as a person advances in meditative life he may arrive at that stage where the three wines on which he lives may be kept away, and yet he feels he lives, and so he becomes convinced that he exists without these three intoxications. Verily, this conviction of existing independently of these three wines, which brings man the realisation of eternal life, is the central theme of the Divine Message and the essence of all religions.

CHAPTER XVIII

The Meaning of Life

AFTER A great enquiry into the depths of life one finds that the only seeking of all souls is to know The Meaning of Life. The scientist looks for it in his search in the realm of science and the artist finds it in his art. In all their different interests, whatever people are interested in, the only inclination behind it is to find The Meaning of Life. This shows that it is the nature of the soul, that the soul has come here for this purpose, that it may realize, that it may understand The Meaning of Life. Therefore either through a material or a spiritual way every soul in its particular way is striving to seek what all the time is its longing.

One can see this even in the life of an infant. The desire of an infant to look at a thing, to tear it to pieces and see what is in it shows that it is the soul's desire to look into life, to understand life. No doubt the effect and the influence of life on earth is intoxicating, and through this intoxication man becomes so absorbed in himself and his own interest that he, so to speak, loses the way, the way that is inborn in man. This desire is not only to be found in man, but even in the lower creation one finds the same attitude. In animals, in birds, the deepest desire is not looking for food or seeking a comfortable nest; the deepest tendency is to understand the nature of life - which then culminates in man. In the life of the youth who continually asks his parents questions - "What does this mean, what is the meaning of that?" - one sees that continual longing to know The Meaning of Life, a longing which continues all through life.

What does this teach us? It teaches us the principle that, the source and the goal of the universe being one and the same, the Creator created all in order to know His own creation. How does the Creator see and understand His own creation? Not only in its highest and deepest aspect, but also through every thing and every being He is continually knowing and understanding His creation. For instance, if a person were to ask me, "What is art? Is it not made by man?", I would answer, "Yes, but made by God also, through man". And if that is so, then what is this whole mechanism of the universe doing? It is working. Working for what purpose? Working for the understanding of it.

What is this mechanism of the world? Is it living or is it dead? All that we call living is living, and all that we call dead is living too. It is for our convenience that we say "thing" and "being". In reality there are no things, they are all beings. Only there is a gradual awakening from the witnessing aspect to the recognizing aspect. And no science, however material, will deny the truth of this, for this truth is to be realized from all things, from religion, from philosophy, from science, from art, from industry, from all things. Only the difference is that one takes a shorter way and the other a longer way; one goes round and about and the other takes a straight way. There is no difference in the destination, the difference is on the way: whether one goes on foot or whether one drives, whether one is awake or whether one is asleep and is taken blindly to the destination, not knowing the beauties of the way.

If destiny may be divided into two parts, it is in this way, that one part is the mechanism that works the destiny and the other part is the soul that knows. The mechanism is the machine and the soul therein is the engineer who is there in order to work this mechanism and to produce from it what is to be produced.

There are many methods, there are many systems, there are many ways man adopts in order to know and understand, and the mind is the vehicle, the tool by the help of which, taking it as a medium, man experiences life in the accomplishment of this purpose. In Sanskrit the mind is called *manas* from which the English word *man* is derived. This means that man is his mind, not his body. As the soul has the mind as its tool, according to the readiness of its tool it experiences and it knows life. It is the condition of the mind which enables the soul to see life clearly. The mind is likened to water. When water is troubled there is no reflection to be seen; when water is clear then it shows the reflection.

But as it is said in the Bible "Where your treasure is there will your heart be also", man in his pursuit of material gains which he values most, has absorbed himself in the material life and has lost the benefit of life. At the present time when one explains civilization as commercial or industrial progress - when that is called civilization - then that becomes the ideal of every soul, and it becomes difficult to keep that tranquillity needed to accomplish the purpose for which the soul was born. Do I mean by this that industrial or commercial development is not necessary for the life of man? Not at all, as long as it does not ruin life's purpose, as long as it does not hinder the purpose for which man was born. Otherwise, in spite of all his progress, he has wasted his life, he has not attained the purpose for which he was born.

There are superstitions in the East and also in the West that animals such as horses, dogs and cats and birds give warning of a person's being ill or of death, and many may have found that there is some truth in these superstitions. If one were to investigate the truth of this and to ask why man does not understand and perceive life as the animals do, the answer is that the animals live a more natural life; they are nearer to nature than man who is taken up by artificial life. No thinking person will deny how many things one does, says and thinks are far from what is true, from what is natural. The more he will be one with nature and one with the deeper life, the more he will realize that one is in a continual state of agitation against reality - not only in doing wrong or evil, but even in doing good. If the animals can know, man is more capable of knowing, and it is knowledge alone which is the satisfaction of his life, not all external things. As it is said in the Bible, "The spirit quickeneth, the flesh profiteth nothing".

A man with all his wealth - what is his wealth? It is in his knowledge. If it is only in the bank and not in his knowledge he has not got that wealth, it is the property of the bank. All good things and great things, values and titles, position and possession, where are they? Outside? No, outside is only that which covers[3] that knowledge which one has within, and therefore the real possession is not without but within. Therefore it is the self within, it is the heart which must be developed. It is the heart which must be in its natural rhythm and at its proper pitch. When it is tuned to its natural rhythm and pitch then it can accomplish the purpose for which it is made.

There are five different ways by which the knowledge of life is perceived. One way which is known to many of us - to woman perhaps more than to man - is impression. Often a person comes in our house or we meet someone and before we have spoken to him we get a kind of impression, pleasant or unpleasant, a certain knowledge of that person's being. Sometimes at the sight of a person we get the feeling "Keep away", and sometimes at the first glance we feel drawn to a person without knowing the reason. The mind does not know, but the soul knows it. It is not only that we get the impression of a person we meet, but if we are more sensitive to impression we can also feel the impression of a letter that comes to us from a stranger. Many say that they can tell people's character by physiognomy or phrenology, but if they do not have the sense of impression in their heart, even if they read a thousand books on physiognomy or phrenology they will never get the impression in their heart. What does this show? It shows that true knowledge, from beginning to end, does not belong to the material realm.

Then there is another way, the intuitive way, by which one knows before one does something whether there will be success or failure. We can often find - it is not rare - that there are many intuitive people who before doing anything, before undertaking anything know what will be the result.

Then there is a third way and that is the dream or the vision. Some will say that a dream has a meaning and many will say that there is no meaning in a dream. But in point of fact there is nothing in this world which has no meaning; there is no situation, no action, no word that does not have its meaning. All that one does with intention and all that is done without intention, all that has a meaning behind it, if one can only understand it. There is a reason why one should see more clearly in the dream than in the wakeful state: when a person is in a dream his mind is naturally concentrated and when he is in his waking state all that is perceived through his senses calls his attention at every moment.

No doubt one finds that impression or intuition or a true dream is not manifested to every soul, and is manifested to one soul more than to another. Also one finds that it is not everyone who always lives in the rhythm and tune for receiving impressions and intuitions. At different times man's impression differs and this shows that in accordance with his evolution he is able to experience the knowledge of life. The more evolved he is spiritually, naturally the more he receives from within the knowledge of life.

The fourth form in which one perceives the knowledge of life is what may be called inspiration. It may come to an artist, it may come to a musician, it may come to a poet. At the time when it comes he can write or compose or do something that afterwards he will be surprised at. Did he really do it, or did someone else do it? If it were not for that inspiration the same poet might strive for six months and not be able to write that verse which he wrote in three minutes'time. What is the explanation? Is it the development of man's mind by which he receives inspiration? No, it is the receiving quality of mind, it is the purity of mind, it is his absorption in his art, the direction to which he has devoted his life. Great souls whose inspirational works have become immortal, where did they get them from? They got them from inspiration. And how did they get inspiration? By forgetting themselves, by being absorbed in the object of their love. That is the meaning of sacrifice: sacrificing to the beauty of the ideal. One has the ideal standing before one - that is the way to get inspiration.

Then one step further comes the realization which may be called revelation. When the soul is tuned to that state, then the ears of the heart are open, the eyes of the heart are open to see and hear the word that comes from all sides. In point of fact every atom of this world - either earth or heaven - speaks, and speaks aloud. It is the deaf ears of the heart and the closed eyes of the soul that make man not see it and not hear it. There is a verse of a Hindustani poet which says,

O self, it is not the fault of the divine Beloved
that you do not see Him, that you do not hear Him.
He is continually before you

and He is continually speaking to you.
If you do not hear it and if you do not see it,
it is your own fault.

It is for this purpose that every soul has been created, and it is in the fulfilment of this that man fulfils the object of God. When that spark that every heart has, that spark that may be called the divine spark in man, is blown and the flame arises, the whole life becomes illuminated and man hears and sees and knows and understands. In a verse of a Sufi it is said that every leaf of the tree becomes as a page of the sacred book when the heart is open to read it and when the soul has opened its eyes.

CHAPTER XIX

The Inner Life

THERE IS one aspect of life which is known to us, which we call our everyday life. The consciousness of doing all that we do in our everyday life is called the outer life. And there is a part of our life of which we are very often unconscious; it is that part which may be called inner life.

To be without inner life means to be without an arm or a leg or an eye or an ear, but even this simile does not sufficiently illustrate the idea of the inner life. The reason is that the inner life is much greater and nobler and much more powerful than the outer life. Man gives great importance to the outer life, being absorbed in it from morning till evening and not being conscious of another aspect of life which may be called inner life. It is therefore that all that matters to man is what happens to him in his outer life, and the occupation of his outer life keeps him so absorbed that he has hardly a moment to think of the inner life.

The disadvantage of not being conscious of the inner life is incomparably greater than all the advantage that one can derive from being conscious of the outer life - which one is always. The reason is that the inner life makes one richer, the outer life poorer. With all the riches and treasures that the earth can offer man is poor; and very often the richer, the poorer, for the greater the riches, the more limitation he finds in his life. The inner life makes one powerful, whereas the consciousness of the outer life makes one weak. It makes one weak because it is the consciousness of limitation. The consciousness of the inner life makes one powerful because it is the consciousness of perfection. The outer life keeps one confused; however intellectual or learned a person may be, he is never clear. His knowledge is based upon reasons which are founded upon outer things - things that are liable to change and destruction. That is why, however wise this person may seem to be, his wisdom has limitations. What to-day he thinks right after four days he thinks perhaps wrong.

The inner life makes the mind clear. The reason is that it is that part of one's being which may be called divine, the essence of life, the pure intelligence. The phenomenon of it is that, wherever the light of pure intelligence is thrown, things become clear. Absorption in the outer life without that which the inner life gives makes one blind. All one says, thinks or does is based upon outer experiences and no one can realize to what extent the power gained by the inner life enables man to see through life. There existed a belief in the third eye. In reality the third eye is the inner eye, the eye that is opened by one's awakening to the inner life.

Inner life therefore may be called in other words spiritual life. One can see it in the forest: it is the rain from above that makes the forest beautiful. This means that what the forest needs is not all that it has, but that it needs something that comes from above: the light, the rain. It is the sun and the rain that make the forest complete. In the desert there is no rain; there is only one aspect: the earth, but no water, no water from above. The water that gives life to the forest is not to be found in the desert. The desert is unhappy, as the man in the desert is unhappy looking for some shade from the hot sun, because the desert is longing, and the man in the desert is longing too for something he cannot find; whereas in the thick forest there is joy, there is inspiration, the heart is lifted up, because the forest is the picture of the inner life: not only the earth, not only the trees and plants - something which the forest needs has been sent upon it.

So it is with man. The man who is solely occupied with the things of the world is in the outer life. In the midst of the world he may be, but he is in the desert. It is the inner life which produces in him - not artificial virtues, not man-made qualities, but such virtues which can only arise from the inner life, besides that insight which makes the eyes see more than mortal eyes can see.

Now the question is: how are we to be sure that there is an inner life? What proof is there? And the answer is: there is not one moment in our life when we do not see the proof of the inner life. Only, we do not look for it. All the different means of communication, telegraphy, telephone and new communications that are coming, radio and X-rays and all new inventions which make a person wonder how much mankind has accomplished - if only he saw that all these machines, all these inventions are nothing but a little imitation, a poor imitation of what the human body is, if only he knew what the human being is! Man is the centre of joy, the centre of happiness and of peace, the centre of power, the centre of life and light. The phenomenon that can be vouchsafed to man is much greater than that of any machine, if only he had the patience and perseverance to explore himself. But what we do is to explore others. When it comes to analysis we think that it is a great study to analyse things, and when we analyse human nature we call it psychology. We analyse all others except ourselves, and therefore true psychology is never reached, because real psychology is to analyse oneself first. And when one's self is analysed, then one is able to analyse others.

If one only knew that besides what one says, does or thinks and their effects which are manifest to one, there is another action of the same person which creates something in that person's life and makes his world. And perhaps in a week, in a month, or perhaps in a year or ten years that which he created one day comes before him as a world, a world created by him. Such is the phenomenon of life. How insignificant a human being appears to be, just like a drop in the water, and at the same time what effect does he create by every thought, by every feeling, by every act! And what influence these spread, what influence they have on the lives of others! If one only knew this, one would find that the outer life and the results of all one thinks, says or does in the outer life are much smaller, incomparably smaller than the results produced by anything one thinks, says or does in the inner life. It is therefore the inner life that makes man more responsible than the consciousness of the outer life. The responsibilities of the outer life compared with those of the inner life are much smaller; for the moment they might appear to be heavy burdens, but they are nothing compared with the responsibilities one has with one's inner life. If one sees what one creates, the responsibility is much greater. There is a saying in the East that the donkey seems to be much happier than the *chacor* which is supposed to be the most intelligent bird.

Man in the outer life seems quite pleased because his responsibilities are less, his outlook is small, his horizon narrow; what he sees of the world is very little. But when the horizon is opened, when the heart has penetrated through the barrier that divides the here and the hereafter, when one begins to see behind the veil and all that appears on the surface becomes a screen behind which something else is hidden, then one experiences life quite differently. The view of the one who stands on the top of the mountain is quite different from the view of the one who stands at its foot. Both are human beings, both have the same eyes, but the horizon of the one is different from the horizon of the other. Inner life means the widening of the horizon and the change of the direction of seeing.

In English a mystic is called a seer, the one who sees. In the East there is a quotation of a great Yogi who says, "In order to see what is before you, you must see within yourself". This means that within yourself there is a mirror, and it is that mirror which may be called the inner world, the inner life. In this mirror all that is before you is reflected. When the eyes are looking outward then you have turned your back to the mirror which is inside, but when the eyes are turned inward then you see reflected in this mirror all that is outside. By this process all seeing is so clear and manifests to such fullness that compared with it the vision one has before one's eyes is a blurred and confused vision.

Two persons may live together for twenty-five years, for forty or fifty years, and may not be able to understand one another because of the lack of inner life; whereas the inner life would enable them to understand one another in one moment. When it is said that the twelve apostles began to understand the language of all nations, did they learn the grammar of all nations at that moment? No, they learned the language of the heart. The language of the heart speaks louder than words can speak. If the ears of the heart were open to hear that language, outer words would not be necessary.

With all the progress it is making humanity is still most limited, and the more we see the limitation of this progress, the more we find that it is because of the absence of inner life. When we hear in the traditions and histories of the past how many thieves and robbers and murderers there used to be and how many murders were committed, we think, "What a horrid time!" And yet, the present time is much worse; the time of robbers and murderers was much milder. One or two persons in a village were murdered; now towns and countries are swept away. One war has swept away a large part of humanity. Imagine, if another war comes, what will be the result? They say people have progressed, they are more thoughtful. But with all this thoughtfulness we have progressed to cause all the destructions and disasters that we find in a much greater degree. Does it mean that humanity is not progressing? It is progressing - but in which direction? Downwards.

The condition of going the path of the inner life is to be free first in order to walk in that path. If the feet are pinned and the hands nailed by beliefs, by preconceived ideas, by thoughts, then one stands still. A person has every desire to go, but is not going because he is holding on to something. He is holding on to certain beliefs he believed in or to what he thought; he is not going on, he is not going forward. And therefore many people with many good qualities, high ideals and religious tendencies, with a devotional temperament, with all the spiritual qualities they may have, can still remain standing in the same place. Either their ideas are holding as pins or nails in the feet, or their hands are somewhere leaning on the railing and holding it, not going further.

What the inner life requires first is freedom in proceeding. The old meaning of freedom is very little understood, although everyone is seeking freedom and so much is said about freedom. One can be free of all things, except one and that is the self - the last thing one thinks about. The conception of freedom is quite different at this time. Therefore while seeking freedom man becomes anything but free because he is caught in the trap of his own self. That is the greatest captivity there is; there he remains as the *jinn* in the bottle.

The inner life requires sacrifice. As man considers his learning, his qualifications, he sees that everything in his life tends to better qualify him to gain all that he can in the world - power, possessions, wealth or anything - and that sacrifice is a way quite contrary to gain. Therefore he develops the nature of gaining instead of sacrificing. Besides, sacrifice requires a large mind, sacrifice requires deep sympathy, great love, sacrifice is the most difficult thing.

Inner life is something which is within oneself; it has been called a chamber of divine light in one's own heart. The door remains closed until an effort is made to open it, and that effort is sacrifice. In terms of the Bible there is the word self-denial, but people often misinterpret it. What people think generally is that self-denial is to deny all that is good and beautiful, all that is worth attaining. In reality self-denial is not denying all that is good and beautiful to the self, but denying the self - and that is the last thing one wishes to deny. The automatic action of this denial opens the door of the inner life.

Now coming to the path of the sages: the sages who have realized the inner life have realized it by the method of contemplation. Man from his infancy is unaware of something in him which is more than a faculty. By experiencing life through the outer senses this faculty which is the faculty of inner life becomes closed, because he does not use it; just as if a door to a chamber of joy and light and life were closed. And as from infancy man has not experienced the joy, the life and the light of this chamber which may be called a celestial chamber in the heart of man, he remains unaware of it, but for a feeling he sometimes has and which he is unconscious of. This feeling remains, and sometimes when one is deeply touched or has deeply suffered, sometimes when life has shown its hideous face, or after an illness or by the help of meditation, this feeling which is unconsciously working as a longing to unfold itself becomes manifest. In what way? In love of solitude, in sympathy for others, in a tendency to sincerity, in the form of all that is good and beautiful. It may manifest in the form of emotion, love, affection, in the form of inspiration, of revelation, vision, art, poetry or music; in whatever form one allows it to express itself or with whatever one happens to busy oneself, in that form it begins to manifest.

All is spiritual once the door of the chamber of the heart is open. If a man is a musician then his music is celestial; if he is a poet then his poetry is spiritual; if he is an artist then his art is a spiritual work; whatever he may do in life, that divine spirit manifests. He need not be a religious person, he need not be a philosopher, he need not be a mystic. It is only that now begins to manifest to view what was hidden in him and was keeping him incomplete in life. That makes life perfect, it enables man to express life to its fullness.

Every attempt made to-day to better the conditions of humanity by politics, by education, by social reconstruction and many other ways, all these excellent plans can only be fulfilled if this something which was missing is added to them. But in the absence of it all efforts of many many years will prove to be futile, for this something wich is missing is the most essential of all things. The world cannot remain a world without rainfall. The world cannot progress without a spiritual stimulus, a spiritual awakening. If that is not the first thing it is natural; still it can be the last thing, and if it is not even the last thing then it is a pity.

Now I should like to explain how the meditative souls are awakened, how they experience the inner life. In the first place the adept should value his object of attaining the inner life more than anything else in life. As long as he does not value it, he remains unable to attain it. That is the first condition: that man values the inner life more than anything else in the world - wealth, power, position, rank or anything. It does not mean that in this world he should not be in pursuit of things he needs. It means that he must give the greatest value to something which is really worthwhile.

The next thing is that when one begins to give value to something, one thinks it is worthwhile to give time to it, because to-day in the modern world time, as they say, is money, and money means the most valuable thing. If a person gives that time which is money, which is precious, to something he considers most worthwhile, more than anything else in the world, then that is no doubt the next step towards the inner life.

And the third thing is that the condition of his mind is relieved of that pressure which is always in a person's heart thinking, "I have not done what I ought to have done towards my fellowmen". Be it his father or mother, child, husband, wife, brother, friend, whoever it is, he thinks, "What I was expected to do towards the persons with whom I am placed, or in the condition I am in, that I have not done". If that pressure is troubling the mind then that mind is not yet fit. A person will give time to contemplation, spiritual life - it is most valuable, but at the same time his mind is disturbed, his heart is not at rest feeling, "I have not done my duty, I have a debt to pay to someone". It is a most essential point for an adept to consider that any debt to be paid in life does not remain unpaid.

When we look at life, is it not a market place? The give-and-take is to be seen in everything, and for what one has not paid just now, the bill will be presented afterwards. Who thinks, "I have gained without paying", must wait till he realizes that he will have to pay with added interest.

In what form does man take, in what form does he give? Man is seldom aware of it. In giving it may be that he gives service, sympathy, kindness, his money, all he has to the north, and from the south it comes back to him; when he takes from the west, to the east he has to pay. Only man does not know in what form he has to pay, in what form he takes. Very often he does not know when he takes or what he gives, but in give-and-take every moment of his life is occupied and in spite of all the injustice in the world it all adjusts itself in the end. It is the clear idea of this condition that shows that it all balances.

If there were no balance the world would not exist. This ever-moving world, turning round and round, what holds it, what makes it stand? It is balance. It is not only the world that is going on, but everything is going on, the whole of life in its own way. What keeps it existing? It is balance that holds it. Being occupied with our worldly life we do not know that balance, but when the inner eye is open and we see life keenly, we will find that it is a continual balancing process going on, we as the particles of one mechanism are constantly busy keeping this balance.

Once the heart is at rest by the thought that one has paid or is paying one's debts, then one has come to a balanced condition which brings about balance in life. That balance creates a condition in which the heart which is likened to the sea, becomes - not a restless sea as it is in a storm but a calm sea, its water undisturbed; and it is that condition which enables man to experience inner life better.

Do we not see in our everyday life what influence has the presence of persons who do not have that tranquillity, that peace, that calmness? It is a terrible influence upon themselves, a disastrous influence upon others. One realizes it in one's everyday life if one sees it; one may be sitting in an office with someone, one may be standing in a certain place, one may be staying in a house where other people are standing or sitting, and one can realize by their atmosphere whether they have reached a state of balance, tranquillity, calm and peace, or whether they are in a state which is not rhythmic, not balanced. This again gives us the idea that what we call happiness or unhappiness is a balanced state or an unbalanced state. When a person is in the normal state in which his mind and heart ought to be, he need not seek for happiness, he is happiness itself, he radiates happiness. When that state is disturbed he is unhappy; it is not that unhappiness comes to him, but he himself is unhappiness.

A Hindu term, a Hindu idea is that self means happiness; the depth of the self is happiness. This means that all this outer structure, the physical body, the breath, the senses of perception, all these which make man stand out, but man's inner being can only be called by one name, and that is happiness. It is natural therefore that everyone is seeking for happiness, and not knowing where to get it, is always seeking for it outside himself. Therefore instead of finding that happiness which is his own he wants to take away the happiness of another. And what happens is that he can neither get the happiness of another nor can he give it. By trying to get it from another he causes sorrow to the other and the sorrow comes back to him.

There are few robbers who go into the houses of others to steal, but there are many robbers of happiness, and they seldom know that they are robbing others of it. The robber of happiness is more foolish than the robbers who are after wealth, for when they are successful they get something, but the robber of happiness never gets anything, he only gives sorrow to others.

Inner life therefore must not be considered, as many have thought it to be, a life spent in the forest or in the caves of the mountain or a retired life. Yes, there is a need for a certain person who seeks for solitude, who prefers to be away from the midst of the world, whose inspiration is stimulated by being alone, who feels himself when he is by himself, but it is not a necessity for attaining that happiness. One can be in the midst of the world and one can stand above the world. Life has many woes, and the only way of getting rid of them is to stand above them all. This can be attained by one thing only, and that is the discovery of the inner life.

CHAPTER XX

The Inner Life and Self-Realization

IT IS by the inner life that self-realization is achieved. Life can be divided into two parts. One part is attending to our worldly needs, toiling, earning money, serving in different capacities in order to live ourselves and to look after our families. That is one side of life. The other side is to think that there is something besides the worldly life, that there is a higher ideal, a greater happiness, a deeper insight into life and a greater peace. That is another life. By inner life I do not at all mean a religious life, for one may be religious and at the same time very worldly.

There is a story of Aurangzeb's reign in India, that he issued a royal command that everyone inhabiting his dominions must attend each of the five prayers of the faithful in the mosque. A sage lived there of whom no one knew that he was a sage; he used to live in solitude. The sage also received this command but he forgot it or did not think about it. The police was sent to bring him to the house of prayer and naturally he came and joined the congregation. The man who leads the prayers began to pray and the others followed him, but after five seconds the sage ran away from the congregation. The police went after him and he was brought before the judge, for he had not only violated the first law but disturbed the whole congregation by running away. He said to the judge, "I would like to know what is meant by leading the prayers". The judge said, "Religion teaches that your thoughts must be united with the thoughts of your leader". The sage answered, "That is what I did! The leader's thought went to his house; he had forgotten his keys. So I could not stay in the house of prayer; I ran for the keys. Wherever the leader's thought led me, there I went". In the end it was proved that it was true. He was a great sage and to him was known all that was going on in the minds of others. To be religious, to be orthodox or to be pious does not necessarily mean to be spiritual. To be spiritual is quite different from being prayerful, as they say.

Now the question arises: how does one proceed in the inner life? One first takes the inner life as a journey, a journey to a desired goal. There are certain conditions of this journey which one must know. In the first place the journey is hard because there are no electric trains; it is a journey we have to make on foot. This at once changes the character of the journey and makes it different from a traditional journey. There is no equipment as we have to-day, and we have forgotten how one journeyed in the past. To go through the wilderness, over mountains, to cross rivers by swimming to the other side, risking all sorts of dangers on the way, that is the kind of journey we have to make in spiritual attainment. The outer journeys are made easy to-day, but the inner journey has its difficulties just the same.

The first condition of this journey is to be conscientious of the customs of the journey. When we have to walk long distances we give up unnecessary burdens, and so we have to give up many things in life in order to make the journey. We unconsciously make our life so heavy for ourselves. Outwardly it may not seem difficult to make it heavy, yet when we begin to journey inwardly we realize how difficult it is to carry a heavy load. When we have to go on foot every little responsibility we take up, every little habit we form, all weigh upon us - little things which in everyday life we never think about. We become more and more addicted to comforts, more and more intolerant to surroundings, more and more sensitive to jarring influences. Instead of becoming stronger we become weaker every day, and when it comes to journeying and facing the difficulties which will rise during the journey, it becomes very difficult.

You must remember that at every time of the world's history everyone who has tried to go further in the spiritual path has met with difficulties. The moment he started on this path he had more difficulties than the average person, greater and greater temptations came on his way, temptations which perhaps had never come before, which were always far away. The moment man takes this path temptations of all kinds come. He is tested and tried at every step he takes. Besides, he is taken to task very seriously if he does not take himself to task. Others are not taken to task so seriously, and that is natural also. When a child breaks a glass one overlooks it, one says, "Why, it is natural". But when the maid breaks a glass one asks, "Why did you do it, did you not see it?" A grown-up person is responsible, the one who takes the spiritual path is responsible. Therefore more is exacted from him; he has to answer for everything he does, either to himself or to life.

Besides, we have many debts to pay in our lives, debts we do not know of. We only know our money debts, but there are many others: of the husband to his wife and of the wife to her husband, of the mother to her child and of the child to its mother, the debts to pay to our friends and acquaintances, to those who are close to us, near to us, to those who stand above us and to those who are dependent upon us. There are so many different kinds of debt we have to pay, and yet we never think about them. In ancient times even those who did not take the spiritual path, noblemen, knights, had the law of chivalry which was very much about paying debts. The ancient people thought in this way, "My mother has brought me up from my infancy, my childhood; she has sacrificed her sleep, rest and comfort for me and loved me with a love which is beyond any other love in this world, and she has shown that mercy which is the compassion of God".

The child thought much about the debt it had towards its mother. Someone went to the Prophet Muhammad and asked him, "Prophet, you said there is a great debt to be paid to one's mother. Suppose that I gave my mother all that I have earned, would that pay her back?" The Prophet said, "No, not in the least. If you served her your whole life, even then you could not pay the debt of what she has done for you in one day. She brought you up with the thought that even when she was gone you would live; she has not only given her service and heart and love to you but also her life. That you will live after her, that was all her thought. And what is your thought? If you are a kind and good person your thought is, 'So long as my poor mother is living I will take care of her to the end. One day she will die and then I shall be free'. It is a different thought compared with hers".

This is only one example; but there are many other debts: to our neighbours, to strangers, to those who depend upon us or who expect from us some help, some counsel, a word of advice, some service, it is all a debt we have to pay. There is much to pay to God - but God can forgive. But before going on the spiritual path the debt to the world must not be forgotten. The spirit, as it goes further, feels a great release when it pays its debts. Do we think about these simple things these days? As soon as we turn our thoughts to spiritual things the first question is, "What occult books should we read?" We never think about those little things and how much depends upon them. When we think of spiritual things, we think, "If only I could get the key to that way". But there is a condition that must be fulfilled, and that condition is our consideration for every soul.

We may ask, "What if people do not deserve it, if they are not worthy of it?" It is not our concern whether they deserve it or not; we do not think about it. When there is money to be paid to a money-lender, it is his due, whether he deserves it or not. So it is on the spiritual path. Those we have to pay we have to pay - in the way of attention, service, respect; all that is due to them we have to pay. In the first place, spiritual realization apart, one feels such a release at having paid one's debt to everyone to whom it is due. This also opens the light of the soul, making the way straight and illuminating it, so that the confusion one always feels when striving for spiritual progress disappears. Otherwise there is always this confusion.

We can now understand what next is necessary on the spiritual path. It is to develop our tendency to trust. A person who wants to go along the spiritual path must have a greater desire to trust than the average man. No doubt the world is going from bad to worse to-day. Promises have no value. A ten cents stamp is valued more than a word of honour, because the stamp is sure. Since this is the state of the world it is difficult to develop the tendency to trust. But once you begin to tread the spiritual path trust is the first thing necessary. Very often a person says, "Well, I would like to trust people, but people are not worthy of trust". Yes, it is practical to think so in business, but when it comes to another kind of life, social life or a life of spiritual attainment, you must not look at it in this way. There you can only develop the tendency of trusting others by being ready to undergo every loss.

It is not always foolish to trust. On the contrary, it is the wise one who trusts more than the foolish one. Besides, it is not a weakness to trust, it is a strength; the one who has less trust is weak, and every day makes him weaker. The one wo does not trust outsiders, cannot trust his own relatives, his own friends, and then that distrust develops to such an extent that he does not trust himself. That is the end.

There is a story of a great Sufi who in the first part of his life was a robber. There was a man travelling through the desert in a caravan. He had a purse full of coins which he wanted to entrust to someone because he heard that robbers were coming. He looked around and found at some distance a tent where a most distinguished man was sitting. He said, "Will you please keep this purse for me, for I am afraid that if robbers come they will take it. The man said, "Give it to me, I will keep it for you". When the traveller came back to the caravan he found that robbers had come and had taken all the money. He thanked God that he had given his purse to someone to keep. But when he went back he saw all the robbers sitting in that tent, and this most dignified man was dividing what they had stolen. Then he realized that this man was the head of the robbers and thought, "I was more foolish than all the others, for I gave my money to the thief ! Who can be more foolish than me !" He was also frightened and began to step back. But as soon as the chief in the tent saw him go back, he called him and asked, "Where are you going? Why did you come here?". He said, "I came here to get my purse back, but I found that I had given it to the very party from whom I wanted to keep it away". The chief said, "You gave me your purse, is it not so? You entrusted it to me; you were not robbed of it. How can I take it away? Did you not trust me? How can you expect me to take it from you? Here is your purse, take it". This act of trustworthiness impressed the robbers so much that they followed the example of their chief. They gave up robbery. It moved them to the depth of their hearts to feel what trust means. In his later days this chief did great spiritual work.

By distrusting people we perhaps avoid a little loss, but the distrust that we have sown in our heart is a greater loss still.

The third step in the inner life is to find someone in whose guidance you can trust. You may find a spiritual teacher as great as an angel, and yet if you have no trust he can do very little for you. Besides, if you found someone in your life, a spiritual guide, who did not prove trustworthy to you, your loss would be smaller than the loss of that teacher; the loss of the teacher would be greater. Nevertheless, the whole spiritual progress under the guidance of a teacher depends upon the extent of your trust in his guidance. Without this trust you may learn all the many teachings and practise occult laws, and it will amount to nothing. Trust is the one thing.

People seeking after truth must know the place of the teacher in their lives, the importance of a spiritual guide and of his guidance; they must value it and consider it sacred. If that consideration is not there, then nothing is there, then a person is like a lost sheep. This tendency of going from one thing to another, from one teacher to another is an offence to the teacher, to God and to oneself. In this way one accomplishes nothing.

In my youth my interest in the spiritual path was great, and I came into contact with the teacher in whose hands I was destined to be initiated in the spiritual path. The first thing my teacher said was, "No matter how great a teacher may come, once you have received this initiation, this blessing from my hands, your faith may not change". Having had a modern education I wondered how to understand this. I did not doubt, but I thought, "What does it mean?" And with every step further in my life I found out that this alone is the right way. When the mind is disturbed, when a person distrusts, when he goes to one teacher and then goes over to another method, what can he find? There is no ideal there. In a university one may study first under one professor and then under another, and so on. That is all right for a university; it is a different kind of education. But when it comes to spiritual education idealism is necessary.

In a village there was a young peasant who was known to be a great seeker after truth. Once a great teacher came to that village, and it was announced that whoever would come into the presence of this teacher, for him the doors of heaven would open and he would be admitted without having to account for his deeds. The peasants were very excited about it, and they all went to be in the presence of the teacher except the young man who was known to be a great seeker after truth. The teacher said, "Everyone from the village has come to me except that young man; I shall go to him myself". So he came to the cottage of the young man and said, "What is it? Is it that you are antagonistic to me or that you doubt my knowledge? What is it that has kept you from coming to see me?" The young man said, "There was nothing that kept me back except one thing. I heard the announcement that everyone in your presence would be admitted to heaven without question. I do not seek this admission, because I had a teacher once and I do not know where he is, in heaven or in hell. If I went to heaven and he was in the other place all would be different for me. Heaven would become hell for me. I would rather be with my teacher, no matter where he is".

That is the ideal the seekers after truth have about their spiritual teacher, and it is with that idealism that they are able to go further and gain the confidence of their teacher. To-day the tendency is different. A pupil begins to weigh and measure the teacher before he has started on the spiritual path. He wants to know whether or not the teacher fits in with his ideas, and if the teacher does not fit in with his ideas he does not come to learn. But when it comes to teaching it is an absolutely different idea. It is that which keeps thousands of people back. They say they are seeking a teacher, but they think they are teachers themselves.

Going still further it is not only the faith and devotion one has for one's teacher, but also the effacing of one's self, because the teacher's work is like that of a goldsmith who melts the gold and turns it into an ornament. Therefore the teacher has to test and to try, to mould and to melt before he can use the pupil for a better purpose. If a pupil cannot give himself to that moulding, then he will have a difficult time.

Once, for instance, the king of Buchara, seeing the futility of life, gave up his kingdom and went to Afghanistan to find spiritual guidance. The first thing his teacher gave him to do was to dust the rooms of all the pupils. There were all kinds of pupils, poor and rich, but none was a king. They all felt very sorry for this man who once was a king and who now had to dust the rooms, a work he had never done before. They said nothing, but one day they could no longer keep back the feeling, "It is a pity that this man should do that work. He is so nice and kind and gentle, such a fine man, and he should do that work?" They went to the teacher and said, "Teacher, would you not give this work to one of us? It pains us to see this man who has been a king, who lived in palaces, dusting rooms". "My pupils", answered the teacher, "you must wait. I do not think the time has come". They said, "It gives us great pain". "Well", the teacher said, "I will tell one of you what to do, and then we shall see". One day the man who had been a king was carrying a little basket, a wastepaper basket, and one of the pupils pushed it so that it fell over and everything fell on the floor. So he had to gather it up again. He looked at the pupil and said, "Well, if I were what I was before I would have shown you what it means to do such mischief". Then he gathered it all up and went away. This report reached the teacher who said, "Did I not tell you that the time is not yet there?" Then again another pupil did a similar thing, and the man who once was a king stood and looked at him, wanting to say something, but did not. The report went to the teacher who said, "Not yet". A third time something of a similar kind was done. The man did not even look up; he went his way. And the teacher said, "Now the time has come".

One might ask, "Is it not weakness to be so passive?" Yes, if one were so passive from weakness it would be weakness. But if one is so passive through thoughtfulness then it is strength, because it requires great strength to dominate one's own self. Such a one has a silent influence, just as in the story of Daniel, where it was the power he had over himself that tamed the lion. It is easy to tame a lion, but difficult to tame one's self. One's self can be horrible, more horrible than a lion. One may say, "How gentle, how molten, how thougtful I have become!". But then there may be moments when, to one's own astonishment, one acts quite differently. Really to dominate that crude nature is a melting process. Then when the gold has melted you can turn it into any ornament you like.

When we go still further on the spiritual path it is the path of power, of concentration. The mind is just like a restive horse that will not stay in order, that cannot be controlled. Once a person begins to practise concentration he finds an even greater difficulty in making his mind obey. As long as he does not begin he does not know it, but the moment he begins to try he realizes how very difficult it is to concentrate the mind.

There is a story of Farid whose mother sent him to the forest because he wanted to meditate, to communicate with nature, to find God. He developed the nature of concentration and then went to a teacher. The teacher asked him, "Is there anything in your domestic life that you love or like?" Farid said, "I have no friends, I have always been in the wilderness. At home there is a cow; it is the only being I like". The teacher said, "Well, I will ask you to think of this cow". All the other pupils had different objects to concentrate and meditate upon. While doing their work they sat by themselves for five minutes and then went out. This was their way of practising. Farid sat by himself a long time. One day when the teacher wanted to speak to his pupils he asked, "Where is the new pupil?" They said, "We have not seen him all these days when we were playing together". The teacher said, "Perhaps he is still sitting where I told him to practise", and he went himself and asked Farid to come out. The first time he called him, Farid did not answer. The second time he answered making the sound of a cow. The teacher again asked him to come out, but he said, "I cannot, my horns are too long". The teacher showed his pupils and said, "This is called concentration. You are all playing. If he, by concentrating on a cow, can turn into a cow then there is nothing he cannot turn into".

That is the secret of all things. What is meant by concentration is to change the identification of the soul, that it may be able to lose the false conception of its identification, and identify itself with the true self instead of with the false self. This is what is meant by self-realization. Once a person realizes his self by the proper way of concentration, of contemplation, of meditation, he has understood the essence of all religions, because all religions are only different ways that lead to one truth, and that truth is self-realization.

Question: What part of God do animals express? In what do the souls of animals and vegetables differ from man's soul?

Answer: Their bodies and minds make the difference. The soul is the ray; as rays they are one and the same. But the body adorns itself in accordance with its fineness, be it greater or smaller, with more or less intelligence. The degree to which animals and vegetables differ from man apart, among men you will find the same differences: some have vegetable qualities, some have animal qualities, some have human and some angelic qualities.

Among Hindus there used to be a custom that when two persons wanted to marry, their friends showed their horoscope to a Brahmin. The Brahmin did not look so much at the horoscope, but he was a psychologist and thought about the category of both persons: were they angelic, human, animal, or still denser? If he found that there was a vast distance between them, and it would not be right to marry them, the Brahmin would say, "The planets do not accord". In this way he avoided many disasters by knowing psychology - not by thinking about the pose and position of the stars.

Question: If the one who is of lower evolution cannot love a person of higher evolution, will the person who is highly evolved lose the love of those of lower evolution?

Answer: I would like to say in a few words that, spiritually speaking, when a person of higher evolution loves a person of lower evolution, his love will perhaps become greater, his heart larger, his feeling more intense; his love reaches far. Who would have thought that Christ could have such love and such friendship for the fishermen with whom he had dinner, and that he could pour his love on all those he met? The higher you advance the greater is your love, and it has to spread somewhere. You just spread it.

And now the question whether a person of lower evolution cannot love a person of higher evolution. There are some reasons for it. A person is very often too blind to appreciate a beauty which he cannot reach. Therefore a person may have in his neighbourhood a most beautiful personality, a saintly soul with all virtue and goodness, and yet he may not appreciate this, because he is not evolved enough. It is therefore said in *In an Eastern Rosegarden** that a person of lower evolution cannot love a person of higher evolution. If sometimes he loves a person of higher evolution, it is because he is held, bound by that person's power; it is not from the bottom of his heart. He cannot resist it , but at the same time he has no love because he cannot admire the beauty which rises beyond his view.

Question: Why should it be necessary to seek the guidance of a personality other than oneself in order to arrive at spiritual attainment?

Answer: If a person is self-sufficient, if he is satisfied and guided by the light within, he must not seek another personality. But I have never seen a child who at his birth had already learned a language and who never needed help from his mother or father. And just as it is necessary for an infant to learn from someone, so we have to learn the heavenly language from someone who knows it. But at the same time, if a person is satisfied with his inner light, that is the best way to be.

Question: What is the difference between concentration, contemplation and meditation?

Answer: Concentration is focusing of mind on form.

Contemplation is focusing of mind on an idea.

Meditation is raising of the consciousness.

* See Vol. VII of this series, Chapter 1, Love, Harmony and Beauty.

CHAPTER XXI

The Interdependence of Life Within and Without

1

IT IS the lack of knowledge of the interdependence of life within and without which brings life into a confusion, a mist. One asks for the cause of everything, one does not know that cause. The first thing to understand in connection with this subject is that the individual is a mechanism as well as an engineer. There is a part of his being which is merely a mechanism, and there is another part which is an engineer. If the part which is a mechanism overpowers, in other words governs that part which is the engineer, then that person becomes a machine working under the influence of all that he comes in touch with.

The influences of the finer world and those of the grosser world, influences of all kinds acting upon that person keep him every moment of the day in working order, whether they are acting in his favour or in his disfavour, whether they work against his will or according to his will. If it is according to his will it is a good accident, if it is against his will it is a misfortune. Will has a great part to play in life, and if the will is hidden under the mechanism then the will has no more power over it; the mechanism works automatically, influenced by different forces coming from the finer and the grosser worlds.

Why are there in this world many persons with whom something is wrong, and why are there very few who think that all is well? Even among ten thousand persons there is hardly one who says, "All is well with me". All the others say, "Something is wrong with me". It is very easy to attribute it to destiny, to call it misfortune or ill luck. But by calling it by these names it cannot be remedied; on the contrary it grows with the years. Besides, that part in a person which may be called the engineer never has a chance; the more the mechanism takes hold of his life, the more that part which is called engineer is suppressed. A person with his little will, with few desires and wishes is pushed downwards by the force of this automatic working of life. This automatic working he calls conditions, circumstances. He sees some reason for it and when it is seen from a logical point of view an answer comes, but it is never satisfactory. It does not give the fullest satisfaction because behind it one can find some solution and some meaning in every problem.

Everything one sees, hears, and perceives through any sense and experience has a distinct and definite effect upon one's soul, upon one's spirit. What one eats, what one drinks, what one sees, what one touches, the atmosphere in which one lives, the circumstances one faces, the conditions one goes through, all these have a certain effect upon one's spirit. Sometimes out of bad experiences a benefit is derived; out of good experiences sometimes comes a loss. Sometimes the result is similar: out of good experiences something good is received and out of bad experiences something bad is taken in.

For instance, a person had a bad experience in his friendship and what it has brought to him is a kind of coldness, a pessimistic view on life; a kind of indifference has developed in him, he shows despise, hatred, prejudice, unwillingness to associate with anybody in the world. He has derived the bad side from his experience. There is another person who has been disappointed and has learned something. He has learned how to be tolerant, how to be forgiving, how to understand human nature, to expect little from others and to give more to others, how to forget himself, how to be open and to sympathize with another. It is one and the same experience thet makes one go to the North and another to the South. The effect of the experiences of life is different on a person. A certain drug or herb has a certain effect, favourable to one and unfavourable to another. So it is with the outer experiences of life; on one person they have a certain effect, on another they have quite a different effect.

We are placed in the world in a condition where we are always subject to outer influences. It is as if a soul were thrown into life with the susceptibility to move to the South, North, East or West. Depending absolutely on the way in which the wind blows, the soul turns accordingly. If there were not this little spark in our soul which may be called the engineer and which we recognize as free will or self-will, we would never think for one moment that we are a being. There would be no difference between things and beings. The more we realize the existence of will in us and the more we are conscious of it, the more we are able to stand in the north wind, south wind, west wind or east wind; whichever side the wind comes from, we can stand it.

Even from a material point of view the strength which enables a person to stand on the earth, on this ever-moving earth, is not his mechanical body. It is his will, and if he lost the will that holds the body man could not stand on the earth. As we do not know what is the will and where it is, therefore very often we overlook its existence in us and become absorbed in the causes that stand outside, causes of all things that bring us joy and distress. The outer conditions move the spirit and the condition of the spirit moves the outer conditions of life. Never, therefore, be surprised that good luck and ill luck, rise and fall - all are directed by the will behind it. Man accustomed to take all things according to reason and logic sees them in another form than they actually are. The saints and wise wish to find that faculty which is called the wlll, and on finding it they work with it. When one becomes able to work with it properly one gains mastery over it.

Very often a thinking person asks whether there is free will or destiny, because the two things cannot exist at the same time. These two things are likened to what we call light and darkness. In reality there is no such thing as darkness. There is less light or more light; when they are compared then only do we distinguish them as light and darkness. In the same way we can see free will and destiny. Destiny is always at work with free will and free will with destiny. They are one and the same thing; it is a difference of consciousness.

The more you are conscious of your will, the more you see that destiny works around it and that destiny works according to it. And the less conscious you are of that will, the more you see yourself subject to destiny. In other words, either a person is a mechanism or the engineer. Yet if he is a mechanism then in him there is a spark of engineer, and if he is an engineer, then the mechanism is a part of his being.

In spiritual realization we do not need to renounce things. Self-denial as described in the Bible has a different meaning. Self-denial means to deny the self its false conception of itself. In other words, to take away from the self that false conception it has of itself; that is the true self-denial. Once man recognizes that part which is called will as a divine spark in his heart and blows on it with the hope to turn it into a flame and then into a blaze - it is he who gives a life to himself, a life which may be called the birth of the soul.

It is not true that there is no destiny. There is a plan of an individual and there is a plan which may be called a divine plan. Mostly the plan of an individual is not different from the plan of God, but it is not true that destiny does not change. As we change our plans, the Creator changes His plans also. For instance, an artist paints a picture on a canvas and while painting the picture, drawing lines and giving different colours to it, he looks at it and inspired by the picture he has already made he feels like changing lines and colours. He could even change it to such an extent that it no longer remains the same picture which he had first made in his thoughts. So it is with an individual and so it is with God. All we make inspires us to complete it. We may make a wrong thing or a right thing, a good thing or a bad thing, its effect upon us is to complete it in a certain way. So we complete our good fortune or our ill luck. If we make ill luck for ourselves we complete it. We may be against it, still we make it complete. Such is the tendency of man: to complete what he has made. He may not know it and when the will is hidden behind the mind, then he sees himself in the hand of conditions; what little power the will gives is to fulfil the mission of the conditions around and to complete that destiny which may be called good luck or ill luck.

In conclusion: it is in the consciousness of the self-will and in the understanding of the definite plan which one really wishes to complete, to fulfil, that one can find life's ultimate purpose.

2

The subject of the interdependence of life within and without can be considered from different points of view. In the first place our physical body should be considered: how it expresses all that it partakes of as food, as drink, as medicine. If a person has grosser or finer food, if he has purer food, it is manifested outwardly, and if he has no consideration for this it is also manifested outwardly. The body shows the nature it has inherited from the earth to which it belongs, for the nature of this earth is such that when it takes the seed of flowers it produces flowers and when that of fruits it produces fruits, and when it takes the seed of poison it produces poison. All kinds of things are produced but it is that which it has taken that is the result. There is nothing one eats or drinks or that this body takes which will be so assimilated together that the body will not manifest it outwardly. In this way we can see the meaning of the interdependence of life within and without when considering our physical body.

When we think still further we shall find the action of the body on the mind and the action of the mind on the body. This must be understood first by considering how intoxicants have a reaction on the mind, how something which is quite material, physical, when taken in, affects the mind which is not material. The mind in point of fact is much greater than the brain. The word mind comes from the Sanskrit word *manas* and from this comes the word 'man'. Therefore really speaking, what is man? What is his mind? In the words of Jesus Christ man is as he thinks. Man is his thought, man is his mind. Therefore it is not always the body, to which man attributes himself so much and which is his identification; his true identification is his mind.

All that one partakes of physically in the form of food or intoxicants has an effect not only upon the body but also upon the mind, and also what the mind partakes of through the senses has its influence upon the body. For instance, all that one sees is impressed upon the mind. One cannot help it; mechanically that impression is recorded. All that one hears, smells, tastes or touches has not only an effect upon the body but also upon the mind. This means that man's contact with the outer world is such that a continual mechanical interchange is going on; every moment of his life he is partaking of all that his senses allow him to take in.

Therefore very often the man who is looking for the faults of others, who is looking at evil, though he may not be a wicked person, is yet without knowing it partaking of all that is evil. Then the result, for instance, may be this: someone is impressed by a deceitful person; the result of this impression is that even when he will cast his glance upon an honest person he will have the impression of deceit, and it is from this that the pessimistic attitude comes. A person once deceived is always on the look-out; even with an honest person he looks for deceit, he holds that impression within himself. A hunter who has come from the forest with a slap given to him by a lion, when he comes home even the caress of his kind mother frightens him; he thinks the lion came.

When we consider of how many impressions, agreeable and disagreeable, we partake from morning till evening without knowing the consequences of them, we understand how a person may become wicked without meaning to. In point of fact nobody is born wicked, for although the body belongs to the earth, yet the soul belongs to God, and from above man has got nothing but goodness. With the wickedest person in the world, if you can touch the deepest depth of his being, there is nothing but goodness. Therefore if there is any such thing as wickedness or badness, it is only that man has acquired it, and not acquired it willingly but only by being open to all impressions as it is natural that every man is open to impressions.

No doubt the secret of what may be called superstition, the superstition of the omen which exists in the East and sometimes also in the West, lies in impression. For instance, there have been beliefs that if you hear the sound of a certain bell there will be a death in your surroundings; or if you see a certain person good luck or bad luck will come to your family. People have sometimes believed these things blindly and have gone on believing them for many, many years. Then other ones, intellectuals, thought there was nothing in those superstitions and have ignored them. But at the end of a study one will find that the secret of all those superstitions is nothing but the impression: what the mind has taken in through the senses has its effect not on the body alone, but also upon man's affairs.

The science of physiognomy or phrenology goes as far as saying that what one acquires helps to form the different muscles of the features and head, according to what one has taken in one's mind. It is written in the Qur'an that every part of man's being will bear witness to his actions. I should say that it does not need to bear witness in the hereafter, it bears witness every hour of the day, for if one will examine life one will find that the mind and the body are formed from what one takes from the outer world. There are the words of Christ, "Where your treasure is there will your heart be also". All that one values - it is that which one makes in oneself; one creates in oneself all that one values. No doubt when a person is an admirer of beauty, he will always partake of all that he sees as beauty: beauty of form, of colour, of line, and beyond that the beauty of manner, of attitude which is a greater beauty still.

In the actual condition of the world man ignores very much the beauty of culture and fineness. No doubt this gives a warning that the world instead of going forward is going backward, for the reason that civilization is not only an industrial development or a material culture. If that is called civilization it is not the right word for the right thing. The explanation of civilization is not very difficult to give: it is progress towards harmony, beauty and love. When one goes back from these three great principles of life one may be very creative, but at the same time it is not civilization.

No doubt every race and every creed has its principles of right and wrong, but there is one fundamental principle of religion, and one in which all creeds and all people can meet. That principle is to see beauty in action, in attitude, in thought and feeling. There is no action which can be stamped as wrong or right, but what can be wrong or wicked is what our mind is accustomed to see as wrong or wicked because it is void of beauty. The one therefore who seeks beauty in all its forms, in action, in feeling, in manner, will impress his heart with beauty.

All the great ones who have come in the world from time to time to waken humanity to a greater truth, what did they teach, what did they bring? They brought beauty. It is not what they taught, it is what they were themselves. As to the intellectual understanding of beauty or talking about beauty, one cannot speak enough about it; yet words are too inadequate to express either goodness or beauty. One can say a thousand words and yet one will never be able to express it, for it is something which is beyond words. The soul alone can understand it. And the one who will always in every little thing he does follow in his life the rule of beauty will always succeed, and he will always be able to discriminate between right and wrong, between good and bad.

Now coming to the point of religion and looking at the interdependence of life within and without from the spiritual point of view we should remember the story told in India of the magic lantern which Aladdin saw. What is this magic lantern? It is a magic lantern which is hidden in the heart of every soul. Only, for the time being its light becomes covered and all the tragedy of life comes from this covering of the light. Why does man seek for happiness? Because happiness is his own being. It is not because he loves happiness or would like to be happy, but he is happiness himself. And why does he seek for it? He seeks for it because he is happiness and when he finds this happiness closed he wants to look for it. Only the mistake he makes, and that perhaps every man makes, is that he looks outside for that happiness which could be found inside.

The most powerful words Christ has spoken are, "I am the truth and I am the way". This sentence shows that there are two things: there is one thing, truth, and there is another thing, the way. When people confuse these two they become perplexed and they cannot find the way. In the first place man always makes a wrong use of the word 'truth', for he always calls fact truth. But truth is something which uproots fact altogether. Then what is fact? Fact is the illusion of truth, but fact is not truth.

Now you may ask, "What is truth?" It is the one thing you cannot express in words. During my travellings I was very often asked, "Tell us something about the truth". When very much urged by people I sometimes thought, "If only I could have some bricks and write on them TRUTH, and say: now hold it fast for this is the truth". If truth were so small that our human words could speak about it or could contain it, then it could not be truth. Therefore the Sufis have always named truth *Haqq* which is another word for God Himself. It is that truth which is the seeking of us all, and the most wonderful thing one can see in the world is that a person, however false he may be, does not want another to deceive him or to be false to him. A man whose profession may be to lie may be lying from morning to evening, but when he comes home he does not want his wife to lie to him.

However, we satisfy ourselves and are contented with facts supposing that they are truth. And it is through this contentment that so many creeds exist in this world, so many faiths and beliefs which fight with one another. But nothing can satisfy the craving of our soul which is continually in search of the truth that no words can speak.

As to the other part, "I am the way", there is a great problem to consider. The one who wants to find the truth at the first step is very often mistaken. He may find it, but it is not always so. It is very strange to see how man gives years and years to the study of grammar, music or science, but when it comes to truth he wants a direct answer. If it were lack of patience on his part he would be excusable, but it is not often so: he considers truth so little. If he were too eager, if he were too impatient it would be possible that in one step he might reach the truth, for there is every reason to be hopeful. Whereas it is difficult to get gold, it is not so difficult to find the truth if one really wants it; for gold is something which is outside, the truth is something which is within ourselves. But how man wanders about all his life in search of something which can only be found within himself!

There is one thing to be considered: the way. Why is there a way? It is not so that a way is not already made between man and God. There was a way between man and

God, but man has gone astray. Therefore he is shown the way by his elder brother. If there was not a way it would certainly be unjust to the birds, the insects, to all the creatures, that there was a bliss only given to man. God is the perfection of justice in whom no injustice is to be found. He has not excluded any soul, however small, from this bliss. It seems that even the birds and beasts have their times when they concentrate; they meditate in their own way and offer their prayer to God. There is no being on the earth, however small, who does not contemplate for a moment. And if man's sight were keen he would also see, by sitting in the solitary woods, sitting in the caves of the mountains, that the mountains and trees all have their prayer and all have their at-one-ment with God. Why do the great ones, the souls who do not find rest and peace in the midst of the world, go to the wilderness? It is in order to breathe the breath of peace, of calm that comes to them in the heart of the wilderness.

Man who is the most intelligent of all creatures is the most astray and lost the way, in spite of all the pride he takes in having created an artificial world as an improvement upon nature. But in creating this artificial world he has lost his way. And is he happy in this artificial world that he has made as a paradise? Does he not cause bloodshed every time more and more, and every time even worse than before? Is he not unjust, is he not deceitful towards his fellow-man? A world which can give him that intoxication and can absorb all his mind, time and efforts in that intoxication, how can it give him the happiness which is the craving of his soul?

It is therefore that the way has from time to time been shown and will be shown to him who for a moment lifts his head up from this world and asks for the way to be shown. And although the way seems to be very far off, yet the distance cannot be compared with the distances of the earth. The way can be so short, even shorter than an inch, and it can be as long and as distant as thousands of such worlds as the one where we are. This way contracts and stretches according to the attitude of the soul. However, there is one hope, and that is in what God says in the Scriptures, "The one who comes to me one step, I go forward to him a hundred steps".

There are many different opinions as to how the conditions of the world should be bettered; some think that the world can be bettered by religious reform, by educational reform or by social reform. Every reform made with the idea of doing some good is worth while, but the reform which is most needed to-day is spiritual reform.

To-day the hour has come when narrowness should be abandoned and we may rise above those differences and distinctions that divide men. It is this rising which will raise our fellowmen. The Lord is not pleased when some children of His are considered our brothers and sisters, and other children of His are considered as separate, for no father is pleased at seeing some children of his favoured and others neglected. What we need to-day is to train ourselves to tolerance towards one another.

By spiritual reform I do not mean looking for wonder-working or talking about metaphysical problems. The problem which is to be solved is solved by itself; we have only to wish and it is solved. The problem we have to solve to-day is the problem of reconciliation and reconstruction which neither the politicians nor the statesmen have been able to solve. It can only be solved by a spiritual awakening. The way to spirituality is the expansion of the heart, the widening of the heart. In order to accommodate the divine truth it is the heart which must be expanded, and it is with the expansion of the heart that divine bliss is poured out. True spirituality is the raising of the consciousness to that plane which is the abode of the divine Being.

CHAPTER XXII

Interest and Indifference

VERY OFTEN spiritual people speak about indifference, giving preference to it, and many who have not reached that stage begin to wonder whether interest is preferable or indifference. Very often people lose their interest because they think that in principle indifference is the best thing. But in reality it is a subject one must study: what is gained by interest and what is accomplished by indifference. By interest all that is there is to be gained, and by indifference all there is is to be lost, and one must first find out if one wants to gain or to lose. If a person is hungering after gain he must have interest, but if he feels relief in losing he must have indifference. In other words: either keep your coins locked in the safe or throw them away and feel relieved. Both things are nice; it is only as we wish.

Interest can be divided into four parts. The first is interest in the self. If a person is not interested in anybody or anything, he is certainly interested in himself. No person is loveless. When a person boasts, "I love no one", then you must be sure that he loves himself. Love must be used somewhere; it can just as well be used for oneself.

Then there is interest in another. It has a different character, because it is chiefly based upon sacrifice.

The third interest is in science or art or in the attaining of a material object, wealth or power or possession. This interest has nothing to do with a person; it is for something which is to be gained. This needs sacrifice also.

The fourth interest is interest in spiritual things. That again brings one to interest in oneself, but this is the higher self-interest. The first self-interest is lower selfishness, the other is higher selfishness.

When we come to indifference, this can also be divided into four classes. The first is indifference to oneself. When a person says, "I do not care whether I eat or do not eat, or how I look. I do not care what people say. I am not interested in myself. I have something else in my thoughts" - that is one kind of indifference.

The next indifference is to a person or to persons. You do not mind whether they live or die; you do not mind what happens to them; you do not mind if they love you or hate you. What does it matter! You do not mind if you profit by them or do not profit by them. If they are happy or unhappy, it is just as well.

The third aspect of indifference is: "what do I care if I am rich or poor, whether my rank is high or low, if I gain this or that in the world. I am quite indifferent to it".

Then there is a fourth kind of indifference: "what does it matter if I pray or do not pray. Whether in the hereafter it is good or bad - who knows? Whether I am received in paradise or not - it matters little!" This is the fourth kind of indifference.

Remember that the people we see in everyday life each have either the one or the other, interest or indifference - indifference to these four things or interest in connection with the four aspects just mentioned.

One might ask which is desirable and which is undesirable. All that is natural is desirable, all that is unnatural is undesirable. When you are interested in something and say, "I do not want to interest myself in it. Although I am captivated by it, although I am drawn to it, tempted by it, attracted to it, I do not like to take an interest in it", that is not right. When a person feels, "I must look after myself, I must feed myself, I must clothe myself, I must look as nice as I can, I must live as nicely as I can" - if there is that inclination, then to say, "But in principle it is not good", and then not to pay attention to oneself, that is wrong. When a person says, "All earthly things are unimportant, of no value compared to the spiritual principle, we must not take notice of them, we must think differently", and yet is attracted to the things of the earth, inwardly wishing for them, he must not say so. His interest is preferable to his indifference. One must evolve naturally. One must not think, "Because it is in principle greater, better, to be without interest, to be indifferent to the things of the world, I must lose my interest". That is not right, but if by nature one is indifferent one may just as well be indifferent. Even if the whole world said, "You are indifferent", it does not matter. Such a person says, "I am indifferent to your opinion too".

Often people say, "By indifference I mean a philosophy". The Yogis, ascetics, adepts, mystics say that indifference gives a great power, but I must add that interest gives a great power too. The whole manifestation is the phenomenon of interest. All that we see in this world of art and science, the new inventions, beautiful things, beautiful houses, all this world that man has made, where has it come from? It has come from the power of interest. The power of interest is behind it and it is this power which has enabled man to create it.

When we go still further, it is the interest of the Creator which has made this creation. Even the Creator would not have been able to create if there had not been interest; it is the power of interest of the Creator which has made it. The whole creation, every object and all in it is the product of the Creator's interest - the Creator as a Spirit or as a human being or as any living being. So it is the interest of the bird to build its nest, and so it is the interest of man to make all that he makes. Imagine, if man did not have this faculty of taking interest the world would never have evolved.

Therefore the secret of manifestation and the mystery of evolution is to be found in interest. But at the same time I do not deny the power of indifference. The power of indifference is greater if the indifference is not an artificial one. When a person follows the principle of indifference by saying, "It is a good principle", then it is no virtue. Besides that, there is no power, because man is captive: on one side he is drawn by interest, on the other side he wants to show indifference. Therefore it is wrong on his part; he neither accomplishes something by the power of interest, nor does he gain the benefit that can be derived from indifference.

Now I should like to explain why from the point of view of metaphysics the power of indifference is greater than the power of interest. It is because motive has a power, and motive limits a power. Man is endowed by his birth with much greater power than he ever imagines, and it is motive, any motive, every motive, that makes this power limited. Yet it is motive that gives man the power to accomplish his object; if there were no motive there would be no power to accomplish it. But when you compare the original power of man with the power he gets from motive, you will find that it is just like the difference between the ocean and a drop. The motive makes the power as a drop. Without motive the power of the soul is like an ocean, but at the same time that ocean-like power is of no use. If power is there without a motive, it is not used for a purpose; as soon as you want to use it for a purpose it becomes less.

Indifference releases that limitation automatically. With indifference a limitation is released, it is broken and the power unconsciously becomes greater. You will see even in wordly things how there are people who run after money and people after whom money runs. I do not mean that they are spiritual people; sometimes they themselves do not know it. Some people are worshippers of beauty, and there are others before whom beauty worships. There are some who wish to hold power, any little power they can get, and there are others, on whom power pours, who do not want it. We have so many examples in this world to see how interest often limits man's power and how indifference makes it greater. But at the same time indifference must not be practised unless it naturally springs from your heart.

There is a saying in the Hindi language "Interest makes kings, but indifference makes emperors", and there is a story of a great sage who lived near Delhi. One day the emperor Akbar, hearing his name, wanted to visit him to pay homage. The sage was sitting on a rock with legs stretched out and arms folded. The emperor had Birbal, his wise prime minister, with him. The prime minister did not like the way the emperor was received by the sage, for the sage knew that it was the emperor and still remained sitting in the same position. So Birbal asked the sage, "For how long have you been sitting this way?" He wanted to make it look nice to the emperor. If the sage was accustomed to sit in that way perhaps that was why he was sitting like that. What was the answer of the sage? "Since I have taken my hands back." This meant that as long as his hands were forward in need, his legs were standing up. But since his arms were folded, his legs were stretched; it did not matter. If a king came or the emperor, it did not matter. In other words, "As long as I had interest my legs were in order; since the time I have no interest any more I sit in any way I like to sit". Everyone may come to the sage, regardless of what he is. That is the indifference of the sages.

How does this indifference come to the sages and how is it practised? Sooner or later there comes a day in the life of a person when he no longer thinks about himself: how he eats, how he is clothed or how he lives, how anybody treats him, whether anybody loves or hates him. Every thought concerned with himself goes away. This time comes and it is a blessed day when this comes to man. It is on that day that his soul begins to live independently, to live a freer life than it had ever lived. As long as man is bound to the thought, "I am treated badly or wrongly, people do not love me or do not like me, people do not treat me justly or fairly", so long he is poor. Whatever be his life's position he is poor, and the moment he begins to forget this his power becomes great.

From a worldly aspect there may be a man who looks after himself, who is self-conscious, thinks of himself, concerns himself with himself. You can see the good points in that person, you can see something good in him, but at the same time that is all you can admire. But there is another person who has given up the thought of himself. You cannot help respecting him. The respect comes by itself as soon as a person has come out of that thought of self. When someone has lost the interest of holding, of possessing others then his charm is such that without his holding and possessing and owning all becomes his own. You can feel that person to be above average in the world.

From the point of view of sages no one really belongs to oneself. In the East they say that it is to the displeasure of God when parents think that their children are their own. God is never pleased with that idea of owning, the idea, "I possess this". All are the creatures of God; He has created and providence has brought about situations in which we are connected with them as parents, as master, as servant, as friend, whatever the relationship may be. When we think that we possess them, own them, hold them, God is not pleased, and so human beings are not pleased either. One arrives at that stage where one does not possess, does not own anything or anyone. That also is a stage of indifference.

Then one comes to the stage of indifference where even all rank, position, honour and power do not matter very much because all these are false claims. In order to occupy a certain position, in order to keep some rank for oneself one has to deprive others of it, and when one has reached the stage where a position or a rank makes no difference, then one has reached a higher stage. And when one arrives at the stage where even paradise has no more attraction - whatever will be the hereafter he will see it, he will meet it - then this point of view becomes that of a sage, of a master.

Now arises the question: how can one learn indifference? By learning interest. If in your life you do not learn interest you cannot learn indifference. A person who is born with no interest in life is merely an idiot. The child who does not stick to the toy he has in his hand and will not keep it, that child has no promise of progress. It is natural for the child to hold on to the toy and claim it to be his own. This is the first lesson for him to learn in that way. It is normal when a child stands up for his toy and says, "It is mine", and wants to keep it. In this way one develops interest, interest in one's well-being, in one's welfare, in one's progress in life, in accomplishing one's purpose in life. All this is natural and normal. Interest in other persons, in their affairs, in those one loves and likes - it is this which develops the character.

Then there is the interest in things of the world. By this interest one helps the world, one contributes one's service to the world. If one had no interest one would not render one's service to the cause of the nation or to the cause of the world.

Therefore evolution is going step by step, not hurrying, and indifference is to be attained by developing interest and by developing discrimination in one's interest, instead of going backward, going forward in one's interest. And you will naturally find that a spring will rise from the heart when in the path of interest the heart has touched the zenith. Then the fountain of indifference will break out gradually, and when this natural breaking out of indifference comes, then follow it, so that in the end you have known what interest means and what indifference means.

CHAPTER XXIII

From Limitation to Perfection

1

THE ROCKS, the trees, the animals and man, all in their turn show an inclination to seek perfection. The tendency of rocks is to form mountains reaching upwards, and the waves are ever reaching upwards as if they were trying to attain something beyond their reach. The tendency of birds is the same; their joy is flying in the air and going upwards. The tendency of animals is to stand on their hind legs, and when they do so they are most pleased. And man who is the finishing of creation has from infancy the tendency to stand up. An infant who is not able to stand moves his little hands and legs showing his desire to stand. It all shows the desire for perfection.

The law of gravitation is known to the world of science in a half measure: the earth attracts all that belongs to it. This is true, but the Spirit also attracts all that belongs to it, and that law of gravitation has always been known to mystics. So the law of gravitation is working from two sides: from the side of the earth which draws all that belongs to the earth, and from the side of the Spirit which attracts the soul towards it. Those who are unconscious of this law of gravitation are also striving for perfection, drawn by this law. Their soul being continually drawn to the Spirit, they are striving for perfection just the same. In the small things of everyday life a man wants more and more. If a person has made a name or has fame he is never satisfied with what he has; he always wants more, be it a higher rank or position. He is always striving for this. It shows that the heart is a magic bowl: as much as you pour into it, so much deeper it becomes, it will always be found empty. Whatever man strives after, he strives after it more and more and is never satisfied. The reason is that unconsciously he is striving for perfection. Only, those who strive after perfection consciously have a different way.

Nevertheless each atom of the universe is supposed to

struggle and strive in order to become perfect one day. In other words, if a seer, a thinker with an evolved soul happens to be in the mountains he will hear the mountains cry continually, "We are waiting for that day when something in us will awaken. There will come a day of awakening, of unfoldment. We are silently waiting for it". If he goes into the forest and sees the trees standing there they seem to to be speaking, waiting patiently. You can feel it; the more you sit there the more you get the feeling of the trees waiting for the time to come when there will be an unfoldment. So it is with all beings, but man is so absorbed in his everyday actions and his greeds that he seems to be more unaware of that innate desire for unfoldment. It is his everyday occupation, his avariciousness, his cruelty to other beings that keep him continually engaged and busy with things. Therefore he cannot hear that continual cry of his own soul to awaken, to unfold, to reach upwards, to expand and to go towards perfection.

One might ask what I mean by perfection. Is it possible for man to reach perfection? When one sees how limited man is one can never think for one moment that man is entitled to perfection. There is no end to his limitations and one cannot even comprehend what perfection means; one becomes pessimistic when it comes to the question of perfection. Yet we read in the Bible the words of Christ, "Be ye perfect even as your Father in heaven is perfect". This shows that there is a possibility. Our philosophy, our religious and sacred teachings are intended to bring about that realization which is called perfection. Any philosophy or religion that does not show this path to perfection has been corrupted and fails; there is something missing in it. If we look at religion as one and the same in all ages, given by different masters of humanity inspired by one and the same Spirit of Guidance, one and the same light of wisdom, we see that all have given the same truth. It is only interpreted differently in order to suit people of different ages, periods and races. In this way religions differ, but the underlying truth of all religions is one and the same. And whenever a religious preacher teaches that perfection is not for man, he corrupts the teaching that is given in religion; he has not understood it. He professes a certain religion but he does not understand it, for the main object of every religion is to attain perfection.

Many people seeking for knowledge say, "What we want in the world to-day is greater harmony, greater peace, better conditions. We do not want spiritual perfection; what we want is what we need to-day". But Christ has said in the Bible, "Seek ye first the kingdom of God and all these things shall be added unto you". The tendency of every man is to seek everything else first and to keep the kingdom of God to the last. That which should be sought first is kept for the last. That is why humanity is not evolving towards perfection.

Occupations such as war and preparation for war are not to be called civilized occupations. It is a pity that in this period of civilization men should have war - and yet we think that we are more civilized than the people of ancient times! Ages before Christ Buddha taught, "*Ahimsa paramo dharma ha,* harmlessness is the essence of religion". He taught people to be friendly even to the smallest insect, the brotherhood of all beings - and we occupy ourselves with wars day after day, and with the condition as it is to-day we can expect war anywhere in the world! Where does it all come from? It all comes from seeking perfection in the wrong way. Instead of seeking spiritual perfection earthly perfection is sought. What everybody is seeking is earthly perfection, the earth, but all that the earth holds is limited, and when everyone struggles for earthly perfection the earth will not be able to answer the demands. Whether we get what we want or not, there will always be struggle.

Now I want to explain what religion means. It is the main knowledge by which perfection is sought. Religion has five different aspects. The first and principal aspect, the foundation of religion is belief in God. What is God? Many say, "If there is a personal God I do not care for it. But if you think that there is an abstract God - yes, it can be". They forget that something abstract cannot be a living being; abstract is nothing. You cannot call space God. Space is space. Neither can you call space God nor can you call time God. Space is our conception; we have made its dimensions - so many yards. In the same way time is a conception. In reality space and time do not exist. What is unlimited cannot be comprehended, and what cannot be comprehended is without name. To what is intelligible we can give a name; if it is unintelligible we cannot give it a name because we do not know it. When we consider those who believe in a personal God, many of them merely have a belief. They worship God and believe in a certain law given in the name of God; they do good works for the sake of God, but at the same time they have no more knowledge than a belief that there is a God somewhere.

Neither of these believers in God has a conception of the real meaning of the God-ideal. They merely have a belief in God and this does not take one much further. In reality the God-ideal is a stepping-stone towards the knowledge of spiritual perfection. It is through the God-ideal that higher knowledge can be gained. And those who wait to see if they will be shown a God before their eyes or who want a proof of the being of God are mistaken. That which cannot be compared cannot be named and cannot be shown.

For instance, you see light. Light is intelligible to you because there is darkness as its opposite. Things are known by their opposites. Since God has no opposite God cannot be known in the same way as the things of the earth can be known. Besides, to explain God is to dethrone God; the less said the better. Yet the knowledge of God is necessary for those who seek after perfection.

Different religions have different conceptions of God; but not only religion, every man has a conception of God. You cannot think of any being without making in your mind a conception of that being. For instance, if someone told you a fairy tale, the first thing you would do would be to make a conception of a fairy, what it looks like. If someone talks to you about an angel you make a conception of it. It is a natural tendency to make a conception according to one's own experience, very near to one's own self. A human being does not think of an angel, a fairy as being like a bird or an animal, but as something like himself. If this is true then it is not a fault if someone has his own idea of God, and it is a great fault on the part of those who want to take away that idea and wish to give that person another idea. It is not right. No one can give to another his own conception of God, because each one must make it real for himself. The prophets of all ages have given some ideal to help man to form a conception of God. As a philosopher has said, "If you have no God, make one", for that is the proper way, the easiest way of realizing the unlimited truth.

There is a story about Moses who saw a shepherd boy sitting near the river and telling himself, "O God, You are so dear. If once You appeared before me I would do everything for You. I would bathe You in the river and cover You with my blanket. I would put You to bed in my hut. I would give You sweets and delicious things to eat. I would take care of You and protect You from all wild animals. I would love You so much and care so much for You, if once in my life I could see You". The prophet said, "What are you saying, young man? Have you any idea? God, the Protector of all beings - you say that you will protect Him? The One who bestows all gifts and who is the sustenance of all beings - even the smallest creature is looked after by God - you would cover Him? How could you! He is unseen, unlimited". The boy became frightened; he thought, "What have I done, what a terrible thing! I said something I should not have said!". He was terrified. When the prophet left him a voice arose within him, the same voice which used to come to him every day in the solitude. "What have you done, Moses? We sent you to bring our friends together, to bring My friends to Me, and you have separated them".

Everyone, every lover has his own idea of his beloved, and no other person knows what he thinks of his beloved. It is told about the Eastern Romeo and Juliet, Leila and Majnun, that someone said to Majnun, the young lover, "Leila is not beautiful. What is she? Why do you love her so much?" And Majnun said humbly, "In order to see Leila you must borrow my eyes". In every person the conception of God is different, distinct, and one person cannot give his conception of God to another.

There is another story, told about a housewife who had

prepared a great feast. When her husband came home he said, "My good wife, why have you prepared a feast? Is it a holy day, a birthday? What is it?" She said, "It is greater than a birthday, it is better than a holy day. It is a great day for me". But he asked, "What is it?" She replied, "My husband, I never thought that you believed in God" - "And how did you find out?" - "One day while turning over in your sleep you uttered the name of God. I am so thankful". He said, "Alas. This something which was so sacred and secret in my heart has to-day been opened. I can no longer sustain it and live". He dropped down dead. His conception of God was too sacred for him. There is outer expression and inner expression and we do not know. We may think that many are removed from the God-ideal and we do not know that they may be much nearer to God than we ourselves.

It is difficult for anyone to judge who is near to God and who is away from Him. It is difficult to know in our lives what pleases our friend and what does not please him. The more conscientious we are in pleasing our friend, the more we find how difficult it is to know what will please him and what will not. Not everyone knows it, for not everyone has kindled the light of friendship. Sometimes it is only a word in the dictionary. The one who has learned friendship has learned religion. The one who has learned friendship has come to spiritual knowledge. The one who has learned friendship needs learn very little, for in the Persian language morals are called friendship.

There is another story that explains this idea of the pleasure and displeasure of God. There was a man who was very pious and lived a very religious life. One day he said to Moses, "All my life I have tried to be a good man and to be religious. I have always been in terrible difficulty, but I don't care. I would only like to know what is in store for me. Will you ask God?" Moses consented, and as he went further he saw a drunken man who said, "Where are you going? Will you ask God about me too? I have never known prayers or fastings. I have never done good works, as they say in this world. What I know are these: my great friends bottle and glass. Go and ask what is in store for me". When Moses came back after his meditation on the top of Mount Sinai his answer to the religious man was, "For you there are great rewards, beautiful things". "Just as I expected", was the reply of the religious man. Then the drunken man asked, "What is the answer?" Moses said, "For you there is the worst place possible". The man stood up and danced and was most joyous. He said, "Oh, I don't care what place is given to me. I am so happy that God thought of me. I am such a humble man, such a sinner. That I am known by God! I thought nobody knew me". He was most happy. In the end the places for both were changed.

Moses was surprised and he asked God within. The answer was, "The first man, in spite of all the good he did, did not deserve Our favour, for Our grace cannot be bought by good deeds. What are man's good deeds? His whole life's good deeds cannot be compared with one moment's favour of God. And the other man pleased Me, for he enjoyed everything given to him. His contentment won Me".

When we cannot understand the pleasure and displeasure of our friend in the world, how can we understand the pleasure and displeasure of God? Who on earth can say that God is pleased with this or with that? No one ever has the power to make rules and laws: by this God is pleased, and by that God is displeased.

Another aspect of religion is the aspect of the teacher: for instance, there are some who see divinity in Christ. They say, "Christ was God, Christ is divine", and there are others who say, "Christ was a man, one like us all". When we come to look at this question we see that the one who says, "Christ is divine", is not wrong. If there is any divinity shown it is in man. And the one who says, "Christ was a man" is not wrong either. In the garb of man Christ manifested. Those who do not want Christ to be a man drag down the greatness and sacredness of the human being by their argument, by saying that man is made of sin, and by separating Christ from humanity. But as to those who have called Christ God or divine, there is nothing wrong with it. It is in man that divine perfection is to be seen. It is in man that divinity is to be manifested.

Then there are Christ's own words, "I am Alpha and Omega", and this is the one idea to which many close their eyes. But the one who said, "I am Alpha and Omega" was before the coming of Jesus too, and the one who says, "first and last", must be after Jesus too. In the words of Christ there is the idea of perfection. He attributed himself to the Spirit of which he was conscious. Christ was not conscious of his human part but of his perfect being, when he said, "I am Alpha and Omega". He did not attribute this to his being known as Jesus. He attributed it to the Spirit of which he was conscious, the Spirit of perfection that lived before Jesus and continues to live to the end of the world, for eternity.

If this is so then what does it matter if some say, "Jesus inspired us", and if millions are inspired by Buddha? It is only a difference of name. It is all one "Alpha and Omega". If others say "Moses" or "Muhammad" or "Krishna", what were they? Where did the inspiration come from? Was it not from one and the same Spirit? Was it not the "Alpha and Omega" of which Jesus Christ was conscious? Whoever gives the message to the world and has illuminated human beings and raised thousands and millions of people in the world, cannot but be Christ whom the one calls by this name and the other by another name. Yet human ignorance causes wars and disasters on account of people's different religions, different communities, because of the importance they give to their conception, their own corrupted conception which differs from that of another. Even till now either there is materialism or there is bigotry. What is necessary to-day is to come to the first and last religion, to come to the message of Christ, to divine wisdom, so that we may recognize wisdom in all its different forms, in whatever form it has been given to humanity. It does not matter if it is Buddhism, Islam, Judaism, Zoroastrianism, Hinduism. What does it matter? It is one wisdom - that call of the Spirit which awakens man to rise from limitation and to reach to perfection.

The third aspect of religion is the manner of worship. There have been many in different ages who have worshipped the sun, but they believed in God just the same. The sun was only a symbol. They thought, "This is a light which does not depend upon oil or anything else, something which remains night and day". Then there were others who worshipped sacred trees and holy places, rocks and mountains of ancient tradition, and others who worshipped heroes of great repute, teachers and masters of humanity. Nevertheless all had a divine ideal, and the form in which they worshipped does not matter. The Arabs in the desert where there was no house, no place of worship stood in the open air and bowed in the open space at sunset and sunrise. It was all worship to God; it was given in that form. The Hindus made idols of different kinds in order to make man focus his mind on particular objects. These were all different prescriptions given by the doctors of souls. These peoples were not pagans or heathens; they were only taught differently by the wise. Different thoughts, different ways were given to them just as a doctor would give different prescriptions to different patients in order to come to the same goal. Therefore difference in worship does not make a different religion. Religion is one and the same in spite of a thousand different kinds of worship.

The fourth aspect of religion is the moral aspect. Different religions have taught different moral principles, but at the same time there is one human moral principle on which all is based, and that is justice. This does not mean justice in principles and rules and regulations, but it means the one law which is the true religious law that is in man, that is awakened in man. As his soul unfolds itself that law becomes more and more clear to him: what is just and what is unjust. The most wonderful thing about it is that a thief, a wicked or unrighteous man may be most unjust to others but if someone is unjust to him, he will say, "He is not just to me". This shows that he too knows justice. When he is dealing with others he forgets it, but when it comes to himself he knows justice just the same. Therefore we are each responsible to ourselves according to that religious law. If we do not regard it, it naturally results in unhappiness. Everything that goes wrong, goes wrong for the reason that we do not listen to ourselves.

The fifth aspect of religion is self-realization. This is the highest aspect. And everything we do - prayers, concentration, good actions, good thoughts - everything leads to that one object which is self-realization. How is it gained? Some say that we realize God by self-realization, but this is not true. We realize the self by the realization of God. Whenever a person tries to realize the self omitting God, he makes a mistake.

It is very difficult for man to realize the self, because the self he knows is a most limited self. The self to which he is awakened from the time of birth, this self which has made within him his conception of himself, is most limited. However proud and conceited he may be, however good his idea of himself, yet in his innermost being he knows his limitation, he knows his small being just the same. He may be a successful general, he may be a king, yet he will know his limitation when the time comes when he runs away from his kingdom. Then he knows that he is not really a king. Earthly greatness does not make man great. If there is anything that makes him great it is only the effacing of himself and the establishing of God in that place. The one who says, "Begin with self-realization", has many intellectual, philosophical principles, but when he tries to do so he gets into a muddle and arrives nowhere. This is the wrong method.

There are people to-day who say, "I am God". This is insolence, it is stupidity; it is foolish to say such things. It spoils the ideal of others, it is an insult to the greatest ideal that the prophets, the saviours of humanity have always respected. By that affirmation, by such intellectual studies people will never reach spiritual perfection. In order to reach spiritual perfection the first thing is to destroy that false self. This delusion must be destroyed first. And how must it be destroyed? By other ways, taught by the great teachers, ways of concentration and meditation, by the power of which one is taught to forget one's self, to take one's consciousness away from one's self; in other words, to rise from one's limited being. By this way a person effaces himself from his own consciousness, and instead of his limited self he places God in his consciousness. It is by this way that he comes to that perfection which is the seeking of every soul.

2

Every kind of striving man has in life, whether for a material thing or for a spiritual object, shows his natural inclination to reach from limitation towards perfection. Whatever it may be, wealth or rank, name, comfort or pleasure, it is its limitation which keeps man discontented. Also in learning, studying, practising, acquiring, attaining we see that the striving of man is to go from limitation to perfection. The Scriptures say that God alone is rich and all others poor, and this can be seen in everyday life. The greater the riches a man has the more want he feels, and it is most interesting to find, when we study the life of a poor person, that he is more content with what he has than a rich person with his wealth. Sometimes we also see that a poor person is more generous in giving than a rich person in parting with his wealth.

We may also see another picture of life. A person who is learned in a small degree thinks that he has learned, that he has read, and wishes to show it. A more learned person who has really learned begins to find that he has learned very little and that there is very much to be learned. Then there is the picture of the foolish and the wise. The foolish one is ready to teach you without a moment's thought, ready to correct you, ready to judge you, ready to form an opinion about you. The wise one, the wiser he is the more diffident he is to form an opinion about you, to judge you, to correct you. What does this mean? It means that whatever man possesses in a smaller degree - he thinks he has something, and when he possesses in a greater degree then he begins to feel the need, the want of perfection, of completion.

There is a story of olden times that a sovereign was very pleased to grant a dervish his desire. The desire of the dervish was to fill his cup with gold coins. The sovereign thought that this was the easiest thing to do and he was looking forward to the pleasure of seeing the cup filled. But it was a magic cup, it would not fill. The more money was poured into it the emptier it became. The sovereign began to be very disappointed and disheartened. The dervish said, "Sovereign, if you cannot fill the cup you only have to say, 'I cannot', and

I shall take my cup back. I am a dervish, I will go and will only think that you have not kept your word". The sovereign with every good intention, with all his generosity and with all his treasures could not fill the cup. He asked, "Dervish, tell me what secret you have in this cup. It does not seem to be a natural cup, there is some magic about it. Tell me what is the secret of it". The dervish answered, "Yes, sovereign, you really have found out. It is true, it is a magic cup. But it is the cup of every heart, it is the heart of man which is never content. Fill it with whatever you may, with wealth, with attention, with love, with knowledge, with all that is there, it will never fill. It is not meant to be filled".

Not knowing this secret of life man goes on in pursuit of every object or any object he has before him, continually. The more he gets the more he wants, and the cup of his desire is never filled. The meaning of this can be understood by the study of the soul. Appetite is satisfied by food, but there is another appetite behind it which is the appetite of the soul and that is never satisfied. It is this which is at the back of all different hungers, all different thirsts. Since man cannot trace that innermost appetite he strives all through life to satisfy these outer appetites which are satisfied and yet remain unsatisfied. If a person is searching for things in the objective world he may go on gaining a great deal of knowledge about them and yet there is never an end to it. The one who searches for the secret of sound, the one who searches for the mystery of light, the one who searches for the mystery of science, they all search and search and search and there is never an end to it, there is never satisfaction. And a thoughtful person wonders if that satisfaction could be found anywhere, a satisfaction which answers, so to speak, the promise of the soul.

The answer is, yes there is a possibility for satisfaction, and this possibility is to attain to that perfection which is not dependent upon outer things, a perfection which belongs to man's own being. This satisfaction is not attained, this satisfaction is discovered. It is in the discovery of this satisfaction that lies the fulfilment of the purpose of life.

Now the question arises: how does one arrive at this

perfection? Religion, philosophy, mysticism - all these will help, but it is by the actual attainment of this knowledge that a person will arrive at this satisfaction.

Life can be pictured as a line with two ends: one end limitation and the other end of the same line perfection. As long as a person is looking at the end which is the end of limitation, however good, virtuous, righteous, pious he is, he has not touched what may be called perfection. Are there not many believers in religion, in a God, many worshippers of a deity - more among simple people than among the intellectuals, the educated? Do they all by their belief in a deity or by their worship arrive at perfection before leaving this earth? Others learn from books. I myself have seen people who had written perhaps fifty or a hundred books themselves and had read perhaps the whole library of the British Museum, and they still stand in the same place where they were. As long as the face is not turned away from the end which is the end of limitation and as long as the ideal of perfection, which is the real *Ka'aba* or place of pilgrimage, is not taken before one's view, one will not arrive at perfection.

What keeps this perfection, which belongs to his own life, which is his own being, hidden from man? A screen put before it, and that screen is his self. The soul conscious of its limitation, of its possession with which it identifies itself, forgets its own being and becomes, so to speak, captive in its limitation. Religion or belief in God, worship, philosophy or mysticism - all these help to attain this perfection. But if one does not search for perfection through these, even they will only be an occupation, a pastime, and will not bring man to the proper result.

One might ask: is there any definition of this perfection? What sort of perfection is it? Can it be explained in any way? The answer is that it is perfection itself which can realize itself. It cannot be put into words, it cannot be explained. If anyone thinks that truth may be given in words he is very much mistaken. It is just like putting water of the sea into a bottle and saying, "Here is the sea". Very often people ask, "But where is the truth? What is the truth? Can you explain it?" But words cannot explain it. Often I thought it would be a good thing to write the word TRUTH on a brick and give it in the hands of a person and say, "Hold it fast, here is the truth".

There is a difference between fact and truth. Fact is a shadow of truth. Fact is intelligible, but truth is beyond comprehension because truth is unlimited. Truth knows itself and nothing else can explain it. What little explanation can be given is in the idea of expansion. There is a man who toils all day in order to earn his livelihood, to give himself a little comfort, a little pleasure, and so his life goes on. There is another man who has a family, who has others to think about, who toils for them, works for them. Sometimes he forgets his pleasure and comfort for the comfort and pleasure of those who depend upon him. He has hardly time to think about his comfort, to think about himself. His pleasure is in the pleasure of those who depend upon him, his comfort is in their comfort. And there is another man who thinks of being useful in his town, to improve the conditions of his town, to help the education of the people of his town. He is engaged in it and very often he forgets himself in the striving for the happiness of those for whom he is working. There are also those who live for their nation, who work for their nation, their whole life is given to it. They are only conscious of their nation, their consciousness is expanded and is larger. There is very little difference between the frames of men, but there is a great difference between the expansion of men's consciousness. There is one man who seems as large as he seems to be; there is another who seems as large as his family; another who seems as large as his town; another seems as large as his nation. And there are men - believe me - who are as large as the world. There is a saying of a Hindustani[4] poet, "Neither the sea nor the land can be compared with the heart of man". If the heart of man is large, it is larger than the universe. Therefore, if perfection can be explained in any terms, if perfection can be defined, it is in the expansion of man's consciousness. The man who strives after this perfection need not know or learn what is selfish or unselfish. Unselfishness naturally comes to him, he becomes unselfish.

The last few years humanity has gone through a great

catastrophe; all nations have suffered and have partaken of it. Every individual, even every living creature on this earth has been affected by it. One might ask what was lacking. Was education lacking? There are many schools and universities. Was religion lacking? There are many churches still and many different beliefs still exist in the world. What is lacking is the understanding of the true meaning of religion. What is lacking is the understanding of the real meaning of education.

Now the question arises: Those who have found out that perfection is attained by realizing the self within, how have they attained it? It was not only by what man calls external worship, but it was by self-abnegation in the true sense of the word. It is by going into that silence where one can forget the limitedness of the self, that one can get in touch with that part of one's being which is called perfection. And this can be attained best by those who have realized The Meaning of Life.

CHAPTER XXIV

The Path of Attainment

1

THE ATTAINMENT of every soul is different. One person may say, "I care only to attain to spirituality, to God. That is the only thing that is worthwhile". Another may say, "All I care for is fame, wealth, position, power. That only is worth attaining". The first one will say, "Money or position is not worth gaining. I desire only spirituality, God". The other will say, "By your spirituality you have nothing yourself and nothing to give to another. You may keep your spirituality in the temple. To gain money is what is of use to humanity".

One person is content if he has a place where he can draw a little money and has a cottage to live in. Another says, "I will give my life, but I must be Secretary of State", and another says, "I must be Prime Minister". A King may have a slave and wish to make him minister, and the slave perhaps finds that, if he has good clothes, good food and a horse to ride, if he can go here and there, that is quite enough; he does not want to be a minister.

Why do not all want fame, why do not all want all the money in the world, why do not all want to be prime minister? Because each soul's attainment is according to its evolution. Therefore we should never say, "Why does that person strive for an object which is not worthwhile?" Our work is to be silent and by our kindness, by our sympathy, to help each one towards that attainment that he is aiming at, not judging it from our standard, but looking at it from his point of view.

A person may say, "I desire only God", and his hand is held out behind his back; if money comes in it he is very glad. Then it is better to desire all the money in the world, because he who desires money and says so is at least frank and open before the world.

In Sanskrit, Prakrit and Hindi there is the word *sadhu* which comes from *sidhi,* meaning mastery. *Sadhu* is the master who in Islam is called *wali*. *Wali* or *vali* comes from the same root as *vilayat* which means will, and I should not be astonished if the English word "will" comes from the same root. It may seem curious that in the East, where we read in their literature so much about renunciation and acquiescence in the will of God, he who attains is called master, and not renouncer.

To renounce what we cannot gain is not true renunciation, it is weakness. When the apples are so high up on the branch of the tree that we cannot reach them, if we try to and cannot and then say, "The apples are sour, I don't want them", that is not renunciation. If we climb the tree and get the apples and cut them in half, then we may say, "They are sour", and throw them away. If we say, "I cannot have my wish; it is not intended by the will of God; I am resigned to the will of God", that is not resignation. Why should it not be meant for us to have our wish? Behind our will there is the will of God; God desires it through us. Christ said, "If ye desire bread, He will not give a stone". By this we see that it is natural for us to have our desire, it is natural for us to have health and riches and success and all things. It is unnatural to have illnesses and failures and miseries. But if, after gaining all the wealth in the world, position and titles, we then give them up, that will be true renunciation.

There are several things by which we prevent ourselves from attaining what we desire.

First, if there are three or four aims before us, if there are three or four thoughts, then we cannot succeed in any one. We must be singleminded; there must be one aim before us.

The second thing is that by doubts and lack of self-confidence we weaken our will and frustrate our attainment. If a person is going to see a friend and thinks, "Perhaps I shall not find him, perhaps he has gone out", very often, psychically, by that thought his friend is driven out of the house, while otherwise he would have been at home. If someone is going to see an official and thinks, "Shall I see him? Perhaps I shall not be well received, I have no letters of recommendation", by this he prevents his own success; reason stands in the way of success. If a person begins to reason, "Perhaps it will be", or, "It will not be", or,"If it will be, how can it be", or, "If it can be how should it be", he goes from one reason to ten and a hundred reasons, and spoils and loses his purpose in the reasons. His mind becomes all reason.

Reason is a gift given to us like any other faculty of mind, like memory, like imagination. But it is a part of mind; if it becomes all the mind, it spoils all. In the state there are so many different parts; there is the military part, the administrative, the judicial part. If the military becomes the whole state it is harmed; if the judicial part becomes all, the state is spoiled. There must be a balance. In a house there is a drawingroom, a diningroom, a kitchen. If the whole house became a kitchen it would be terrible; if the whole house became a diningroom it would not be good.

The great minds, the masters think that behind their thought, their will, there is the will of God. They have confidence in that will, and whatever they think is done. I have myself seen this. At Sekunderabad there was a dervish living in retirement. In the East people have a great trust in a faqir. Whether they have all other means or none, they go to him in their difficulties and say, "I have all other means", - or, "I have none" - "but your blessing is the greatest source of help in my time of difficulty". There was a man who was to be tried in a court of law and he had no money even to pay a lawyer to defend him. He went to this dervish and said, "I am a poor man, and now my case is coming up. If I am condemned there will be no one to support my family. Pray help me". The dervish wrote a few words on a piece of paper and gave it to him saying, "Now go home and be quiet". He had written on the piece of paper, "I have examined the charge against this man and I find that it is groundless. Therefore I dismiss the case". When the man's case came before the judge, the judge wrote these same words, and the man was released. Such is the power of the master mind.

The masters, the founders of religions, have been called fanatics, but the words spoken by them are thought by thousands to-day. The words of Moses, of Christ, of Muhammad after thousands of years are thought by millions of people. This may be called fanaticism, yet its power is much greater than that of those who reason.

The third thing that prevents our attaining our wish is lack of patience. Many Suras of the Qur'an begin with, "O men of patience". By this we see what importance patience has. Patience strengthens the will, it makes all attainment possible. The lack of patience makes people commit suicide, it makes them call for death to come, it makes them lunatics. Patience is needed in all relations of life, in all things: patience with the servant, with your subordinate, with your wife, your husband, your son, your daughter, thinking that he or she may improve and may become as your ideal-patience with your friend.

Patience is fed on hope, it stands on the feet of hope. As long as there is hope there is patience, and when hope is gone then there is no more patience; we say, "I have no more patience, it is finished". Hope is needed in all things, the hope that, "If I have not attained my desire now, I shall attain it". We live on hope. In all our affairs hope is the foundation: in our undertakings, in friendship, in love affairs. In the East there is a beautiful saying, "Brahma extracted honey from all flowers, and it was hope". This means: Brahma, God, extracted the essence from all things in the world. The essence is wisdom. The things, all objects in the world, are flowers that attract us, and they attract us by hope. Hope is life and without hope life ends.

A small child, if he is given a sham gold chain, is happy with it; an older person is satisfied only with the real gold. The look is the same, the colour is the same, the difference is only that the sham gold does not last, the real gold is permanent, it is everlasting. He who does not value the permanence, the everlastingness, is pleased with the sham. Of all attainments only that which is everlasting can satisfy us in the end. Until we attain to that, it is right for us to have all desires, all wishes, and to rise from each attainment to the higher, until we attain to the highest.

It may be asked whether all things cannot be attained by psychic power alone without any physical means. This has been experimented with by the ancient Yogis. They left the world and retired to the caves of the mountains, to the wilderness, and led a life of asceticism. You would be astonished to know what hardships they went through, some of them not sleeping for years, others not speaking for years at a time. Not only in ancient times: my father had seen a saint who had been standing for years and years, always standing; he never slept or sat. By this the Yogis strengthened their will and gained control, and what they thought was done. But as we exist on the physical plane and have the physical body, it is better to work with the physical means also, to work by the thought and with the body. In this way the aim is attained by all means.

If we can gain what is greatest we should not content ourselves with little. It would be like someone who might take all the money from the Bank of England and who takes twenty pounds. If one can take from the Bank of England one should take millions and millions. If we wish for a palace and are sitting in a cottage, we should not think, "How could such a miserable person as I ever have a palace?". We should think that the wish to have it is the sign of our being capable of having it. Behind our wish there is God's wish, who has all might, all greatness, all wealth.

2

Spiritual attainment cannot be reached in the same manner as material attainment; it must be seen from quite a different point of view. What discourages is that after striving for a year one does not seem to have arrived at anything. The person who strives to attain things of this world finds the proof of having attained them by holding them. He says, "This is mine", because he possesses it. Spiritual attainment, on the contrary, wants to take the possessions away; it does not even allow you to possess yourself. This becomes a great disappointment for a person whose only realization of having attained is in possession. Spiritual attainment comes by not attaining.

There is the question what difference there is between the spiritual person and the person who possesses nothing. The difference is indeed great, for the spiritual person, in the absence of any possessions, is still rich. What is the reason? The reason is this: the one who does not possess anything is conscious of limitation - the spiritual person, in the absence of even possessing himself, is conscious of perfection. Then one may ask, "How can a limited man be conscious of perfection?" The answer is that the limited man has limited himself, he is limited because he is conscious of being limited. It is not his true self which is limited; that which is limited is what he holds, not man himself. That is the possibility that made Christ say, "Be ye perfect as your Father in heaven is perfect".

Spiritual knowledge is not in learning something, it is in discovering something, so to speak in breaking the fetters of the false consciousness and allowing the soul to unfold itself with light and power. What does the word spiritual really mean? Spiritual is spirit-conscious. When a person is conscious of his body he cannot be spiritual. He is like a king who does not know his kingdom. The moment he is conscious of being a king he is a king. Every soul is born a king - afterwards he becomes a slave. Every soul is born with kingly possibility - by this wicked world it is taken away. This is told in symbolical stories, as in the story of Rama from whom his beloved Sita was taken away. Every soul has to conquer this, has to fight for this kingdom. In that fight the spiritual kingdom is attained. No one will fight for you, neither your teacher nor anybody else. Yes, those who are more evolved than you can help you, but you have to fight your battle, your way to that spiritual goal.

An intellectual person thinks that by adding to knowledge he may attain spiritual knowledge. This is not so. The secret of life is boundless, knowledge is limited. Eyes see a very little distance; just so limited is the human mind. How far can it see? Those who see can see by not seeing, learn by not learning. The way of spiritual attainment is contrary to the way of all attainment concerning matter. In material attainment you must take, for spiritual attainment you must give. In material attainment you must learn, in spiritual attainment you must unlearn. Material attainment is one side, spiritual attainment the other side, the opposite direction.

The word spiritual simply means spirit-conscious. If a person is conscious of his body and thinks this is all that can be known of himself, the spirit is covered. It is not that he does not have a soul, but his soul is obscured. In English one says, "He has lost his soul". No, it is only covered. Can anything that is possessed be lost? If a man thinks so, he is limited. Neither objects nor beings are lost; they are covered for a moment, yet they are all there. No one made can ever be destroyed; it is only covering and uncovering. All relations and connections, nothing is separable. The separation is outward; inwardly they are never separated. They are separated from one's consciousness, but when the consciousness is accommodated, then nothing in the world can separate them. What does one learn from this? That spiritual attainment is to be reached by the raising of the consciousness from limitation to perfection.

There is another side to this question. There is no one, wise or foolish, who is not progressing, slowly or quickly, towards the spiritual goal. The only difference is that the one is attracted to it facing his goal, making his way towards it, while the other has his back turned to it; he is held and is drawn without being conscious of it. Poor man, he does not know where he is being taken, but he goes just the same. His punishment is that he does not see the glory he is approaching, and his torture that he is being drawn to the pole opposite to the one he desires. His punishment is not different from that of the infant who goes into the water of a lake and whose mother pulls him back by his shirt - but he is looking at the lake! From a religious point of view it is very unjust towards the perfect Judge to be deprived of that perfect bliss which is spiritual attainment, but from the point of view of metaphysics, no soul will be deprived of this knowledge some time or other through eternity.

What does Sufism teach on this subject? Sufism avoids words - words from which differences and distinctions arise. Words can never fully express truth. Words promote argument. All the differences between religions are differences of words; in sense they do not differ, only in words, for in sense they all have come from one source, and to the same source they return. This very source is the store, is life, light and power for them. How then can differences be made? By man's limitations. This is the way of the Sufi: if he does not meet somebody in one particular idea, he takes a step higher instead of differing in the lower plane. Therefore for the wise person there is no difficulty. The main thing that Sufism teaches is to dive deep within oneself, and to prepare mind and body by contemplation so as to make one's being a shrine of God, the purpose for which it was created.

3

The path of attainment is likened to a narrow path, to a steep path that one finds on a mountain to climb to the top. Therefore the path of attainment is difficult because it is up-hill. There is another path which leads to the goal that follows after the attainment. It cannot very well be called down-hill, but at the same time the journey on this path is as easy as it is to come down from the top of a mountain. The path that is up-hill towards the attainment requires a continual sacrifice. The one who is not ready to sacrifice must stay either at the foot of the mountain or at the place where he is standing on the way. He cannot go further because he cannot sacrifice.

The path that is after the attainment of arriving at the goal requires renunciation. Very often there is confusion between sacrifice and renunciation, but to muddle these two words up is like confusing words such as pleasure and happiness, as intellect and wisdom. The one who has not made sacrifices in his life, who has not yet gone through the path of sacrifice, must not use the name renunciation, for it is quite a different thing. Everything is good in its own time. When sacrifice is needed, and one makes a renunciation, one goes backwards. When renunciation is necessary, and one makes a sacrifice, one goes backwards too, for these are two distinct and different things.

Apart from the spiritual path, even in things of worldly life, such as starting a new business, going into a new profession, making one's career, treading the path of love and friendship, working for name and fame, whatever be the nature or character of the object one wishes to attain - what it asks is sacrifice from beginning to end. We are apt to forget this and therefore each of us thinks, "Our life asks for so many sacrifices! Look how that professional man is happy, how that businessman is enjoying his life, how that man who is making a career in government is going on in his life". But we do not see the sacrifice that each one of them has to make in order to arrive at that object which they wish to attain. A lazy man is preferable to a man who is unwilling to make sacrifices. By laziness a man shows that he does not care enough to attain something. He enjoys his comfort, his convenience, he is quite content in his life. But the man who wishes to attain something and is not willing to make sacrifices will have a difficult time, for he wants to purchase things without paying the coins.

The sacrifice one has to make is of different character, of different nature, according to the object one has in view. The greater the object of attainment, the greater is the sacrifice asked for it. But sacrifice must be understood rightly. It is not always that one has to sacrifice what one possesses, but one has to sacrifice what one is. It is here that a great difficulty arises. As a miser holds on to his last penny, so a man disinclined to sacrifice holds himself tightly thinking, "Anything may be stolen but not myself". It is a natural inclination in man. And what does the spiritual path ask you for? For this very thing: self. Give the false self, and gain the real self. If this mystery is understood, then attainment is at the next step. But man is not easily inclined to give himself up - anything else, but not himself!

Now what is meant by this? One says, "My idea is my idea, my wish is my wish, it is mine. My thought is my thought, my inclination is my inclination, my point of view is my point of view". One makes all these things greater possessions than those one has outwardly, and so it becomes easier to give away what one possesses than to give up what one thinks and feels. If you say to someone, "This is a wrong thing to do", he replies, "Yes, but I am that way, I think like this. I know that it is wrong, but I feel like it, although it is wrong. I cannot do otherwise". In other words, he holds his possession thinking that it is himself. But it is not himself, it is his false self.

However small be the object of your attainment, it matters little, and however great a sacrifice it asks from you, it does not matter. If you have attained a small object by paying a greater price, even then you have attained something.

As to renunciation, very often a person sees it in a wrong light. He thinks, "I am not willing to make that sacrifice, therefore I renounce that object of attainment". This is a wrong conception of renunciation and many, often in their lives renounce objects only because they are unwilling to make enough sacrifices. They value themselves, or they value the sacrifice it asks more than the object they wish to attain, and because they cannot attain it they say, "I renounce it". It is very easy to renounce! The great heroes and the souls who have really done something worthwhile in the world and have left some impressions which can never die, began their life with sacrifices: sacrifice of comfort, sacrifice of convenience, sacrifice of pleasure, of merriment, of joy. There is hardly one to be found among them who did not have to pay a great price to arrive at that attainment.

The higher the attainment, the greater the sacrifice it asks, but the one who understands keeps his object always higher than the sacrifice he makes. The one who does not understand wishes to see the object of attainment much less than the sacrifice it asks for, and he thinks that this is practical, that it is common sense. No doubt, when the object is material, it is practical and it is common sense to only pay the price of the object. But the high-minded person who has an ideal in him will show this tendency; even if one calls him unpractical also in material things he does not mind. The diamond ring that he likes - he will pay any price for it. The object of antiquity that he wishes to possess - he does not mind what price is asked for it. Others will mock at him, call him unpractical - he does not mind. The pleasure he gets out of the thing he has bought is greater than the money if he had it in the bank. After all life is but four days. Sa'di, the great

Persian poet says, "Who has earned and who has spent and who has lived is greater than the one who has earned and has collected at the sacrifice of the joy that one gains by sacrifice".

When it comes to higher things, such as friendship, as love, as kindness, there one can never make enough sacrifice. For the one who has the ideal in his heart sacrifice is always small; whatever sacrifice he makes is always small. It is the one who has no ideal who will weigh and measure and see if it is even or uneven, if "what I give is even with what I take, or whether it does not balance". There is his practicality; he calls it wisdom. It is not wisdom, it is cleverness. Wisdom stands higher, above it all; wisdom does not come through this practicality. The one who says, "I will guard my interest against every attempt made by others", is a different person. That person is greater who trusts, who risks, and who can make sacrifices.

When we come to the spiritual path it needs a greater sacrifice than anything else. It asks for one's time, for one's thought. When you are concentrating it does not even allow you to think of anything else; you must think of the object you concentrate upon. The further you go the greater sacrifice is wanted. The difference between those who go more quickly on this path and those who go slower is in their capacity for sacrifice. Sacrifice teaches resignation, and there is no other way of self-effacement than sacrifice. The one who knows the path of friendship, the one who knows what real friendship means, need not be told what sacrifice means. He knows it, for friendship does not mean a good time, a pastime. Friendship means sacrifice, and when once by friendship sacrifice is learned, then one begins to know what sacrifice is necessary in the path of spiritual attainment.

CHAPTER XXV

Stages on the Path of Self-Realization

WE SEE that in the words of philosophers, mystics, sages, thinkers and prophets great importance is given to self-realization. If I were to explain what self-realization is, I would say that the first step to self-realization is God-realization. The one who realizes God, in the end realizes self; but the one who realizes self, never realizes God. And that is the difficulty to-day with those who search after spiritual truth intellectually. They read many books on occultism, esotericism and mysticism, and what they find emphasized most is self-realization. Therefore they think that what they have to do in the world is to come to that self-realization, and they think it is just as well to omit God. God in reality is the key to spiritual perfection. God is the stepping stone to self-realization. God is the way which covers the knowledge of the whole being, and if God is omitted then nothing is reached.

The wrong method carried on to-day in many different so-called cults often proves to be a failure, when the beginner in the spiritual path is taught to say, "I am God" - a phrase of thoughtlessness, words of insolence, a thought which has no foundation, which leads him nowhere except to ignorance. The prophets and thinkers, the sages taught their followers the ideal of God; it had a meaning, a purpose. To-day people do not recognize this and being anxious to find a short-cut they wish to omit the principal thing in order to come to that realization.

Once a man went to a Chinese sage and said to him, "I want to know some occult laws. Will you teach me?" The sage said, "You have come to ask me to teach you something? We have so many missionaries in China who come to teach us". The man said, "We know about God, but I have come to ask you about occult laws". The sage answered, "If you know about God you do not need to know anything more. God is all that is to be known. If you know Him, you know all".

In this world of commercialism there is a tendency, an unconscious tendency, even of persons who promote the spiritual truth, to cater for the taste of the people. Maybe owing to a commercial instinct or with a desire for success they have a tendency to cater for what people want. If people seem tired of the God-ideal, they want to give them occultism, they want to call it mysticism, to make a mystification of anything, perhaps because the God-ideal seems so simple. And as to-day there is one fashion and to-morrow another, even in belief there is a fashion. People think that the ideal of God is old-fashioned, something of the past. In order to set a new fashion they mar the method which was the royal road made by all the wise and thoughtful ones of all ages, the road which will surely take a person to perfection. There is safety and success on that path; on that path he is sure.

Now I want to discuss a most vital point on the subject of God. There is a man of devotion and of simple faith, of a religious belief, who believes in a God whom he calls the Judge, the Creator, the Sustainer, the Protector, the Master of the Last Day, the Lord, the Forgiver, and so on. And there is another person, perhaps an intellectual who has studied philosophy, who says, "God is all and all is God. God is abstract and it is the abstract which is God". Now in point of fact the one has a God, even if that God be in his imagination, and the other has none. He has the abstract; he calls it God because others say "God", but in his mind he has only the abstract. For instance, when you say "space" there is no personality attached to it, no intelligence recognized in it, no form, no distinct individuality or personality. It is the same thing with time. When you speak about time you do not imagine time to be a man or Lord. You say it is time, which means a conception you have made for your convenience. A man who says that the abstract is God has no God; he has the abstract. What is it? The same as space or time.

By this I do not mean to say that one or the other is right; I am explaining to you that from a mental point of view the one has a God, even if it is in his imagination, but the other has not. He may admit it or not, as soon as he identifies God with the abstract he has the abstract. When we come to the question of who is right, my answer is, "Both are right and both are wrong". One is in the beginning and the other is at the end. The one who begins with the end will end at the beginning, and the one who begins from the beginning will end at the end.

We might think, "Why in this short life must we create for ourselves a kind of illusion? Why should we arrive at the truth in the end, why not begin with it, as everyone is so anxious to find the absolute truth just now?" But if truth were such a thing that it could be said in words I would have been the first person who would have given it to you just now. But truth is a thing that must be discovered; you have to prepare yourself to realize it, and it is that preparation which is called religion or occultism or mysticism. Whatever you may call this, it is that preparation: you prepare yourself by one way or the other in order to realize truth in the end. And the best way, which all the thinkers and sages have adopted, is the way of God.

The next question is belief in God. There are four stages of belief in God. Each stage is as essential and important as the other, and if one does not go stage by stage, gradually evolving towards the realization of God, one does not come to anything. It must be remembered that belief is a step on the ladder. Belief is the means and not the end. Belief leads to realization; it is not that we come to a belief. If a man's foot is nailed to the ladder, that is not the object. The object is that he must step on the ladder and climb upwards. If he stands on the ladder he defeats the object with which he journeys on the spiritual path. Those therefore who believe in a particular creed, in a religion, in God, in the hereafter, in the soul, in a certain dogma, are no doubt blessed by their belief and think they have something, but if they remain there, there is no progress.

If a religious belief was the only thing needed then thousands and millions of people in the world to-day who have a certain religious belief could have been most advanced people. But they are not. They go on year after year believing something that people have believed perhaps for many generations, and they still continue in it and remain there just like the man standing on a step of a staircase, a place not made for him to stand but to go on. He stayed there and came to nothing.

The first belief is the belief of the masses. If one person says, "There is a God", then everybody repeats, "Yes, there is a God", because the others say so. If one person is religious then everyone says, "Yes, we too go with him". You might think that to-day at this stage of civilization people are too advanced to have a mass-belief, but that would be a great mistake. People are the same to-day as they were a thousand years before, or perhaps worse if it comes to spiritual questions. When someone is called "the man of the day" in a nation, one day the whole nation has a favourable opinion of him and is with him. Thousands and millions lift him up, hold him high; and for how long? Until a powerful person says, "No, it is not so". Then the whole country throws him down.

Just before the war I visited Russia. In every shop was a picture of the Czar and Czarina. They were held in high esteem; it was sacred for the people. The emperor was the head of the church and there was a religious ideal attached to him. People used to be filled with joy when they saw the Czar and Czarina passing in the street; it was a religious upliftment for them. But not long after I heard that they had processions in the street where at each step they struck the crown with hammers. It did not take one moment to change their belief. Why? Because it was a mass-belief. This is a very powerful belief. It changes nations; it throws them down and raises them; it brings wars. But what is it after all? A mad belief. And yet no one will admit it. If you ask an individual, he says, "I am not one of them". At the same time all move together when an impulse comes for good or bad.

Then there is a second step towards belief, and that is belief in an authority. People believe in a leader. They say, "I will not believe in the ordinary man, in my neighbour or in my colleague, I believe in that man whom I trust. This belief is one step higher, because it is a belief in somebody in whom one has trust. When a person says, "I am a Christian", he has a belief in Jesus Christ and his teaching. It is a belief in someone, not in everyone but in the one in whom he believes. The belief in authority is the second step towards belief. One might say, "We do not even care for belief in authority to-day", but this is not true. Everybody accepts a discovery made by a scientist before having made investigations about it. When a person comes forward and says, "I have discovered something", everybody accepts it. May-be another scientist will produce another thing to believe in, but the one who speaks with authority is believed by the multitude.

Then there is a third stage of belief, a further stage, and this belief makes man still greater. It is the belief of reason: one does not believe in authority nor in what everybody else believes, but one has reasoned it out, one sees its reason. This belief is stronger still, for of the beliefs I have explained before one cannot give proof; there is only a scientist who says, "It is such and such" or many people who say so. But in this case one can stand up and say, "Yes, I have reasoned it out". However this has its limitation just the same, since reason is the slave of the mind and reason is as changeable as the weather. This reason obeys your impulses. If you have an impulse to insult a person or to box with him, you can produce many reasons for it. It may be that afterwards there will be contrary reasons, but at the time when you have this impulse, right or wrong, there is always a reason for it. Do you think that criminals put in jail have committed crimes without a reason? No, they have a reason. It does not fit in with the law perhaps, it does not satisfy society, but if you ask them, they have a reason. At the same time the reason you have to-day, you may perhaps change next week. Nevertheless this third belief makes one stand on one's own feet for that moment if not for ever, and gives a greater power to defend one's belief.

And then there is a fourth belief. That belief is a belief of conviction which stands above reason. There is a sense of conviction in man which is not discovered for some time in life; but there comes a time when it is discovered and that is a blessed time. Then there arises an idea, an idea which no reason can break, a feeling which is not a passing feeling but a conviction. However high the idea may be, you seem to be an eye witness of the idea; you are as strong, as powerful as a person who has seen it with his own eyes. Something in you says, "Yes, I have seen it". You can be convinced of ideas so fine that they cannot even be expressed in words, and you are more convinced of them than if you had seen them with your own eyes. It is this belief which is called by Sufis and Persian mystics *iman* which means conviction.

I remember the instance of my spiritual teacher, my *murshid* who gave me a blessing every time I parted from him. That blessing was, "May your *iman* be strengthened". At that time I had not thought about the word *iman* which in the East means belief or faith. On the contrary I thought as a young man, "Is my faith so weak that my teacher wants it to be strong?" I would have preferred it if he had said,"May you become illuminated", or "may your powers be great", or "may your influence spread" or "may you rise higher and higher" or "may you become perfect". This simple thing, "May your faith be strengthened", what is it? I did not criticize, but I pondered and pondered upon the subject. In the end I came to realize that no blessing is more valuable and important than this, for every blessing is attached to conviction. Where there is no conviction there is nothing. The secret of healing, the mystery of evolving, the power of all attainments and the way to spiritual realization, all come from the strengthening of that belief which is conviction, that nothing can ever change.

Now we come again to the question of God. This is the first important question we must make clear in our mind before we take a step further in spiritual progress; although I must say that to analyse God means to dethrone God. The less said on the subject the better, but at the same time the seekers after truth who want to tread the spiritual path with open eyes and whose intellect hungers for knowledge must know something about it just the same.

There is a Hebrew story that once Moses was walking near the bank of a river where he saw a shepherd boy speaking to himself. Moses was interested and halted there to listen. The shepherd boy was saying, "O God, I have heard so much about You. You are so beautiful, You are so lovely, You are such a dear. If ever You came to me I would clothe You with my mantle, and I would guard You night and day. I would protect You from all the cruel animals of this forest, and bathe You in this river, and bring You all good things, milk and buttermilk. I would bring You a special bread and love You so much. I would not let anyone cast his glance upon You. I would be all the time near You. I love You so much. If only I could see You once, God, I would give all I had". Moses said, "What are you saying?" The boy looked at Moses; he trembled and was afraid. "Did I say anything wrong?", he asked. Moses said, "God, the Protector of all beings, you think of protecting Him, of giving Him bread? He gives bread to the whole universe. You say you would bathe Him in the river ! He is the purest of all pure things. And how can you say that you will guard Him who guards all beings?" The boy trembled; he thought, "What terrible things I have done - such wrong things!" He seemed to be lost. As Moses went a few steps further there came a voice, "Moses, what did you do! We sent you to bring Our friends to Us, and now you have separated one from Us. No matter how he thought of Us, he thought of Us just the same. You should have let him think the way he was thinking about Us; you should not have interfered with him.".

Everyone has his own imagination about God. It is best if everyone is left with his own imagination. In our daily life we hate someone and that same one is loved by another; we criticize someone and the same one is praised by another. If that is so then the conception of everyone about everyone is different. The same person is considered saint by one and Satan by another. If that is true then the God we know or can know is nothing but our conception, a picture that we have made of God for our own self, our own convenience. It is the greatest mistake for anyone to interfere with another's conception of God or to think that another should have the same conception of God as he has himself. It is impossible. So many different artists have painted the picture of Christ and each one is different. And since we allow every artist to have his own conception of Christ, so we should allow every person to have his own conception of God.

Therefore we need not blame the old Chinese and Greeks and Indians who believed in many gods. Many gods is too small a number. In reality each one has his own God. Besides, all these different conceptions are nothing but covers over one God. Let them call that God by any name, think of Him with whatever imagination they have. It is after all the highest ideal, and the ideal of each one is as high as his imagination can make it. Forcing upon someone that God is abstract and formless and pure and that God is nameless, all these things do not help a person to evolve, because the first step on the path of God is to make a conception of God. It is only to help the seekers after God that the wise in all ages perhaps have made a little statue and called it God or Goddess and said, "Here is God. There is a shrine, go there". And to the one who was not satisfied with it they said, "Walk two hundred times around the shrine before you enter, then you will be blessed". When he tired he naturally felt exaltation because he walked in the path of God.

Now I come to the idea of self-realization. In relation to the belief of God you might ask: if we leave everyone with his particular imagination or ideal of God, will he then progress and one day come to the realization of the self which is the highest attainment taught by all the great teachers of humanity? I say yes.

There are three stages towards spiritual perfection. Those who are unaware of the possibility of spiritual perfection are greatly mistaken when they say, "Man is imperfect, man cannot be perfect". They are mistaken for the reason that they have seen in man only man. They have not seen in man God. Christ has said, "Be ye perfect even as your Father in heaven is perfect". This shows that there is the possibility of perfection. It is also true that man cannot be perfect. But man is not alone man; in man there is God also. Therefore man remains imperfect, but the God part in man seeks for perfection. That is what the world was created for. Man is here on earth for this one purpose: that he may bring that spirit of God in him to discover his own perfection.

Now I will explain the three stages towards this perfection. The first stage is to make God as great and as perfect as your imagination can make it. It is in order to help man to perfect God in himself that the teachers gave different prayers, prayers of God, calling Him the Judge, the Forgiver, most Compassionate, most Faithful, most Beautiful, most Loving. All these attributes are our limited conceptions. God is greater than whatever we can say about Him. When we form all these conceptions and when by our imagination we make God as great as we can make Him, it must be understood that by making God great He cannot become greater than He is. We cannot bring God pleasure by making Him great. The only thing we do is that by making God great we come to a certain greatness; our vision widens, our spirit deepens, our ideal reaches high, before us we create a greater vision, a wider horizon for our own expansion. It is therefore by the way of prayer, by praise, by contemplation that we try to make God as great in our idea as possible.

The truth of this is that a person who sees good points in others, and wants to add to them what is lacking, becomes nobler every day. Imagine, by making others noble, by thinking good of others, he himself becomes nobler and better than those of whom he thinks good. And the one who thinks evil of others in time becomes wicked, because he covers the good in him and the vision of evil is produced. Therefore the first stage and the first duty of every seeker after truth is to make God as great as possible for his own good, because he is making an ideal within himself, he is building within himself, which will make him great.

The second stage is the work of the heart; the first that of the head. To make God great intellectually with thought and imagination is a painter's work. In the work of the heart it is our love that forms that ideal. In our everyday life we see the phenomenon of love. The first lesson love teaches us is, "I am not, thou art".

The first thing to think of is to erase yourself from your mind and to think of the one you love. As long as you do not come to this idea, love is a word in the dictionary. Many speak about love but very few know it. Is love a pastime, an amusement, a drama, is it a performance? The first lesson of love is sacrifice, service, self-effacement. There is a little story of a peasant girl who had passed through a field where a Muslim was offering his prayers. The law was that no one should pass by such a place. After a time the girl returned by the same way, and the man said, "O girl, what a terrible thing you have done to-day". She was shocked and asked, "What did I do?". He said, "You passed by this way. It is a great sin. I was praying". She asked, "I would like to know what you were doing". He answered, "I was praying, thinking of God" - "Were you thinking of God? I was going to see my young man, I did not see you. How did you see me when you were thinking of God?".

To close the eyes for prayer is one thing, and to produce the love of God is another thing. That is the second stage in spiritual realization, where in the thought of God you begin to lose yourself, in the same way as the lover loses the thought of self in the thought of the beloved.

And the third stage is different again. In the third stage the beloved becomes the self, and the self is no more there, because the self as we think it to be no longer remains. The self becomes what it really is. It is that realization which is called self-realization.

CHAPTER XXVI

Man, the Master of his Destiny

1

IT IS said in the *Gayan*, "The present is the reflection of the past and the future is the re-echo of the present". Destiny is not what is already made, destiny is what we are making. Very often fatalists think that we are in the hands of destiny, driven into life in whatever direction destiny drives us, but in point of fact we are the makers of our destiny, especially from the moment we begin to realize this fact. Among Hindus there is a well-known saying that the creation is Brahma's dream; in other words: the manifestation is the dream of the Creator. I add to this that destiny means the materialization of man's own thought. For success and failure, for rise and fall man is responsible, and it is man who brings these about, either knowingly or unknowingly.

There is a hint of this in the Bible. In the principal prayer taught by Christ are the words, "Thy will be done on earth as it is in heaven". It is a psychological suggestion to mankind to make it possible for the will of God which is easily done in heaven also to be done on earth. And the English saying that man proposes and God disposes supports this; it suggests the other side of the same idea. These are two contrary ideas, but at the same time they explain the same theory that what is meant by destiny is changed by man, and that destiny changes man's plans.

The question of destiny can be better explained by the picture of an artist meditating on a certain design or picture that is in his mind. To create what he first had made in his mind is one stage. Then he wishes to bring the picture onto the canvas, and when he draws it on the canvas this picture suggests something to him that he had not thought when he made the design in his mind. And when the artist has finished his picture he will see that it is quite different from what he had thought. This shows that our life stands before us as a picture, and when all that has been designed beforehand is brought about, this picture suggests something else to our soul. It suggests a certain improvement to be made; that what is lacking might be put in. In this way the picture is improved. So there are two kinds of artist: one artist designs the plan that comes to his mind on the canvas, the other takes suggestions from the picture itself as he goes on painting. The difference is that the first is merely an artist and the other is a master; whereas the latter is not bound by a plan, the former has designed something and is bound by what he had once designed; he is limited.

One sees the same thing with a composer of music. A composer thought a certain melody in his mind; he contemplated upon it and wished to put it on paper. When he played his composition on the piano the music suggested improvements to him. He played the same idea he had in his mind and that melody became perfect and finished once he had heard it with his own ears.

This is the picture of our life. There is one man who is driven by the hand of destiny; he does not know where he comes from, he does not know where he is going. He is placed in a certain condition in life, he finds himself busy somewhere, occupied, attached and sees no way of getting out of it. He may desire something different but he thinks, "I must go on". That is the man who has not yet understood the meaning of this secret*. But there is another man who after a hundred failures still makes up his mind to be successful at the next attempt. That man is the master of his success.

What is man? We read in the *Gayan*, "When a glimpse of Our image is caught in man, when heaven and earth are sought in man, then what is there in the world that is not in man? If one only explores him there is a lot in man". When a person says, "I cannot help it, this is my habit", when he says, "I cannot help being like this. I have always done so; I cannot do things differently", when he is fixed in a situation and cannot alter it, he does not know the meaning of this quotation. There is everything in man, if only one could explore oneself and find what treasure there is within oneself.

Those who have explored the being of man have discovered that man has two aspects: one living, the other

* i.e. the secret that we are the masters of our destiny.

dead. Man is the engineer and man is a mechanism. When the engineer part is buried, the part of man which may be called a mechanism is there. Then man is a mechanism, a machine. He works like a machine from morning till evening. He eats, drinks, sleeps and works. And what is he? A machine which carries on with the oil and steam given to it. This machine part of man is subject to favourable or unfavourable conditions, to climatic conditions, to personal influences which come from all sides. Then there is a side of man which may be called the engineer. This side is living, and it is this side which may be called free will or self-expression, where there is intelligence, where there is power. The greater this part of man's being, the greater the person, for the more a person is conscious of his engineer part the more he is living. In religious terminology this may be called the divine spark. And whereas man has inherited his physical being from this dense earth which has made him a mortal being, there is one part of his being which is immortal. It is that part which may be called the divine spark, and it is that part of his being which is the heritage of God.

In the Bible one often reads "the Father in heaven". This means that man is considered as a child of God, or the son of God. What does it mean? As man has inherited a part of his being from the earth, so he has inherited the most essential part of his being from God. In other words, man is linked with God or more fully said, man is an expression of God. In man is the being of God and that being can especially be distinguished and defined as the Creator. God is the Creator, and man is a creator at the same time. Besides, man by his creative faculty gives the proof of God being the perfect Creator.

Now comes the question: how does one attain to this path which is called the path of mastery? In all times of the world's history, in all periods of the world's tradition one can trace that there have been the wise, there have been those who have searched after truth, and as the outcome of this search after truth have gained mastery. What the prophets of all times - Buddha, Moses, Jesus Christ, Muhammad - in one way or other have shown in their lives was mastery.

In a small way it can also be seen in those who first came to America, a country where they had nothing; and all this is made and created as a great wonder in the world. Many who came from their country far away and settled here had nothing in the beginning, and now they have everything. This is also an example of mastery, but mastery does not end here. To gain the earth is not the only object, there is something further still. There is a larger scope in life and as soon as man begins to see that larger scope, he sees much space to be filled, much to be done besides all that one does materially.

There is the story of Timurlenk, a Moghul emperor in the history of India, a man whom destiny had intended to be great. Yet he was not awakened to that greatness. One day, tired of the strife of daily life and despairing of life's duties in the world, he was lying on the ground in a forest waiting for death to come and take him. There happened to come a dervish who saw him asleep and recognized in him the man whom destiny had meant to be a great personality. Here he was, unaware of it. The dervish struck him with his stick and Timurlenk woke up. He asked, "Why have you come to trouble me here? I have left the world and have come to the forest. Why do you trouble me?" The dervish said, "What is there to gain in a forest? You have the world before you. What you have to accomplish is there, if only you realize the power you have". Timurlenk replied, "No, I am too disappointed, too pessimistic for any good to come to me. The world has wounded me; I am sore, my heart is broken. I will no longer stay in this world". The dervish said, "What is the use of having come to this earth if you have not accomplished something, if you have not experienced something and been happy, if you do not know how to live?" Timurlenk then said to the dervish, "Do you think that I shall ever accomplish something?" The dervish answered, "That is why I have come to awaken you. Awake and pursue the course which is meant for you. You will be successful, there is no doubt about it". This made an impression on Timurlenk which awakened in him the spirit with which he had come into the world. And with every step that he took forward he saw that conditions changed, and all the influences and forces needed for success came to him, as if life which had closed its doors opened before him, and he walked through it and reached that stage where he was the famous Timurlenk of history.

There is another example of the same kind in the history of India: that of Shiwaji who began as a robber. One day he came to a sage, whose name was Ram Das, to be blessed by him. Shiwaji asked him, "Will you bless me?" The sage asked, "Why? What do you want?" He answered, "I am a robber. I am going to rob travellers". The sage who was compassionate and merciful saw who this man was and what would become of him. He did not break his heart. He said, "I will bless you. Go, but become a great robber". And what did he become, this great robber? A king. His attempt then was to be a still greater robber, to be an emperor!

In all walks of life it will be proved to a seeker after truth that if there is a key to success, a key to happiness and a key to advancement and evolution in life, it is the attainment of mastery. The question is how to attain mastery. There are three stages. The first stage of attaining mastery is to gain self-control. And when self-control is gained then the second stage is to control all the personal influences which pull one away from one's path, which push one aside from the way one wishes to take. And if one has been victorious in this second stage, then the third stage is the control of conditions and situations. The man who is responsible, the man who has control over conditions and situations is greater than a thousand men who are qualified and at work. The controller may sit in his chair and do nothing, but he will accomplish more than the one who is doing things all day long and accomplishes very little. Very few can imagine to what extent man can gain power; especially as life to-day is a continual strife for nothing, a busy life without much accomplishment. We cannot imagine to what extent the power of the master-mind can accomplish things. Only, it is behind the scene. Those who do little come forward and say, "I can do so much", and those who really do something say little.

All that is on earth, gold and silver, gems and jewels, are

all for mankind. And all that gives happiness: power, intelligence, harmony, peace, inspiration, ecstasy and joy also belong to man. Man can make a heavenly thing his treasure as well as a thing of the earth. It is not necessary for man to leave all the things of the world and to go away from here. He may just as well attend to his business, to his profession, to his duties in life, and at the same time develop that spirit in himself which is the spirit of mastery. The spirit of mastery is likened to a spark; by blowing continually upon it this spark will grow into a flame and out of it a blaze will arise. The man who will continually keep before him the idea, "All that is lacking outside must not trouble me, for it is all within myself, and if I blow on this spark of mastery by continual contemplation, one day a flame will rise and life will become clear" - his power will indeed be great.

2

The word "man" comes from a Sanskrit word *manas* which means mind. It is symbolical and expressive and shows that man is not his body but his mind.

There are two opposite opinions existing in the world: one belongs to those who are called fatalists, those who believe in fate, and the other is the opinion of those who believe in free will. If we look at life from both these points of view we shall find some reasons for and against each. When we look at life from the point of view of the one who believes in free will we see many instances where there are qualifications, conditions, inclinations and every possibility of progress, and at the same time there is some unknown hindrance and one cannot find out what it is. A man may work for years and years and not succeed. Against fatalism there is also an argument: there are many who hope and believe that all good things will come, but by hoping and believing alone good things do not come. It takes an effort and perseverance, it needs patience to accomplish things. This shows that both possibilities are true, but at the same time the middle way is best, the way to understand how far free will works and also where free will is hindered, what it is that hinders free will from being successful.

According to the mystic's point of view life can be divided into two aspects. One is the preparatory aspect, and the other the aspect of action. The preparatory aspect of life is before a person is born, the other aspect is after his birth. A person is born in a certain condition which becomes the foundation of his life's career; he may be born in surroundings of addiction or in a rich family. This shows that the condition in which a person is born already gives him a foundation upon which to build his life. The credit of what he does with that condition belongs to him, but that condition is something he has not made; from that he has to develop and evolve through life. The question is how this condition is brought about.

Eastern philosophers have had many different conceptions on this question. The way how the wise and the mystics look at it is that man is a ray of the Spirit which is likened to the sun; each soul is a ray shooting forth from that sun. Therefore the origin of all souls is one and the same, just as the origin of the various rays is in one and the same sun. But as these rays shoot forth they pass through three different phases; in other words, they penetrate through three different spheres. Eastern metaphysics recognizes the three spheres as the angelic sphere, the sphere of the *genius* or *jinn* and the physical sphere. When the ray shoots forth the first sphere it passes through is the angelic sphere; the next is called the sphere of the *genius* or *jinn*, the third is the physical sphere.

The nature of each sphere is such that the ray or soul, when it penetrates through a certain sphere, must don the garb of that particular sphere. As a person from a tropical country going to a cold climate must adopt the clothes of that climate, in the same way the soul, which by origin is intelligence and a ray of the sun, the source and goal of all beings, adopts or dons a certain garb with which it is able to enter, to stay and to pass through that particular sphere. Therefore according to Eastern metaphysics man is an angel, man is a *genius* and man is man. In these three conditions the soul is the same but the garb it has taken makes it different. Passing through the angelic sphere the soul is angel, passing through the sphere of the *genius* the soul is *jinn*, passing through the physical sphere the soul is man. Therefore if there is an angel it is man; if there is a *jinn* it is man. It is man's condition in the preparatory stage of *genius* which in the end makes him man.

Then one may ask, "What about animals and other beings and objects which show some part of life, such as trees and plants and rocks?" The answer is that all these are preparatory covers which make the clothes, the garb for the soul to take. There is a saying of a great sage of Persia who lived 500 years before Darwin gave his idea of biology. You can find this saying in numerous Persian manuscripts, "God slept in the rock, God dreamt in the plant, God awoke in the animal, and God realized Himself in man". It tells that this process from mineral to vegetable, from animal to man is the progress of the garb. For instance, in a country where people did not know how to make clothes the first clothes were made of the bark of the tree. Then as they went on making clothes they found better materials and finally came to the finest material. Man is the finest material - his garb, not his soul. His soul is the same as that of the man of a thousand years ago. The material has changed and has progressed with the evolution of the soul which has adorned itself with it. In this way the variety of creatures has come to manifest.

There is another outlook on this subject: as the soul comes forwards to the physical sphere as a ray, so its nature is to go backwards because it follows the law of gravitation. As the body which is made of clay is drawn to the earth, so the soul which belongs to the Spirit is drawn to the Spirit. But one may say, "We see the body drawn to the earth; we see all things of the earth drawn to the earth, but we do not see the law of gravitation working in the soul". We do see it, but we deny it, we do not look at it in that way. There is a dissatisfaction, a discontentment in every soul. In a palace, in a cottage, in whatever condition man lives, there is an innate yearning and longing which he himself does not know. One thinks to-day, "I long for money", and to-morrow one longs for a position, for a friend, for fame or name. One goes from one thing to another, but no doubt one does not long for the thing one wished for yesterday; one does not even want the thing one thinks one wants to-day. It just goes on, and when in the end one has touched the object one wants something else. That something is the Spirit, the Sun. This is what is at the back of the law of gravitation. Therefore in ancient times people worshipped the sun-god as a symbol of the sun within us, of the sun which cannot be seen, which is the source and goal of all beings, from which we have come and to which we are drawn. As it is said in the Qur'an, "From God we all come and to Him we have our return". That means: there is a Spirit, the Spirit of all things, the essence of life from which we come and towards which we are drawn.

Now we have to think about another side of it. There is an action of souls coming forwards from their source to manifestation and there is an action of souls withdrawing from the physical sphere going backwards. The souls who come forward are coming with light and life, with that electricity, intelligence, freedom and freshness which they can impart to those they meet. The souls coming from the manifestation also have things to give on their way: their thoughts of the wickedness of the world, of the goodness of the world, their desire to accomplish things, their experience of life, all the good and evil they have done, their good and bad actions towards others - all these things they take back. There is an exchange as natural as that between people coming from the East and from America who meet in Europe. Both exchange, as they have a great deal to do in their lives. One says, "I give you this introduction, I know a good friend for you". And when that person arrives there is already a condition made for him to begin his life. Another sees that the wrong person sent him to a wrong place.

In Western countries much is made of what in the Hindu philosophy is called reincarnation. In the East people speak very little about it. Sometimes this conception has been so much exaggerated that its real spirit becomes confused. The real meaning of the idea of reincarnation lies in the impression that the soul who has come from the source has received. That impression has made the soul the same person as the one who gave the impression. For instance, the soul of

Shakespeare going backwards towards the source met many souls coming towards the earth, and they became impregnated with all the expressions and thoughts that Shakespeare had developed. When a person comes on earth with those thoughts he is born with the inspiration of Shakespeare. In the same way debts are paid; one has to pay the debts of the other. Because one has the benefit of the other one has the debts also. In the East one says, "You have to look after your children or to pay for your family; it is the debt you have to pay". The more we think about this subject the more we shall find that a preparation is made for man before he is born on earth, and that preparation makes him able to live his life on earth.

Now coming to the question of life on earth: is this life fixed and designed or is there free will? Often people do not understand the meaning of the term free will, and especially those who claim most to have free will have least of it. They are conscious of their free will and do not know where it comes from. They have an inclination to laugh and cry, to sit and move, but they do not know where it comes from. They think, "I did it because I felt like doing it", but they do not know where the thought came from. It may have come from a friend or perhaps from someone they did not know. Do we not feel every day at some time an oppression, a humour without reason, sometimes a feeling of despair, sometimes a desire for action, sometimes a state of lethargy? We think that whatever comes to our mind is free will but free will is quite different from that.

Man has two aspects to his being. One is merely a machine aspect, a mechanism which is made to work, subject to conditions, to influences, climatic and planetary. This is the case of the average man. If there is one part engineer in him there are ninety-nine parts of the machine aspect. When sometimes he thinks of free will it is because of that one part of the hundred he has, but most often he has the ninety-nine parts of the machine aspect. A person gets an impulse suggested by another and he thinks, "It is my impulse". But it was suggested by another. The desire that springs forth in his mind is perhaps the influence of conditions, his wish is perhaps a planetary influence. And there are thousands of influences unknown to man, but as he does not know the influences working behind his vision he thinks, "This is my free will".

The machine part in man's life comes from the garbs he has taken. His body is a machine and there is another finer machine inside which is the mind. But these are both apart from the spirit of free will which is the soul. The more conscious man is of that spirit of free will, the more he awakens mastery in himself. In the East the person who awakens to that spirit of free will is called the master-mind. We are often confused about our two instruments. We have a physical and a mental aspect, the body and the mind, and the person who makes them work according to his free will begins to experience mastery in life.

Great heroes of whom we read in books, inventors, composers, generals, statesmen, whatever they have accomplished in life, they all show that spirit of free will which is the pure essence of the spirit or the soul. That spirit which was developed in them brought about the great accomplishments they achieved in their lives[5]. But if we think about life, we realize that this is not all there is to accomplish. There is much more to accomplish in life than new inventions, great accumulations of wealth and different aspects of civilization. When we ignore this and become contented with all we have, we do not progress any further.

There is a need of the soul to be satisfied, and that is the higher destiny. There are two purposes of life: one is the individual purpose and the other the collective purpose. The purpose of the lives of individuals is different. For instance, in an orchestra the purpose of the clarinet is one and that of the violin another, and that of the cello another again. Each instrument has to take its own place in the orchestra. So there is a purpose, a separate purpose to each individual's life. And then there is the collective purpose, the purpose of all lives. That purpose is to come to the realization of that Spirit which is in man which is the source and goal of all things, the Spirit which was and is capable of producing this whole manifestation. Therefore religious people have called it

"Lord", "the Architect of all", "the Composer of all", in order to express their feeling that this Spirit has all the power of creation. It is the power of the one and only Spirit.

One may think, "How to realize it? Is it not possible to realize this power intellectually?" It seems that with the war there has come upon the world a wave of realizing spiritual truth. No doubt it seems that people are awakening to spiritual truth, but to my mind many are going backwards instead of forwards. Do you think that there is greater peace than before? People thought that war would bring about peace, but first came outward war and now there is inward war; now war is in people's minds. We talk so much about freedom, but where is it? We cannot travel without showing a passport and this becomes more severe than it has ever been. There are a thousand things to-day which show that there is less freedom than fifty years before. The conventionalities, the commercialism and the extreme materialism of to-day have removed man far from that spiritual ideal which was the central theme of civilization. No doubt a majority to-day is wakened to the higher truth or is at least seeking for it. The reason is that man has become so material and life has become so material that now every soul, consciously or unconsciously, yearns for something different to what he has. He naturally has a desire to look for something else.

Politicians are working for better conditions and yet they have not come to see things more clearly. So it is with the scientists to-day. They are inventing many things; yet they think that there is something which still remains to be discovered. The other day I had an interview with a great scientist in New-York. At the end of the conversation I found how greatly scientists to-day desire to find some evidence of inspiration, of power, of light which has not yet been explored. But very often people take wrong ways. For instance, during my visit to the States I have seen seekers after truth who thought that by reading occult books they would come to realization. It is like looking for the moon on earth. One must look in the sky. It is the same thing when people want to find truth intellectually. They can never find it. To reach the secret of life one has to take quite a different way. I do not say that intellectual study is not of great importance to interpret truth to others, but in order to find truth something greater than the study of books is needed.

There was a man who had read perhaps a hundred books on occult subjects and had written fifty books himself. He came to me and said, "Truth I have not yet found". I answered, "You will never find it in books. It is not in learning, it is in unlearning. It is not to be learned or taught, it is to be discovered. It is not something you can get from outside, it is there already. It is not something new that you will learn, it is what your soul has known".

Then there are others who think, "Well, I do not care what truth is. What is worthwhile is to see some wonders, some spirits which others cannot see". They are like children with toys. These persons are out for curiosity. They will go to jugglers who will give them illusions, and after that they will come to some understanding. Others again want to seek in this book and that book, in this school and that school. They are restless people who are amusing themselves. They do not want truth. The seeker after truth has a different rhythm, a different inclination. The wobbling and moving boat will not reach its destination. It is the heavy ship which will reach its destination. Man must first make himself that ship, earnest and serious. How can an insincere person without self-confidence reach that stage, a person who doubts, a person with a weak will?

There are many things one has to overcome before setting forth on the journey to high realization, and at each step one takes towards realization of truth one feels more self-confident. The more one overcomes all doubts and the greater self-confidence one has, the greater becomes one's will; the closer to truth one reaches, the more light one sees. And what is that light? It is the light of self-realization.

CHAPTER XXVII

The Law of Action

TO SAY that results are similar to deeds sounds simple, for almost everyone knows it, but it is not always that everyone follows it. The reason is that knowing a law does not enable man to observe the law. Besides, the nature of life is so intoxicating that, absorbed in the activity of life, one mostly forgets this law. It is natural that the most simple thing is most difficult to practise; for the very reason that it is simple man neglects to think seriously about it. In order to prove the theory that the results of a deed are similar to the deed one need not go far. One can see in one's own life and in the lives of others numberless examples, for it is like an echo: what one does has an echo and in that echo is the result.

Zarathushtra says that actions may be divided into three kinds: deed, speech and thought. One may not do wrong but one may speak wrongly, one may not speak wrongly but think wrongly, and the wrong is done just the same. How many give as an excuse, "I said it but I did not do it" and a person can even say to himself as an excuse, "I did not say it, I only thought it".

According to the idea of the mystics the world in which we make our life is called *akasha* and *akasha* means capacity. It is pictured by them as a dome; whatever is spoken in it has its re-echo. Therefore no one can do, say or think for one moment something that will become non-existent. It is recorded and the record of it is creative. It is not only that what one does, says and thinks is recorded on the memory or in the sphere, but that record creates every line at every moment. Each letter of this record becomes the seed or germ that produces a similar effect.

I once heard a sculptor say - and he spoke truly - that every man is the sculptor of his own image. I would like to add, "Not only this, but every man is the creator of his own conditions, favourable or unfavourable". The difficulty is that man never has patience to wait till he sees the result, for the result takes some time and before it shows he sees contrary effects. For instance, a person who has just robbed another and coming home meets with the good luck of finding in the street a purse full of gold coins, naturally thinks, "A good result after a good work! Now that it is going well I must continue. Those who speak against it are simpletons. It is all profit, it is ready money. I have my experience". Life is so intoxicating that it gives man no time to think that the result is perhaps still waiting, while the lucky find is the result of something else. This saying will always prove true: that the present is the reflection of the past and the future will be the echo of the present.

When we consider The Law of Action we see that it can be divided into five different aspects. One aspect is the law of the community. A law that suits one community may not suit another, for it depends upon the particular development of that community. This law is made for the comfort and convenience of the members of the community.

Another aspect of this law may be called the law of the state, a law by which different classes of people and different communities are governed as one whole. No doubt, as limited as is the mind of man, so limited are the aspects of this law. Naturally therefore many laws are rejected and many new laws are brought into practice. And as time goes on people will see that the members of the community or the state will always wish for changes to be made to the law. This has always been and will always be.

The third aspect of the law is the law of the church, a law which perhaps comes from tradition and which people accept not only because it is a law that governs them, but because it is a law that is concerned with their faith, with their belief, which is sacred to them. It is this law that forms man's conscience more than any other aspect of the law.

But then there is another aspect of the law, which is brought by the prophets from time to time. What is this law? This law comes as an interpretation of the hidden law that the prophet could see. But a law given by a prophet is for the period in which the prophet has come; it is for the people of that period and their particular evolution. When we study the religions given by different prophets to different people in different periods of the world's history we shall find that the truth which is behind the religions is the same. If the teaching differs it only differs in the law that the prophets have given. People have always disputed in vain over this difference of law that the teachers have given to their people, not knowing that the law had so much to do with the people to whom it was given and with the time when it was given.

These four laws which I have just mentioned: the law of the community, of the state, of the church and of the prophets, have their limitations. But there is one law which leads man towards the unlimited, and it is this law that can never be taught, and can never be explained. At the same time it is this law which is rooted in the nature of man, and there is no person, however unjust and wicked he may seem, who has not this faculty in his innermost being. This may be called a faculty of knowing what is proper and improper, a property of discerning whether something is right or whether it is wrong.

Now we come to the question: what determines that something should be called right or wrong? Four things: the motive behind the action, the result of the action, the time and the place. A wrong action with a right motive may be right, and a right action with a wrong motive may be wrong. We are always ready to judge an action and we hardly think of the motive. Therefore we readily accuse a person for his wrong and readily excuse ourselves for our wrong because we know our motive best. We could perhaps excuse another person as we excuse ourselves if we tried to know the motive behind his action too. A thought, a word, an action in the wrong place turns into wrong even if it was right. A thought, word or action at a wrong time may be wrong even if it may seem right. When we analyse this more we shall say, as a Hindu poet has said, "It is no use feeling bad about a wrong deed of another person. We must content ourselves knowing that he could not do better".

There is another side to this question. Things seem to us as we see them. To the wrong person everything looks wrong and perhaps to the right person everything looks right, because the right person turns wrong into right, and the wrong person turns right into wrong. The sin of the virtuous is a virtue and the virtue of a sinner is a sin. Things very much depend upon our interpretation, as on no action, on no word, on no thought there is a seal which decides it to be wrong or right.

There is still another side to this question: how much does our favour or disfavour play its role in discerning right and wrong? In someone whom we love and admire we wish to see everything which is wrong in a right light. Our reason readily comes to the rescue of the loved one; it always brings an argument as to what is right and excuses his wrong. And how readily do we see in the person whom we disfavour his faults and errors! He easily does wrong before us because we easily see it, and it is difficult for us to find a fault, even if we wanted to, in someone we love. Therefore if we read in the life of Christ that he forgave those who were accused of great faults, great sins, we can see that naturally the one who was the lover of mankind could not see a fault; the only thing he could see was forgiveness. We see that a stupid person, a simple person is ready to see the wrong in another and is ready to form his opinion and ready to judge. A wise person you will always find diffident in expressing his opinion of others, always trying to tolerate and always trying still more to forgive.

The Sufis of Persia have classed the evolution of personality into five grades. In the first category is the person who errs at every step in his life and who finds fault with others at every moment. The picture of this is that of a person who is likely to fall or who is on the point of tumbling down and while falling grabs at someone else. This is not a rare case; it is generally to be found if we study the psychology of man. The one who finds fault with others very often is the one who has most of the faults in himself. The right person first finds fault with himself, and the wrong person finds fault with himself last; after having found fault with the whole world he finds fault with himself. Then everything is wrong, the whole world is wrong.

The next grade of personality is that of the one who

begins to see the wrong in himself and the right in the other. Naturally he has the opportunity in his life to correct himself, because he has all his time to find his own faults. The one who finds fault with others has no time to find fault with himself. Besides, one cannot be just, the faculty of justice cannot be wakened, unless one begins to practise justice by finding fault with oneself.

The third type of person is he who says, "What does it matter if you did wrong or if I did wrong? What is needed is to right the wrong". He naturally develops himself and helps his fellow-man also to develop.

Then there is the fourth type, who can never see what is called good without the possibility of its being bad, and who can never see what is called bad without the possibility of turning that bad into good. The best person in the world cannot hide his fault before him, and the worst person in the world will show his merit to his eyes.

But when a person has risen to the fifth category of personality then these opposite words right or wrong, good or bad seem to be the two ends of one line. It is at that time that such a person can say little about it, for people will not believe him. He is the one who can judge rightly and he is the one who will judge last.

There are three different ways that man adopts in order to progress towards human perfection. A person who is not evolved enough to adopt the third or the second way would not be forced to adopt them. If he were forced it would only be a manner taught to him for a certain time, for these three ways are like three steps towards human perfection.

The first degree is the law of reciprocity. In this degree one learns the meaning of justice. The law of reciprocity is to give and to take sympathy and all that sympathy can give and take. It is also according to this law that religion is made and the laws of the state and of the community. The idea of this law is: you may not take from me more than you could give me and I will not give you more than I could take from you. It is a fair business: you love me and I love you, you hate me and I can hate you. If a person has not learned the just measure of give-and-take he has not practised justice. He may be innocent, he may be loving, but he has no common sense, he is not practical.

The danger in this law is that a person may esteem more what he himself does and may decrease the value of what is done by another. But the one who gives more than he takes is progressing towards the next grade. It is easy for us to say that the law of reciprocity is a very hard and fast law. But at the same time it is the most difficult thing to live in this world and to get out of this law. One must ask a practical man, a man of common sense, how it is possible to live in this world and to disregard this law of give-and-take. If the people of the world did no better than observe this law properly, there would be much less trouble in this world. It is no use thinking that people will become saints or sages or great beings. If they only became just, it would be something!

Now we come to the next step. This is the law of beneficence. This law means being unconcerned with what comes to us from another person in answer to what we do to him in love and sympathy. What one is concerned with is what one can do for another person. It does not matter if a favour is not appreciated; even if the favour were absolutely ignored, even then the satisfaction that the beneficent man gets is from what he has done, not from what the other who has received it has expressed. When this sense is born in man, from that day he really begins to live in the world, for his pleasure does not depend upon what he receives from others, but his pleasure depends upon what he does for others, and therefore his happiness is not dependent, it is independent. He becomes the creator of his happiness. His happiness is in doing, not in taking.

Now what do I mean by giving? We give and take every moment of the day. Every word we speak, every action we do, every thought and feeling we have for one another - this is all giving, this is all taking. And it is the one who will forget his sorrow, who will forget his miseries, it is this person who will rise above the pains and miseries of this world.

A step further brings another law, the third law. This is the law of renunciation. To the one who observes this law, giving means nothing, for he is not even conscious that he gives, he gives automatically. He does not think, "I give", he thinks, "It is being given". This is a person who may be pictured as someone walking on the water, for it is this person who will rise absolutely in the face of the disappointments and distresses and pains of life which are so numberless. Besides, renunciation means independence and indifference. Indifference to all things, yet not by absence of sympathy; independence to all things, yet not independent in the crude sense of the word.

Renunciation therefore may be called the final victory. One among millions can live up to this ideal, and the one who has lived up to this ideal is he who may be called elevated, liberated.

CHAPTER XXVIII

The Purity of Life

PURITY OF life is the central theme of all the religions which have been given in all ages to humanity, for purity is not only a religious idea but is the outcome of the nature of life itself, and one sees it in some form or other in every living creature. It is the tendency of all animals and birds to cleanse their coats or feathers and to find a clean place in which to live or sit, but in the human being this tendency is even more pronounced. A man who has not risen above the material life shows this faculty in physical cleanliness, but behind this there is something else hidden, and that is the secret of the whole creation and the reason why the world was made.

Purity is the process through which the life-rhythm manifests, the rhythm of that indwelling spirit which has worked through the ages in mineral and plant, in animal and in man, for its effort through all these experiences is to arrive at that realization where it finds itself pure - pure in essence, pure from all that affects its original condition. The whole process of creation and of spiritual unfoldment goes to show that the spirit which is life and which in life represents the Divine has wrapped itself in numberless folds, and in that way has, so to speak, descended from heaven to earth.

This process is spoken of in occult terms as involution, and that which follows is what is known as evolution or the unwrapping of the divine essence from the folds of enshrouding matter.

The sense of this need of freeing the spirit from that which clogs and binds it is what is called purity, in whatever part of life it is felt. It is in this sense that we may understand the saying, "Cleanliness is next to godliness". In the Arabic language the word for purity is *saf* from which root the name Sufi is derived. Some of the early orders of Sufis were called the Brothers, or the Knights of Purity, and this did not allude to physical purity but to the unfoldment of the spirit towards its original condition : the pure being of the metaphysician or the pure reason of the philosopher. The word *sophia* or pure wisdom has the same derivation.

In the ordinary use of the word pure we find the same meaning. For instance, when we speak of pure water or pure milk, we mean to express the idea that the original substance is unmixed with any foreign element. Therefore a pure life is the term used to express the effort on the part of man to keep his spiritual being untainted by the false values of worldly life. It is the constant search for the original self, the desire to reach it and the means to recover it, which alone can truly be called purity of life, but the term can be applied with the same meaning to any part of man's life.

When it is used for that which pertains to the body it denotes the idea that what is foreign to the body must not be there. This is the first stage of purity. When a person is spoken of as pure-minded, does it not mean that only that which is natural to the mind remains there and that all which is unnatural has been cleared away?

This leads to the question as to what is natural to the mind, and for an answer we cannot do better than to take the mind of a little child. What do we find there? We find first of all faith, the natural tendency to trust; then love, the natural tendency towards friendliness and affection; then hope, the natural expectancy of joy and happiness. No child is a natural unbeliever. If it were so it could not learn anything. What it hears and what it is told is accepted by the mind which is ready to believe, admire and trust. It is experience of life, the life of the world where selfishness reigns, that spoils the beauty of the mind of the child who by nature is a believer, a natural friend ready to smile at every face, a natural admirer of beauty ready to see without criticism and to overlook all that does not attract him, a natural lover who knows not hate.

Such is the original mind of man and such its natural condition. It is not sin that is original but purity, the original purity of God Himself. But as the mind grows and is fed by the life in the world, that which is not natural is added to it and for the moment these additions, as they come, seem desirable, useful or beautiful. They build another kind of mind which is sometimes called the ego or the false self; they make a man clever, learned, brilliant and many other things. But above and beyond all this is the man of whom it can be said that he is pure-minded.

When we think about this there arises the question, "If this is so then is it desirable to keep a child always a child so that it shall never learn the things which belong to the worldly life?" To ask this is to ask, "Is it then not desirable that the Spirit should always remain in heaven and never come to earth at all?"

The answer is that the true exaltation of the Spirit is in the fact that it has come to earth and there has realized its spiritual existence. It is this which is the perfection of the Spirit. Therefore all that the world gives in the way of knowledge, in the way of experience or of reason, all that a man's own experience or that of others teaches, all that is learned from life, its sorrows and disappointments, its joys and opportunities - all these contradictory experiences help us to become more full of love and wider of vision. If a man has gone through all experiences and has held his spirit high and not allowed it to be stained, then such a man may be said to be pure-minded. The person who could be called pure because he had no knowledge of either good or evil would in reality be merely a simpleton. To go through all which takes away the original purity, and yet to rise above all which seeks to overwhelm it and drag it down, that is spirituality, the light of the spirit held on high and burning clear and pure. This is the effort of a whole lifetime, and he who has not known it has not known life.

The first purity is the purity of the physical world in which man has to obey the laws of cleanliness and of hygiene. In doing so he takes the first step towards spirituality. The next is what in general is called purity of life, that purity of life which is shown in a man's social, moral and religious attitude. The national and religious codes are often very rigid as to this kind of purity. Sometimes it is merely an external man-made purity which the individual soul has to break through to find that of a higher plane.

There is however a standard of inner purity the principle of which is that anything in speech or action which causes fear, brings confusion or gives a tendency to deception, takes away that little twinkling spark in the heart, the spark of trueness which shines only when life is natural and pure. A man may not always be able to tell when a particular action is right in regard to circumstances or when it is wrong, but he can always remember this psychological principle and judge as to whether the action or word robs him of that inner strength and peace and comfort which are his natural life. No man can judge another; it is man's self that must be his judge. Therefore it is no use to make rigid standards of moral or social purity. Religion has made them, schools have taught them; yet the prisons are full of criminals and the newspapers are every day more eloquent about the faults of humanity.

No external law can stop crime. It is man himself who must understand what is good for him and what is not good for him. He must be able to discriminate between what is poison and what is nectar. He must know it, must measure it, weigh it and judge it, and this he can only do by understanding the psychology of what is natural to him and what is unnatural. The unnatural action, thought or speech is that which makes him uncomfortable before, during or after it takes place, and his sense of discomfort is proof that in this it is not the soul which is the actor. The soul is ever seeking for something which will open a way for its expression and give it freedom and comfort in this physical life. The whole life is really tending towards freedom, towards the unfoldment of something which is choked up by physical life, and this freedom can be gained by true purity of life.

We have seen what it means to purify the life of the body and of the mind, but there is a further purity which is the purity of the heart : the constant effort to keep the heart pure from all impressions which come from without and are foreign to the true nature of the heart which is love. This can only be done by a continual watchfulness over the attitude towards others, by overlooking their faults, by forgiving their shortcomings, by judging no one except oneself, for all harsh judgments and bitterness towards others are like poison. To feel them is exactly the same as taking poison into the blood; the result must be disease. First disease in the inner life only, but in time the disease breaks out in the physical life, and it is such illnesses which cannot be cured. External cleanliness does not have much effect upon the inner purity, but inner uncleanness causes disease both inwardly and outwardly.

Then after this third stage has been reached and the heart has been attuned by high ideals, by good thoughts, by righteous actions, there comes a still greater purity in which all that is seen or felt, all that is touched or admired, is perceived as God. At this stage no thought or feeling must be allowed to come into the heart but God alone. In the picture of the artist this heart sees God; in the merit of the artist, in the eyes of the artist which observe nature, in the faculty of the artist to reproduce that which he observes, such a one sees the perfection of God. Therefore to him God becomes all and all becomes God.

When this purity is reached man lives in virtue; virtue is not something which he expresses or experiences from time to time, his life itself is virtue. Every moment when God is absent from the consciousness is considered by the sage to be a sin, for at that moment the purity of the heart is poisoned. It is a lack of life which is sin, and it is purity of life which is virtue. It is of this purity that Jesus Christ spoke when he said, "Blessed are the pure in heart for they shall see God".

CHAPTER XXIX

The Ideal

IF ANYONE asks me what is the life of life and what is the light of life, I shall tell him in one word: it is the ideal. If anyone asks me what throws light on the path of life and what gives interest in life, I shall answer him in one word: it is the ideal. A man with wealth, with qualifications, with learning, with comfort, without ideal, to me is a corpse, and a man without learning, without qualifications, without wealth or rank - if he has an ideal, he is a living man. If a man does not live for an ideal, what does he live for? He lives for himself, which is nothing. That man is powerless and lightless who lives and knows not an ideal. The greater the ideal, the greater the person; the wider the ideal, the broader the person; the deeper the ideal, the deeper the person; the higher the ideal, the higher the person. Without ideal, whatever he be in life, his life is worthless.

Now you will ask me what I mean by an ideal. An object, however small, which you love, which you look up to, for which you are ready to sacrifice yourself and all you possess, that is an ideal. I consider that fanatic worth more who says, "For this idol of rock I will give my life. I have worshipped it as a god", than a person who says, "I do not know, I just live on from day to day".

A sincere ideal, however small, is an ideal. There is a person who will go through any sacrifice to serve his nation; he has his ideal. There is a person who in order to keep up the dignity of his family, of his ancestors, will endure troubles and difficulties and yet will keep their honour; he has a certain ideal. However narrow he may seem to be, however conservative, yet he has a virtue; it must be recognized. The records of the world's history show that those who have been able to maintain their virtue very often were able to maintain it because their parents had done so, because their ancestors had dignity; therefore they could not do otherwise. There is something in it, it is not all together to be discarded. A person who does not consider these things will go on living and may even have a profitable life, but it is an ordinary life, a life which has no depth, a life which has no value. There is nothing in life which can make life worthwhile except an ideal.

There are others who have a racial ideal; they think, "These are the qualities of my race which I value, I maintain them and in order to maintain them I shall go through any sacrifice; that is my ideal". There are others who have the honour of their word; once they have given their word it is for ever. There are other idealists who have the honour of their affection, the honour of their love, of their friendship. Once they have given, it is given; to go back upon it is the greatest disgrace to them. In giving their heart and in taking a heart, in both there is character, there is honour. The breach of that stability is worse to them than death. All these things, however small they seem, however childish they may appear, at the same time have value, they are the only things worthwhile and of value in life.

I shall tell you a story about an extreme ideal. Some little girls were playing together when the Maharaja of Jaipur was taking a walk in their street, disguised as an ordinary man. One little girl said, "I am going to marry a millionaire". Another little girl said, "I am going to marry a commander". And there was another girl who said, "I am going to marry the king of this place, the Maharaja". The Maharaja was on the spot and heard it. He was old enough to be her grandfather. He was amused and told the family of the girl that when her wedding came they should apply to him and a dowry would be given by the state so that she could be happy all her life. Days passed, years passed, the king passed away, and there came a time when the parents thought of arranging the girl's wedding. When the question came before the girl she said, "How can it be? I was married already. Did I not give my word ? Is it not enough?" The parents said, "It was a word given in your childhood, it was nothing at all, it was in play. The Maharaja is now dead". She said, "No, never. I will not hear about it. I am a daughter of *kshatryas**, I have given my word, I will not go back upon it".

*the Hindu knightly caste

This is an extreme ideal, it has a fanatical aspect. Nevertheless it is an ideal. There are others. There is the ideal of a general who, when the time of defeat came, still raised the flag of his nation and said, "The nation is not defeated". There are a thousand ideals like these. One could say that they lack wisdom, that they lack balance, that they lack reason and logic. Yet they stand above logic and reason, they stand above what one calls practicality and common sense. Many practical people with common sense came and went. If we remember the name of anyone who made an everlasting impression upon the world it is that of the idealist.

No doubt that ideal in which we all feel that we come from the same source and return to the same source, that ideal is the greatest, because in that ideal we unite with one another and serve one another and feel responsible to be sincere and true to one another. I think that if a man has no ideal, if he has learned any virtue he cannot very well practise that virtue. The ideal naturally teaches virtues; they rise from the heart of man.

There is a story of a king who judged four persons for the same fault. The wise king said to one that he must be exiled, to another that he must stay in prison for his whole life, to the third that he must be given a death sentence, and to the fourth he said, "I am very surprised. I had never expected that such a fault could be committed by you". And what was the result? The one who was sent to prison was quite happy there with his comrades. The one who was exiled built up his business outside the country. The one who was sentenced was sentenced. But the fourth went home and committed suicide.

What prompts man to sacrifice is only one thing, the ideal, and he can only sacrifice one thing, his life, his own life. A man without ideal therefore has no depth, he is shallow. However pleased he may be in his everyday life, he can never enjoy that happiness which is independent of outer life. The pleasure which is experienced through pain is the pleasure experienced by the idealist. But what pleasure is that which has not come out of pain? It is tasteless. Life's gain - people think so much of it, and what is it after all? A loss caused by an ideal is a greater gain than any other gain in this world.

Question: Can one lose the ideal?

Answer: Then to have another ideal. There are two ways of losing an ideal. One loses the ideal by becoming pessimistic or by being disappointed in it. But I think that one must make one's ideal so independent that nothing outside oneself may have the power of breaking it. I think that a person who can see the faults of his beloved friend has not yet loved his friend, because his love should be able to add to his shortcomings all that is necessary in order to complete him. It is not that the beloved is complete, the lover completes him. Many say, "I have loved, but I have been disappointed". I tell them, "You have dug but you did not dig deep; you reached the mud but not the water".

Question: Is idealism catching?

Answer: There is nothing more catching than idealism.

Question: Often people have many small ideals; they are conscious of one at a time and then leave it for another. Is that not also a danger?

Answer: Yes, but at the same time even to have a small ideal and to understand it and to be sincere towards it is something worthwhile. We do not really touch the ideal when we go from one ideal to another.

The Oriental Society produced a play here; it was the old story of Harish Chandra. One part of the play I should like to bring to your notice. Harish Chandra was a king who had as his principle to be faithful, to be truthful, to be true to his word. There came a time when he was sold into the house of a person who made him a keeper of the place where the corpses are cremated. There he saw his wife after a separation of many years. She brought him his dead son to be cremated, but she was so poor that she had no money to pay. There was his struggle: it was his own child, his own wife whom he had not seen for many years had come to him and she was so poor that she could not pay, and here he was appointed by his master to ask money for his work. Therefore, although he recognized the woman, he never said, "I am your husband". He recognized the child but never allowed his heart to show his deep sadness. He did not allow her to enter without paying, for he was appointed for that purpose. He went through a sorrow which was worse than death, yet kept to his principle.

The ideal will always appeal to you however fanatical it may seem, however reasonless, however it may seem to lack logic. Yet an ideal is an ideal. It has a life of its own. The ideal is living and makes the one who is an idealist alive.

Question: To what test could we put an ideal that is true? That it may lead us onward?

Answer: I think that an ideal is an ideal. If it leads you so far and no further then another ideal will come to lead you further. But the ideal is the way to take.

Question: If it is a true ideal will it lead us on and on?

Answer: It is very difficult to distinguish between false and true. It is not only difficult, it is impossible. But I should say that if it is false, then it is as false as it is real, and if it is real, it is as real as it is false. The best way is from time to time just to take as true what appears to us true - not to discuss it with others, not to defend it. We do not know what we find true, how to-morrow we may consider it untrue. Never say that to-morrow you will not say that the same thing is false, for all these terms - good or bad, right or wrong, virtue or sin, false or true - are relative, and through differences of time and space they change; that means that they change, seen from the height and from the position we look at them. In other words in order to simplify I should say: what seems right in the morning, in the evening may seem wrong. What may seem wrong in the day, at night may seem right.

Another picture is that, if there were many stairs and we were looking at things standing on each landing, the right things would seem wrong by looking at them from another step and the wrong things would seem right. It is how we look at them. Therefore the best thing is that whatever for the time being we consider to be right, just, good and virtuous, that is the thing we ought to do. But we must not impose or urge what we consider right or good or true upon others who do not consider it in the same way as we do.

Question: Then what should we do in education?

Answer: Of course for children the question is different. In order to gain freedom we do not begin with freedom. In order to arrive at freedom we begin with discipline. It is always the mistake of this time that in order to come to freedom they give freedom and so spoil things, for if you begin with liberty then you will end in discipline. If you begin with discipline you will arrive at liberty. Freedom is the ideal to gain and the result of your work; it is not to begin with.

Question: Yes, but in life many people are like children before others who are wise. Do the wise then have a responsibility?

Answer: Yes, children may be wise, but at the same time they are dependent from infancy not only for their livelihood, but they are dependent for their culture also.

No one is responsible for anyone else. We are all responsible for ourselves. And many times you may make a great mistake by thinking another person not so advanced as you yourself.

But at the same time if one wants to know how to deal with those, I should say, "In a modified form in the same way as one deals with children".

Question: How can we know that we are on the way which is true? Our upbringing may have its influence upon our ideas.

Answer: Truth is part of our own being, the most essential and important part. Therefore all we consider true at the moment is true for that moment. It is only our sincere discerning that is required, for if we fool ourselves then we shall be fooled. When people go far away from truth it is because they fool themselves, for they are not careful, they are not attentive to keep to that truth of which their own soul says that it is true. What for the moment you consider as true, that is true for you.

Question: We may be limited by principles which we think are wrong, but which we have from our upbringing. One wishes to get rid of thoughts and yet . . . ?

Answer: But as I have said : the principle which you think to be wrong you must not hold to be true. If the whole world says that it is true and you think that it is false, then it is false, for it is false at least for you, and that counts most in your life.

Question: Sometimes it is very hard to know whether it is true or false. One's upbringing is such a strong force that one reasons with oneself and thinks : this is impossible, this is useless. One is handicapped.

Answer: Yes, if one knows that what one has learned is all false then one must unlearn.

Question: By what test can we know this? Can we not take it in the silence and find out the truth? Is there not a place where we can find the truth?

Answer: As long as one is pursuing the truth one is moving in the truth already.

Question: Truth does not change; it is only our point of view that changes. In the silence can we find that light?

Answer: That truth is the absolute truth which cannot be compared with anything else. A distinction must be made between fact and truth. The two things between which you choose one as real and the other as false are facts. But when you come to the ultimate truth it is just like light. In the presence of light there is no darkness. Therefore that truth which is ultimate truth has no comparison, it is not relative. That truth is something which makes all truth.

Question: Can we get it by silence?

Answer: Of course, silence is the chief thing.

Question: What is the meaning of the sentence in the *Gayan*: "The ideal is the means, but the breaking of the ideal is the goal?"

Answer: This is a very subtle question. What is the

breaking of the ideal? The true ideal is always hidden behind a man-made ideal which covers it. For instance, the fragrance is hidden under the petals of the beautiful rose and, when you have to take the spirit out of it, you have to crush it. Thereby the same rose which was to last for twentyfour hours has been turned into spirit, into essence which can last with you for your whole life. That is made by the ideal.

Question: Is it not often necessary to raise one's ideal still higher even before attaining to it?

Answer: It depends upon what the ideal is. If that ideal is such that it could be made higher, no doubt in raising the ideal the soul is certainly raised.

Question: Is it not generally so that the more we approach our ideal the further it goes away? When we come nearer to it we feel still more that we are far from it, because the object becomes greater.

Answer: In different words, the keener your sight becomes, the greater becomes the beauty of the ideal. In that way it becomes larger, but in that way you are not removed further; in reality you are brought closer to it.

CHAPTER XXX

The Journey to the Goal

1

WHEN WE picture life as a journey there are a thousand things which will prove it to be so. We see that on a journey we are with a great many people looking at life and moving forward. Those who have arrived at their station have got out of the train, and the little friendship, sympathy or antipathy that we felt for them only lasted till then. Those who have left have left with us their impression which we carry with us. That impression either makes us happy or unhappy, either makes us still love them in their absence or hate them wishing that we shall never see them again. When we think of yesterday, when we think of last week, of last month, and when we think of the years that have passed in our lives, it only shows that they have passed and we have gone through them. At the same time it is the same sensation that one has in the train: as if the train were standing still and the trees were running. In life we have that sensation that life is passing and we are standing still.

Then we also see in this travelling that some are prepared with all that is necessary in this world, and there are others who are not prepared. Both have to journey just the same, those who are prepared and those who are not. Only the difference is that for those who are prepared this journey is easy.

There is an Indian fable of a monkey and the sparrows. When autumn seemed to come closer the sparrows said, "We must have a nest, we must build it, it must be ready because the autumn is coming nearer". A little monkey also heard this and was very frightened because it was the first time this young monkey had to face autumn. It came with great anxiety to its parents and said, "We must build a home, we must build a nest where we can be protected. I did not know the autumn was coming, but someone told me so". While they were speaking the sparrows had their nest ready, but the monkeys put it off and went from one "to-morrow" to another "to-morrow".

So it is in this world; we find these two kinds of personalities. There is a person who says, "What does it matter? We shall see what will come", and when he is faced with a difficulty, with a need, a want, then he begins to realize that it would perhaps have been better if he had prepared beforehand. And so it is with education. When a young person is learning there is always an attraction to play, to enjoy life, and when that golden age of childhood which gives facility to learn and to acquire knowledge is past, then it is too late to acquire it. It is the same with the youth; these are the days when he should be careful of what he spends, and at the time when he has spent all and has earned nothing, then he begins to feel the loss.

The greatest wealth is health, energy, intelligence and life itself. If from youth this health is not preserved, conserved and looked after, one does not feel it at that time, but there comes a time when one knows that one did not prepare for later. I once asked a person who was old and strong and healthy, "Sir, will you tell me what blessing you have? What is it that keeps you at your age so strong and healthy?" He said, "It is the conserved energy of youth which is now maintaining my life". Very few young people think about it. Youth is an intoxication. When they are in that intoxication, when they are full of energy, they do not think about it: what they have to spend in order to go far in the journey of life.

And then we come to the idea of humanity. To-day what we consider learning or education is mostly made of grammar, history, geography, mathematics and calculations, but the education which we should have as a current coin - a good manner, a strong will, a right attitude of mind - that education seems to be overlooked; we do not find it. And if a man has education, qualifications, rank or position and yet lacks manner, he lacks a great deal in life. If a man has all these things and yet does not have the strength of mind necessary to carry him on all along his life's path, he lacks a great deal.

A man who lacks money misses little, but the man who lacks power of mind misses everything in life. Weakness develops and develops without man knowing it. When one sees a little spark of weakness in oneself one says, "What is it, it is nothing", but one does not know that the spark will turn into a glow, and the glow will turn into a flame one day. And for those who lack manner, who lack strength of mind, who lack a right attitude it is then too late, they cannot be corrected. The nature of life is such that the thoughtless life will pull into thoughtlessness, and the thoughtful also will draw thoughtlessness towards itself. Therefore there is more chance of falling than of rising in life. Besides, among thousands of persons there is hardly one who is taking this journey with open eyes; mostly all journey with their eyes closed. Man so much depends upon his friends, upon his relations, upon those who love him, upon those who admire him, but he does not know that any quality missing in him will be asked of him by those who love him.

Therefore what is necessary in life is to possess oneself and not to think, "Oh, what does it matter! My father was a king and my grandfather was an emperor! Nothing matters to me". Whatever relations you have, how great and good they may be - that is not of any use to you. We each have our journey to make and we have to answer the demands of this journey. How wonderful it is to watch in the little journeys we make how one person comes along in a little group of travellers and gives them all pleasure, puts before them all the good he has, shares with them, gives a good impression to all and wins their hearts. When he has gone, what he has left with his friends is joy, that beautiful impression which they will always keep. And there is another one who hurt or harmed or produced some disturbance among those travelling with him. When he has gone they pray that they will never meet him again.

A maid one day said to her mistress that there was a funeral passing through the street. She was much impressed and said, "Certainly the person who died went to heaven". Her mistress laughed at the maid's authoritative exclamation that this dead person went to heaven. She said, "Did you see this dead person go to heaven?" - "It is simple, Madam, everyone who was walking with the funeral was weeping.

Certainly this person made an impression on those among whom he lived".

Man absorbed in his daily life loses all, not knowing that life passes and the call comes before he thinks of it. Man makes great mistakes, but among all mistakes there is a principal one, which is that he goes on through life thinking that he will stay here for ever. And naturally without preparation the call comes to him as a blow instead of coming as an invitation. When we think of the journey beyond we begin to see how many there are in this world who do not even know that there is a hereafter, and if they know of the hereafter they have their preconceived ideas as to its coming.

There is either a religious or a philosophical belief, but neither can suffice our purpose. What can suffice our purpose is to be acquainted with the road by which we have to pass, and by becoming acquainted with the road we also begin to see that it was the road by which the soul descended to come on earth. This road is the bridge which stands between the physical and the spiritual part of our being, and therefore the nature of this journey is different. The journey we make in the world is outside ourselves. This journey we are making is within ourselves, and it is made by being acquainted with this road that leads to the destination where we are meant to go. It is this that is acquired as a divine knowledge by the help of meditation.

There are many in this world who are curious to know what we shall find beyond this life, and it is this which gives an opportunity to those who wish to attract mankind by falsehood. It gives them scope to make up stories and to satisfy man's curiosity, for who can know of this way but man himself; he is the traveller and his own spirit is the way. It is man himself who must see his way, and it is with his own eyes that he must see what he will find in this way. Therefore the teachers of life's secret do not tell that you will see this or that on your way. They say you will find whatever you will find, and your duty is to open your eyes that you may travel on the way and see for yourself.

Once a *mureed* asked his teacher, "How I should like to see how it is in heaven and what is the appearance of hell!" –

- "Close your eyes", said the teacher, "and you will see it". "Shall I see heaven first?" The teacher said, "Yes". He closed his eyes and went into meditation. "And now", said the teacher, "see also hell in meditation". When the mureed opened his eyes the teacher asked, "What did you see?" He answered, "Neither did I see in heaven that paradise of which people speak, nor those beautiful plants and flowers and all the beautiful things of comfort and luxury. I saw nothing" - "And what did you see in hell?" - "I saw nothing. I had expected to see fire and people in torture, but I saw nothing. What is the reason? Did I see or did I not see?" - "Certainly you saw, but the brimstone and fire of hell or the beautiful gems and jewels of paradise you have to bring for yourself. You do not get them there". This gives us the secret of Omar Khayyam's saying, "Heaven is the vision of fulfilled desire. Hell is the shadow of the soul on fire".

What is most necessary for us to learn and understand is that from a perfect source we come and to a perfect goal we go. But many seek that source unconsciously and most of us seek that source wrongly; few seek that source consciously and fewer still seek that source rightly.

Now we come to the question of the right seeking of that source. The way to seek it is first to learn the psychology of one's own life - what makes man fall, what makes him rise, what makes him fail, what makes him succeed, what gives him happiness, what brings him sorrow - and then to study the nature of pleasure and pain - whether it is lasting pleasure, whether it is lasting pain, or whether it is momentary pleasure or momentary pain - and then to find the deceitful and false nature of one's own impressions: how under a cover of pain there was pleasure, how under a cover of pleasure there was pain; how in the worst person there is some good to be found and how in the best person there is something worse to be traced. This widens the point of view of man and prepares the ground of his heart in order to realize the secret of enjoyment.

The next thing man has to do is to control his activities, physical and mental. He must know that the nature of life is to go on and that therefore the suspension of life gives to that travelling attitude a scope within instead of giving it a scope without. However much a person reads and studies these things, that does not bring him satisfaction; satisfaction comes out of experience, and experience is gained from meditation.

Besides, in this journey no one asks you what family you come from, what nation, what race you come from, what people, what faith you are coming with. What is asked is, "Are you prepared for this journey?" It is your preparation which is your passport, it is your readiness which is your ticket to show on this path of life. No personalities are considered here; what is considered is your evolution in the spiritual path.

In the East the school of the Sufis has existed for thousands of years - a school which had its beginning even before the time of Abraham. It is the message of that wisdom which is now being given here in the Western world, and at this time when the need is felt everywhere in the world the doors of this school are opened in many different countries of the world. It is to serious seekers who do not seek for phenomena or wonder-working, who go after this teaching not for the sake of curiosity but with a serious mind and a steady intention of going on this path - it is to these that this school opens the doors of its heart to welcome them.

2

There are two different stages in human evolution; they may well be called the minor and the major stage. In the Hindu Puranic symbology the characters in these stages are called the younger and the elder brother. Just as there is a stage of childhood when the child only knows what it wants and is only happy when it gets it, no matter what may be the consequence, so the minor stage of the soul is when man in reality desires only what he can see, hear, perceive, touch. Beyond that he does not care; only that is desirable to him, he does not wish for anything else. The major stage is when man has experienced life more or less, has known pleasure and pain, enthusiasm and disappointment, and knows the variability of life. Only then has he reached the stage of majority.

Minor and major do not depend upon a certain age, nor upon a particular education. They depend upon the inner life. When a man has gone into life as far as he could go and when he has passed the limit of the minor state, then he arrives at the major state. In the East there is a custom that has become a kind of religious etiquette: not to wake a person who is asleep, but to let him sleep well. If this is not respected it is considered a crime. In other words, you must treat the world according to nature and not go against nature. Do not force the man in the minor state into the major state; he must first sleep well before he can awaken.

Now as to progress on the spiritual path: there are two different characters. The first is the man who says,"Yes, I like to go on this path, but where shall I arrive?" He wants to know all about it before he travels on this path. He wants to know if his friends are going with him, and if they are not he is not ready to go either. Because he is not sure of the way, he will not go alone and wants to know when and where he will arrive, and if it is safe to journey on that particular path. When he travels on the path he looks back and tries to look forward, asking, "Shall I reach the goal? Is it really the right path?" A thousand times doubt comes, fear comes; he looks back, forward, around. If others could only tell him how far he has journeyed! He is restless, he wants to know how far he is from the goal. Therefore he is still a child although he has a desire to journey. For him there are toys; the mystical hints for mental research keep him busy. He may look at the map of the journey to see where he is going.

About the conditions of the major state of character the Bible says, "Unless the soul be born again it cannot enter the kingdom of God". If I were to tell what the journey is and what its object, I would say that the whole creation was purposed for this journey, and if it were not for this purpose there would be no creation at all. Before a person undertakes this journey he practises in some form or other in play how he will make it, but he has not yet started in reality. For instance, a person desires to be rich and he devotes all his time, his energy, his life, his thoughts to that object and he, so to speak, journeys to that goal. If he desires power he makes for that and gets it, if he wants position he uses all his strength to reach his goal - naturally all this in a playing way. The proof of this is that every activity man pursues to attain the thing he desires brings him to the desire for something else. If he is rich he desires to be famous, if he is famous he wants something else. If he has one thing he strives for another and is never satisfied. It shows that man, outwardly busy in the pursuit of worldly things, is not satisfied in his soul but has a constant yearning in his soul for something more - which keeps him uneasy.

A very good explanation is given by Rumi, the great Sufi teacher of Persia, in his book the *Mathnaavi* where he says,

What is it in the reed flute that appeals to your soul,
that goes through you and pierces your heart?

The answer is that it is the cry of the flute, and the reason for its crying is that it once belonged to a plant from which it was cut apart. Holes were made in its heart. It longs to be united with its source, its origin. So the soul feels a longing for its origin. In another place in his book Rumi says,

So it is with every person
who has left his original country for a long time.
He may roam about and feel very pleased with all he sees,
but there will come a moment
when a strong yearning is in his heart
for the place where he was born.

One sees that those in the world who have really suffered, who have been disappointed and are broken-hearted do not wish to tell anybody of their experiences, do not want any company, but wish to be alone. And it is then as if there was someone waiting with open arms, waiting for that soul to come as a child comes to its mother. This shows that there is somewhere a consoler greater than any in the world, a friend dearer than anyone in the world, a protector stronger than any earthly one. Knowing that the world is not to be depended upon he looks for that great one in himself. A friend who is a friend in life and after death, in pleasure and pain, in riches and poverty, one upon whom you can always depend, who always guides you aright, who gives the best advice - that friend is hidden in your own heart. You cannot find a better one. Who is this friend? Man's own being, his true, inner being. That friend is the origin, source and goal of all.

But the question arises: if that friend is one's own being, why then call him a friend, why not call him oneself? The answer is that no doubt in this friend is really one's own being, but when the greater self is compared with the present realization one finds oneself smaller than a drop in the ocean. Man cannot very well call that friend himself, until he has forgotten himself, until he is no more himself. Until and unless he has arrived at the state of perfection man had better be quiet than insolent, talking about that which he has not yet become. All occult schools all over the world prescribe as the first lesson quietude, no discussion, no dispute, no argument. The conditions for those on the path are altogether different from those of the outer world. The true knowers of life have kept their lips closed on this subject. No method has been successful and profitable other than the method of the prophets of all lands who give man the first lesson of love for God.

Religious authorities of different times have kept humanity ignorant of the knowledge of God and have only given it a belief in God. Absence of knowledge has made the man of reason rebel against that which he could not understand. There remained no link between the two and that is how the reign of materialism came to the world, a reign which is still spreading. In such times of materialism there comes chaos in the world, all is confusion, unrest. All wish to do good but do not know how. Such times Shri Krishna has called the decay of *dharma* when spirit is gone and only form remains No doubt warning in time comes to the soul as intuition, but the intoxication of life, the mist, is so great that the message is not heard, not understood, not received until the messenger has disappeared.

Now coming to the journey: what is the manner and the method of it? We see that when a person rises above all things of the world as power, wealth, possession, all that gives pride

*i.e. knowledge and belief

and vanity, there comes a desire in his heart, a remembrance of his origin, of the perfection of love and peace. No one in the world can pretend to have arrived at this stage, because every moment of his life speaks louder of what he says than of what he really is.

Man's first tendency towards humanity is a loving attitude, a charitable attitude, to such an extent that forgiveness leads every action of his life. He shows patience in his actions, tolerance to humanity and considers that each one has his own stage of evolution. He cannot expect a person to act in a better way than his point of evolution permits. He does not make his own law and want others to follow it; he follows the law for all.

When a man's attitude is a loving attitude, a tendency to serve, to forgive, to tolerate, a reverence for all, good and bad, young and old, then he begins his journey. To explain what path this is there is no better symbol than the cross. No one without courage, without strength of will and without patience can go this path. When a person has to live among people of all natures he must make his own character soft as a rose, make it even finer so that no one can be hurt by the thorns. Two thorns cannot harm each other; the thorns can hurt the rose, but the rose cannot tear the thorns. Think what the life of the rose must be between two thorns!

The journey begins with a path of thorns, and one must go barefoot. It is not easy to be tolerant, always to be patient, to refrain from judging others and to love one's enemy. It is a dead man who walks this path, one who has drunk the bowl of poison. The beginning of each path is always difficult and uninteresting, hard for everybody. Ask the violinist about the first days when he practised the scales and could not even form the tones. Often he does not have patience enough to go on till he can play so well that he is satisfied. The first part of the path is permanent striving, a struggle with life, but as one approaches the goal the path gets easier. The distance seems larger but the path is easier, the difficulties are less. The journey is achieved by first realizing in oneself: what am I? Am I body, mind or what else am I? Do I originate from the earth? Or from where else?

As soon as one has started on the journey one's lower nature rises up. All man's follies and weaknesses want to drag him down to earth and the struggle of breaking these chains requires the strength of a Samson. Then comes the struggle between beauty in matter and spiritual beauty. Beauty in forms is more realistic, spiritual beauty is hidden in mist, until one comes to a stage where spiritual beauty becomes the beauty, which is a shining light.

Another struggle comes when man has acquired knowledge, power, magnetism. He is conscious of having a greater power than others, of knowing more than others, of being able to do more than others. To use those faculties rightly is another struggle; he must not pride himself on these accomplishments. There is an enemy who starts with him on the journey and never leaves him: his pride and spiritual egotism. This enemy stays with him as long as he is on his path. Think of the temptation when, having received inspiration and power, one can think, "I can do, know, understand more than you". This is a constant struggle until the end and every moment one falls and tumbles down. Only the steady traveller will persist in rising up every time, as without patience he may lose the path. Those who journey on this path will get help, as Christ said, "Seek ye first the kingdom of God and all things will be given to you". The goal is the important thing and the right attitude of the soul towards it; not the things you meet on the path.

The inner culture of the Sufi school which is now presented to the Western world is meant as a guidance on this path. Nobody in the world can carry a person on this path. Only a little advice can be given by those who have journeyed on the path to those who really wish to travel on it.

CHAPTER XXXI

Acknowledgment

WHAT GENERALLY happens is that man acknowledges what he must not acknowledge and does not acknowledge what he should acknowledge in life. As a rule it is best never to acknowledge a fact to which one does not wish to give life. For instance, when a person begins to see that his friend is not as kind, not as affectionate, not as pleased as he ought to be as a friend, as soon as he acknowledges it he at once gives strength to something which so far has been a shadow. A person who feels, "Everyone in my family, in my surroundings dislikes me, disapproves of me; I have a tiring effect upon them", certainly gives life to that fact.

Once a friend came to me and said, "I do not know what kind of bad planet has its influence upon me, but for the last three years everything I touch goes wrong. Nothing I touch brings success or pleasure". I said, "I am very sorry you have come so late. Yet it is not too late, but for three years you have given fuel to this fire". The friend asked, "How did I give fuel to this fire?" - "By acknowledging it."

What happens is that every little fact that has a bad effect upon our life - if we acknowledge it - we give it life and thus make it a living thing. So it is with many illnesses. Very often people get into a habit of saying, "Oh, I am so tired !". For them it is not necessary to cut stones or wood, or to carry wood and stones: they will be tired before doing it. They need not wait for an action, for something to make them tired; no sooner do they think of tiredness than it is there. There are many cases where there is no need to be tired; the person is tired because he has acknowledged it. It is the same with sleeplessness. Once you acknowledge to yourself "I cannot sleep", that is enough to keep you awake all night. There are many illnesses of this kind, especially the acknowledgment of depression, to acknowledge, "I am depressed, I am sad". There may be no other reason to be depressed, to be sad; the very fact of acknowledging "I am sad" will make a person sad.

To the one who acknowledges this life to be his friend, this life will prove to be his friend. To the one who acknowledges this life to be his enemy, this life will prove in every way to be his enemy. There are many who take notice of those who are working against them, and especially by taking notice they make them do so more, because they make an impression upon them. But you might ask, "When we do not think about it, does animosity not exist in persons?" Yes, it may exist, but by taking notice of it, by acknowledging it, you give life to it. If you do not acknowledge it, it will die in time, for animosity is fire - but not a perpetual fire. It is the acknowledging which gives the fire fuel; if you do not acknowledge it the fire will go out.

Many might say that it is hypocrisy not to acknowledge a fact, but that hypocrisy is better than the truth. In fact it cannot be called hypocrisy when you know its meaning, its worth, what is to be understood by it. A doctor is not a hypocrite when, seeing that his patient has a high fever, he says, "It is all right, it is nothing". By saying that there is a high fever he will certainly increase the fever of the patient - and many doctors do so. Everything a physician or a religious man does to make a person who is on his deathbed think of death only encourages him towards death; he is pushing him towards death. One could prove a greater friend to the friend who is on his deathbed by not acknowledging his trouble, his difficulty, his coming death. As soon as the doctor has given up hope, the whole family begins to talk about it to the patient and his departure is hastened by six months.

Now coming to the question: what must we acknowledge? That which we always escape from acknowledging: our faults. By acknowledging our faults we shall kill them; when we acknowledge them as our enemies we shall destroy them. But that is the one thing we want to hide, the one thing we want to keep hidden even from our own sight. To look one's own fault in the face is the best thing to do; to analyse it, to weigh it, to measure it and to understand it better. By this one either destroys it or understands it or turns the same fault into a merit.

Very often people think it is wise to tell a person, "No, you are not my friend. You have not been very attentive to me, not very kind". When a person says all these things to someone he inspires him with these things, even if they did not exist.

Besides, all misfortunes, all dangers that threaten, that frighten man, very often are not as great as man thinks. They can be averted if he does not acknowledge them, for how a person feels about a danger depends upon the particular pitch to which his heart is tuned. For instance, if ten persons were standing before the same danger and one could weigh their fear, one would find that the degree of their fear is very different.

There is an interesting story of the Prophet Muhammad. Once when he was exiled his enemies pursued him in the desert. A disciple was with the Prophet. They were standing behind a rock and heard the running of many horses. "O Prophet", said the disciple, "they are pursuing us, they are many, there is an army behind us". "O, they are going somewhere else", said the Prophet. "They are coming here; I hear them." - "They will take some other direction." - "But what shall we do if they come here? How many they are, and we are only two !" - "Are we two? No, three: you and I and God."

Everyone does not look at danger from the same point of view. To one the smallest thing is too great, to another the greatest thing is nothing. It is as one views it. Once you see the danger as great you will make it greater, and by not acknowledging the greatness of the danger you will diminish its greatness.

There is another thing that one must acknowledge. You must acknowledge in your friend, in your companion, in those you wish to help, the good part of their character. By acknowledging it, by noticing it you will fortify it; it will become greater. Do not think that it is against humility even to acknowledge your own merits, for if you are unconscious of your merits the plant is suffering without water. By acknowledging one's merits, one's virtues it is not that one becomes proud or conceited; by recognizing them one certainly waters the plant which is worth rearing.

Now going from the psychological point of view to the esoteric point of view, you can carry the same method from psychology to esotericism. In esotericism you have a problem before you: there is truth which you have to discover, which is covered by fact. If you are accustomed to deny a fact in order to discover a truth, then you are ready in your esoteric work to deny the fact which hides the truth and to discover thereby the truth which is worth discovering. The one who understands this will understand the meaning of all the concentrations and meditations which are studied and practised by the Sufis. It is all for one purpose: to deny fact in order to establish truth.

Question: What kind of fact is it that obscures the truth and that we should remove by meditation?

Answer: Explaining the meaning of the word fact I should like to say that fact is a shadow which for the moment represents something, which has a certain meaning, which we can witness and which at the same time will not continue its reality for ever. For instance a person says, "Sandow* in fact is a strong man". Yes, it is a fact that he is a strong man, but because he will not be eternally strong that is a fact, it is not a truth. Therefore the knowledge of our own existence and the knowledge of the existence of others, all this knowledge that we have, is a changeable knowledge, and since it is changeable it is fact. Truth is behind it. But when we discover within ourselves and in others that something which is everlasting and will never change, that is truth.

Question: In great trouble how is one to dominate one's thoughts?

Answer: Of course when conditions have gone so far that it is most difficult to dominate the trouble, then one has to control one's thoughts. But by causing great excitement over it we shall not make the trouble any less; on the contrary it will be greater. I will tell you a story which is amusing and at the same time explains this.

Not long ago there was a Minister of Hyderabad who was

* Eugène Sandow, famous as a "strong man" and inventor of a system of physical culture.

one of the ancient royal families who carried with them a certain ideal of manner and culture. Once sitting at table entertaining some foreign friends it happened that a part of the palace caught fire. As it was the custom of the palace not to come hurriedly to bring news, the aide-de-camp had to come very gently between courses; he whispered in the ear of the Minister what was happening. To his great surprise the Minister only said, "Yes", and went on with the course which had just arrived. Then when the next course was brought he begged his guests' pardon and said, "I will come back in a moment". Gently he went, as if nothing had happened, giving orders what to do to extinguish the fire, and then came back gently. A great part of the palace had already burned and the guests left after dinner without knowing. The next day they read in the papers that a great part of the palace had burned. They were very surprised to have seen such a thing, such patience, such self-control, such mastery over oneself. It does not mean that the Minister did not feel the loss; he felt it perhaps more than anyone could have felt it, but he did not show it. It was not his manner to jump up, it was not his manner to run and rush, it was not his manner to make a fuss for nothing. Suppose he had done as everyone does, what would he have done? He would have excited the others also and made things worse. It was better that the palace was on fire than that the spirit was on fire.

CHAPTER XXXII

Responsibility

IN THE Arabic Scriptures it is said that God sent His trust to the mountains, and they refused to bear it; then God sent His trust to the trees, and they were unable to bear it. Then God sent His trust to man who readily accepted it. Trust in this case is responsibility. The value of man is as great as his responsibility, for what mountains cannot bear and trees cannot lift up, mankind has carried through life. Naturally therefore a responsible man shows in himself a spiritual quality in all connections, in all relationships. Be he your friend or master or servant or relative, if he is responsible for the trust you give him, it is that which gives him value. Be he a minister or a king or a president of the state, his greatness, his value is according to his responsibility and according to the power with which he carries it out through life.

There is another point of view from which to look at it : that man may become great by his responsibility, his great responsibility, and at the same time he may fall, for there is a stumbling block;the more conscious man becomes of his responsibility the less he recognizes the power of wisdom which is working beside him. It is therefore that at this time of materialism great personalities come who accomplish great things, and yet in the end they show limitation. That limitation comes from being drowned in the responsibility they have taken on, and from having forgotten God, the other power that is working beside them. However great man may be in wisdom, in power, yet he is limited and if his wisdom and power can be compared with divine wisdom and power, they are not even as much as a drop compared with the sea. Sa'di, the Persian poet, has made a remark in his *Rosegarden* in simple words. He says, "The Constructor of this whole universe is active in constructing even my affairs; but my anxiety about my affairs is my illness". By this he means, "It is something I cannot help, but at the same time I recognize that all that I wish to accomplish is already being done by someone else who is far greater, more powerful and wise than me".

Jelal-ud-din Rumi points out in a verse of his *Mathnavi* that the smallest insect receives its proper nourishment; either it is attracted to it or the nourishment is sent to it. Man, who is responsible for himself and who takes responsibility upon himself for other living creatures would never even think of the small insects living at the bottom of the wall of the house, under the earth, hidden under leaves, covered by little grasses. But they receive their nourishment, all that is needed to keep them alive. And so birds and animals receive their nourishment and all they need to build their nests without the help of man. The unfortunate task falls upon man to toil and to make his living. But it is a price that he pays for self-reliance, for self-dependence, for the responsibility that he takes upon himself. In so far as he takes responsibility upon himself he no doubt does a great work for humanity, but if he becomes so absorbed in that responsibility that he only relies upon his limited sources and forgets the source from where his help comes and becomes unaware of that power and wisdom which are beside him, then with the greatest responsibility and with all the power and might he may have, he fails in the end.

Now there is a question which man asks to-day, "Is there not an energy at work, a force void of wisdom?" The answer is that there cannot exist a quality, an attribute without the possessor of that quality, that attribute. Energy cannot exist without the energetic one to whom energy belongs. Might cannot exist without the mighty one whose attribute it is. Intelligence cannot exist without the intelligent one to whom intelligence belongs. A person may say, "Well, is it not an energy, a force, a power from which all this comes?", but he does not call himself energy or force or power. He says, "I am I, an ego, a being". If this being is produced from an object it cannot be a being, it must not claim itself to be a being. This shows that a being has come from a being; there is a being behind it all. That being is perfect in its power and wisdom.

But then a person is inclined to ask, "Is that being a larger being than me?" - because his ego compares that being with himself. He wants to see that other being, how it stands in comparison with himself. The answer to this is that it is a being which includes you and me and all. Therefore there is nothing else that you can compare with this being, nor can this being be explained, for neither is the wisdom of this being like our wisdom nor is its power like our limited power.

Those who have tried to learn the life of dependence upon that being have been saints and sages. They have practised the recognition of the divine power and divine wisdom by becoming passive to it, by becoming responsive to it. By this practice their load of responsibility was taken away from them; their life was made easy and they experienced a great ease and peace in their lives. Very often a thoughtful person envies a little child who is so happy, without cares, without anxieties. The child represents the divine kingdom, as if all that is there belongs to him and all that is beautiful and good is his.

But now the question arises how far one must depend upon divine wisdom and power, and how far one must feel responsible for oneself and for those who depend upon one. What sometimes happens is that man takes a principle and practises it; but in order to practise that principle he must prepare himself. If he is not prepared for that principle he must not practise it. If a person who toils every day for his livelihood sits down and says, "God must supply", the supply will not come so soon; he will be disappointed. In order to practise this he must first of all prepare himself to come to that faith. It is that confidence and faith which will bring supply. But that confidence and faith must first be cultivated gradually, and the principle must not be practised at once. If one has a business affair somewhere and one says, "Well, it will all be done. I shall not go there", that will be wrong, because that person has begun by being responsible for it. He cannot suddenly take himself away like this; he must practise every day that principle of recognizing the wisdom and power which are beside him.

I would never advise anyone to give away his responsibility in recognition of the might and wisdom of

God. I would only advise to be full of courage and confidence in the face of difficulty and seeming trouble by recognizing that there is a mighty power, a perfect wisdom behind you and that all will be well. By this a person will rise above his limitation of power and wisdom and will be able to draw power and wisdom from that unlimited source, which in the end will lead him to success. And then in the case of failure this recognition of perfect power and wisdom working beside him will also give him the strength to bear it and to be resigned to the will of God.

CHAPTER XXXII

The Certitude of Life in the Hereafter

THE QUESTION of the certitude of life in the hereafter occupies every mind. Sooner or later a person begins to wonder if there is such a thing as continuity of life. There are many who in their pessimistic idea think that there seems to be nothing afterwards, and there are others who owing to their optimistic idea think, "Whether there is something or whether there is nothing, it is just as well to think that there is something". Nevertheless, when a person thinks that there will be nothing after death, this thought is most painful, and however many reasons he may have in support of his belief, that belief itself is worse than death. There are some who through different phenomena wish to obtain proof of life in the hereafter, but they meet with ninety-nine disappointments and perhaps one reality.

When we come to the idea of the Sufi, it is that life lives and death dies. In other words, to life there is no death and to death there is no life. But his way of attaining the certitude of life is not only an intellectual one. A person may study all the philosophies, all the metaphysics all through his life, which may in every way prove that there is continuity of life, still this realization gained by the effort of mind will not give that feeling of certitude which one wishes to have. The Sufi therefore practises a process through which he is able to touch that part of life in himself which is not subject to death, and by finding that part of life he naturally gets the feeling of certitude of life. It makes him more certain of life than of anything in the world, because he sees in all things changeability and limitation. Everything that is constructed is subject to being destroyed; everything that is composed is subject to being decomposed; everything born is subject to death. But in finding that life he finds that it is his self and that it is the real life. All else he knows about life begins to lose its importance.

Now you will say: in what way does the Sufi discover that

life in him which was never born and will never die? By self-analysis - but according to what mystics know of self-analysis: to understand what this vehicle we call the body is to us, what relation we have to it, and to understand what this mind, what we call mind, consists of. And then to ask, "What am I? Am I this body, am I this mind?" There comes a time when he begins to see that he himself is the knower of the body and of the mind. But at this realization he only arrives when he can hold body and mind in his hands as his objects which he uses for his purpose in life. Once he has done this then body and mind, these two things, become as two corks which a person puts on himself in order to swim in the water without danger of drowning. The same body and mind which cause man mortality - at least in his thought - this very body and mind then become the means of saving him from being drowned in the waters of mortality.

Really mortality is our conception; immortality is reality. We make a conception of mortality because we do not know the real life. By the realization of the real life the comparison between it and mortality makes us know that mortality is non-existent. Therefore it would not be an exaggeration if I said that the work of a Sufi is unlearning. What he is accustomed to call or to recognize as life he then begins to recognize as death, and what he is accustomed to call death he then begins to recognize as life. Thus life and death both are not for him conditions to which he is subject but are conditions which he brings about upon himself. A great Persian Sufi, Bedil, says, "By myself I become captive and by myself I become free". If I were to interpret this in simple language I would say, "By myself I die and by myself I live". Why does a Sufi say this? Why does everyone not say it? Because for a Sufi it is a condition which he brings about; for another person it is a condition in which he is helpless.

Now you will ask me in what way this realization is to be brought about. In the first place one must learn in every little thing in life the way of unlearning. In my own work I find a great difficulty when a person comes to me and says, "Now I have learned so far. Will you add more to my knowledge?" In my heart I say, "The more you have learned the worse it is for me. If I would like to add to it, it would not be adding, it would be taking away from it, in order that I may unburden you from all you have learned, that you may be able to unlearn first and that, through this unlearning, what will come will be the true learning".

But you might say, "Is it then useless for us to learn all that we learn in life?" The answer is no; it is all useful. But for what? For that purpose for which you have learned it. All is not learned for the purpose for which you are searching. When you wish to search for the secret of life, that which one calls learning is the first thing to unlearn. No doubt this is something which is difficult for everyone to understand. Yet when we read the life of Rumi, a great teacher, and his teacher Shams Tabriz, the first lesson he gave Rumi was, "Unlearn all that you have learned".

Now you may ask, "Is this unlearning forgetting all that one learns?" Not at all; that is not necessary. This unlearning is to be able to say with reason, with logic, the contrary to what you know. When you are accustomed to say, "This is wrong, this is right, this is good and this is bad, this is great and this is small, this is higher and this is lower, this is spiritual and this is material, this is up and this is down, this is before and this is behind", if you can use the opposite words for each with reason and with logic, naturally you have unlearned what you had once learned. It is after this that the realization of truth begins, because then the mind is not fixed. And it is then that one has become alive, for the soul has been born. It is then that a person will become tolerant and it is then that he will forgive, for he will understand both his friend and his foe. Then he never has one point of view, he has all points of view.

You might say, "Is it not dangerous to have all points of view, for then I would not have my own point of view". That is not necessary. You may have one room in the house or you may have ten rooms. You may use each as you like. As many points of view as you can see, so large is your point of view.

But all this is attained by the meditative process, by tuning oneself, by bringing oneself to a proper rhythm, by concentration, contemplation, by meditation and realization, by both dying and living at the same time. In order to rise above death one must die first. In order to rise above mortality one must know what it is. But this is certain: there is one greatest and most important thing that one wishes to accomplish in life, and that one thing is to rise above the conception of death.

Question: How can we rise above the conception of death?

Answer: As I have already said, the most necessary thing is to play death and to know what death is. It is a great lesson to learn how to play death. What we do is a very false thing, and that is: we play life while we are subject to death. If we played death it would be real, it would not be hypocrisy. And it is out of this that we shall discover life, for we experience death by playing life, and we experience life by playing death. What we call death is a death of this body, but if we attach ourselves to this body as ourselves then it is death. A simple man asked a person, "How can I know that I am dead?" "Well", the other said, "it is very easy. When your coat has become torn and worn out, then that is a death". So when the coat was worn out and torn this man thought that he was dead and wept bitterly. A thoughtful person came and told him, "It is your coat that is torn. How can you cry? You are still alive!"

This is exactly the condition of the mystical idea: for the mystic the body is a garment. But it is no use realizing this intellectually, for if you say intellectually, "The body is my garment", then what are you and where are you? As I have said, by the meditative process one finds where one is and what one is. Therefore this does not remain as a belief, it becomes a faith and even greater than faith: it becomes conviction.

Question: In what way can we play death? How can we do it?

Answer: There was a king who thought that he would give up his kingdom and become a mureed; that is to say to become a disciple of a teacher and to give up all worldly things and live in spiritual thought. He went to Bokhara to be under the guidance of a teacher. This teacher gave him the work of a probationer which was to sweep and clean the whole house where all the pupils lived and to pick up the garbage and take it out of the village. The pupils were of course very much in sympathy with this man and were shocked, for he was used to sitting on a throne as a king. They said, "This is something he was never accustomed to doing, it must be terrible for him". No doubt, the teacher, knowing the object he had before him, could not do otherwise. He said, "He must do it, for he is not yet ready". Once all the disciples went to the teacher and said, "Teacher, we are all in sympathy with this man; we think he is so fine and so nice and so cultured. We would so much like you to relieve him of this duty". Then the teacher said, "We shall have a test". One day when the man was taking the garbage pail out of the village, somebody knocked against him and all was spilled on the ground. He looked back and said, "Well, it is not as in the days of the past. What can I say to you!" When the report was brought to the teacher he said, "Did I not say that the time has not yet come?" After some time the test was repeated, and when somebody did the same thing this man looked at him and said nothing. The teacher said, "Did I not say that the time has not yet arrived?" The third time the man was tested he did not even look at the one who had spilled his basket. He picked up all that had been spilled and carried on. The teacher said, "Now is the time, now he can play death".

All the teachings Christ taught: if one strikes you on one side of the face turn the other side; if one asks you to go one mile go still further; if one asks you for your overcoat give your cap also - when we think of all this, what is it? Is it not teaching to play death? Therefore if at any time the teachers of truth have prescribed to their pupils any process of behaviour towards their fellow-men, that process can be called nothing else but playing death.

One might think that it is very hard, very cruel on the part of the teacher, but the instructor had to go through the same cruelty once in a certain period of his life. But sometimes the greatest cruelty is the greatest kindness. It is hard, but the hardest path can be conquered by this. If I were to speak about it in simple words I would say it like this: how many times do we take to heart unnecessary things, how many times do we cause or take interest in inharmony which could just as well have been avoided. How often we resist evil which could just as well not have been resisted. This is all playing life and what I said before is playing death. When we play death we arrive at life; when we play life we arrive at death.

Question: Do we not sometimes become insensitive to the pain of others by just looking at them and not sharing with them?

Answer: But I have said : playing death is rising above sensitive and insensitive, because being sensitive and insensitive has a certain stage. One can rise above that stage; then all is sensitive. Besides you can always find that those who play death or who have played death are the most sympathetic and the most open to the pain of others, for when they are playing death automatically they are playing life too. And therefore, although they are as dead to all the wrong things that come to them, they are alive to everything that can happen to others.

Question: May I ask in what consists that state when at certain days and at certain hours one no longer feels one's body, and only the thought is alive and awake?

Answer: It is a condition. As I say, any condition that comes automatically is not normal, even if it is a high condition. If it comes automatically it is not normal. The normal thing is to be able to experience any condition one wishes to. To be able to experience death, to be able to experience life, that is the right thing. The one who always experiences death and does not experience life, that is abnormal too.

Question: How to have a balance?

Answer: To have a balance everything one does from morning to evening must be balanced.

1. This lecture was concluded as follows: "And now as this is my last address here for some time before I come again to Paris, I would like to say a few words about the work of the Sufi Movement. It is a group of students, of seekers after truth, who come together to read, to study, to have silence together, and think of the same source of which I have just now spoken. And the leader of this group who has done her very best to keep this activity alive in Paris will do everything, and will not leave any stone unturned, in order to keep this activity alive. May I therefore ask the sympathy and cooperation of those who are present here?

In all different ways they can help to further the Cause, to further this work which appeals to them and which interests them there is an opportunity. And this opportunity they can take by keeping in touch with the meetings here and personally with the leader. There is a saying in the Hindustani language, 'There are many friends who are friends when you are present, but there are very few friends who keep friends when you are absent'. And now the time has come to recognize friends in my absence. When they will come here and keep this activity alive, this flame that has been lightened, when I come back and see it kept by my friends, then I will no more think of that Hindustani saying: I will no more believe it. May I also promise before my leaving that my thoughts and blessings will be with my friends - more in the absence than they have been in presence."

2.It is worth noting that in the present lecture, given in 1921, the terms "Sufi Movement" and "Sufi Order" appear as synonymous indications of the structure erected for all the esoteric and exoteric activities of the Sufi's under Pir-o-Murshid Hazrat Inayat Khan's guidance. It was not until 1923 that the name "Sufi Movement" was officially and legally adopted for the whole structure of modern Sufism; simultaneously the term "Sufi Order" obtained its present, more limited meaning of Esoteric School, one of the five main activities of the Sufi Movement. This lecture, as well as articles in the Magazine "The Sufi" during World War I make it clear that Hazrat Inayat Khan has long pondered on the best way to erect an *akasha* for and to give a name to the organization that was needed to spread his Message.

3. In the original report of this lecture one or more words are missing. The original text reads: "No, outside is only that which .... that knowledge which one has within.

4. In older days Hindustani and Hindi were synonymous with Urdu as the main language of Muslims generally and of the cultured class of all the communities in Hindustan (Northern India). In a further derived meaning Hindustani in a simplified form came to denote the language spoken by the educated classes to the uneducated and the British, thereby becoming a lingua franca throughout India. After partition and independence (1947) "Hindustani", continuing to be written in an adapted Arabic script, merged into "Urdu" (*zaban il urdu* - the language of the Horde) to become an official language in both Pakistan and India. Written in the *najari* script and expanded by a Sanskrit vocabulary, Hindustani became the Hindi that has become India's primary and general official language.

5. The following words have been omitted in order to avoid repetition.

"You have a great example in America: a country, a land where there was nothing except forests and deserts, and a few people living there. And what is made of this country by those who came and who had patience and strength of will, who lived there and made it all as it is! It gives a great and wonderful example to all."

List of Lectures that are the Sources of this Volume

The Alchemy of Happiness, England, 1922
The Aim of Life, Brussels, 22nd May 1924
The Purpose of Life (1), New York, 27th December 1925
The Purpose of Life (2), Detroit, 9th May 1926
The Art of Personality, Detroit, 14th May 1926
The Development of Personality, New York, 28th May 1926
The Attitude, Suresnes (France), 4th July 1926
The Secret of Life, Paris, 1st December 1923
What is Wanted in Life, Paris, 21st November 1925
Life, a Continual Battle (1, 2), Paris, 5th and 12th February 1923
The Struggle of Life (1), Paris, 12th December 1922
The Struggle of Life (2), date unknown
Spiritual Attainment and the Continual Struggle of Life, Geneva, 7th April 1924
Reaction, Paris, 13th December 1924
The Deeper Side of Life, on board the SS Volendam between Rotterdam and New York, 22nd December 1925
New York, 22nd December 1925
Life, an Opportunity, New York, 18th May 1926
Our Life, Paris, 9th November 1925
Communicating with Life, Burlingame (Cal.), 10th April 1925
The Intoxication of Life (1), date unknown
The Intoxication of Life (2), Paris, 2nd December 1923
The Meaning of Life, Rome, 15th November 1923
The Inner Life, Geneva, 19th September 1925
The Inner Life and Self-Realization, Chicago, 5th May 1926
The Interdependence of Life Within and Without, Suresnes, 16th August 1925
Interest and Indifference, Suresnes, 20th July 1926
From Limitation to Perfection (1), New York, 24th May 1926
From Limitation to Perfection (2), Paris, 14th December 1924
The Path of Attainment (1), date unknown
The Path of Attainment (2), Geneva, 2nd April 1924
The Path of Attainment (3), Suresnes, 11th August 1925
Stages on the Path of Self-Realization, Chicago, 29th April 1926
Man, the master of his Destinyn (1), New York, 23rd

December 1925

Man, the Master of his Destiny (2), Wichita (Kansas), 20th April 1926

The Law of Action, Paris, 23rd March 1925

Purity of Life, Southampton, 8th May 1922

The Ideal, Paris, December 1924; the 3 last questions and answers after a lecture on "Divine Manner", Suresnes, 9th October 1923

The Journey to the Goal (1), Bern, 22nd January 1925

The Journey to the Goal (2), date unknown

Acknowledgment, Paris, 10th January 1925

Responsibility, Suresnes, 28th July 1925

The Certitude of Life in the Hereafter, Paris, 28th March 1925

INDEX

Index of Words in Oriental Languages

Index of proper names